THE SILVER LINK LIBRARY OF
RAILWAY MODELLING

•

THE LIVING
MODEL RAILWAY

THE SILVER LINK LIBRARY OF
RAILWAY MODELLING

THE LIVING MODEL RAILWAY

Developing, operating and enjoying your layout

Robert Powell Hendry

SLP

Silver Link Publishing Ltd

First published in November 1994

Caledonian Railway No 139, a Pickersgill 'Superheater' 4-4-0, backs on to the turntable at Hillside (South) MPD on the Greenlane & Hillside Railway, shortly after dawn on a summer's day. She is still in full Caley colours, and has come in with the overnight LMS sleeper from Glasgow. She is on a 'lodging turn', and will return to Scotland on 'the Glasgow' the following evening.

British Library Cataloguing in Publication Data

A catalogue record for this book is available from the British Library.

ISBN 1 85794 027 X

Silver Link Publishing Ltd
Unit 5
Home Farm Close
Church Street
Wadenhoe
Peterborough PE8 5TE
Tel/fax (0832) 720440

Printed and bound in Great Britain

CONTENTS

Stanier 'Pacific' No 46241 *City of Edinburgh* heads 'The Caledonian' through Rugby *en route* to Euston in 1958. My father knew these majestic machines from new, and I grew up with them. Although 30 years have elapsed since I last saw a 'Duchess' snake through the maze of tracks around Rugby station, the memory remains as vivid as ever.

Somehow a suitable 'Duchess' never seemed to come our way on the GHR, then in 1991 a *pair* became available in quick succession. No 46252 *City of Leicester* is turned at Hillside (Millbank) MPD after arriving with 'The Hillsider'. The headboard bears a striking similarity to the board on No 46241 in the photograph above.

INTRODUCTION

In drafting the introduction to this book, I am in the position of the man who started to build a model of Stephenson's *Rocket*, but ended up with a Class '50' instead! Being translated, this cryptic remark will tell you that this book changed dramatically between the initial concept and the completed manuscript. I am grateful to Will Adams, of Silver Link Publishing, who commissioned one title and ended up with another, for not only accepting this metamorphosis, but even encouraging it, and providing an important part of the revised title!

The project was first discussed between my father, the late Dr Robert Preston Hendry, Will Adams and myself. Initially, it was to be a book on Model Railway Operation, for we all agreed that while locomotives, rolling-stock and scenic developments have made dramatic strides in the past 30 years, operation has remained the Cinderella, and many fine layouts, whether for exhibition or home use, are seldom, if ever, operated in a realistic or satisfying manner. Sadly my father passed away before this book got off the ground, but as the manuscript took shape it became clear that there was something missing. Chapters covered layout design, prototype practice, selecting interesting operating features, realistic passenger and freight working and so on, yet it did not have the vital spark. An additional chapter on 'X', even if I knew what 'X' was, did not seem to be enough. I felt like Archimedes may have done as he clambered into his bath. History tells us that revelation came to the said gentleman, who thereupon leapt from his bath and ran through the streets crying 'Eureka!'. Such conduct, though eccentric, seems to have been tolerated in classical Greece, but would probably get anyone arrested today!

As my own moment of revelation did not occur in the bath, the citizens of Rugby were spared such drama. Indeed, if truth be known, the idea crept up surreptitiously, for a question gradually shaped itself.

What is it that we try to do when we create a model railway? We are trying to re-create something in miniature in which we are interested. The full-size railway, the prototype as we refer to it, is a living entity. We can create exquisite models, perfect to the last rivet, breath-taking scenery and state-of-the-art electronics, yet unless we can capture that element of life that animates the prototype, our layout remains lifeless. It becomes boring.

It was only when I posed that question that I saw where the early drafts of this book were incomplete. I had always believed that the appeal of my father's layout, which has attracted operators week after week for 30 or 40 years, and which has brought regular team members from 50 miles away, was 'operation', hence the original aim of this book. One who fell under its spell was Will Adams, who is still afflicted! One day, as I was working on the layout, I realised it was not operation, locomotives or scenery. Instead, it was the blending of *all* the elements into a living tapestry that mattered.

The 0-4-0T is not merely an attractive model, but it is doing a job. It is there for a purpose. The 4-6-0 that backs down on to an express is not a show-case exhibit on which we count the rivets, but is there to move a heavy train, and has a job of work to do. A 4-4-0 would be incapable of doing it. The coal wagons that rumble through a wayside station *en route* to the coal-yard are there because they ought to be there, and would be required 'on the prototype'. The grimy retaining walls, the gasworks or granite setts are there, not because we love grimy retaining walls or retort houses, but because they contribute to the *life* of the railway.

In some places, more than I would like, we still have to *imagine* retaining walls, buildings and even ballast, but there does exist the concept of a world in which the trains run for a purpose, not aimlessly. Some of the models are delightful replicas of the prototype; others are less accurate. Some are crude, and would gain few marks from the purist. In the best modern thinking, we have banished derailments, they never happen - but we do suffer wheel-to-rail disorientations! The layout isn't perfect, and there is a lot we would like to do, but it has that living character that has brought team members to operate and help maintain it year after year.

The first person to formulate that idea was one of the team. Appropriately he did so at a Memorial Service held to my father at which the medical, military, railway and family aspects of his life were all apparent. I had invited Philip Ingram to give the appreciation. This is what he said:

'Dr Hendry was a remarkable man. In an age of two-dimensional people and the cultivated image, he was a three-dimensional person, whose image was himself. Whatever your association with him, he had depth. . . During the very hard winter of 1962-63 I became a member of the operating team. To my amazement I found that the procedures for running the railway were all documented so that novices could swot up. For me, the added dimension was atmosphere. We were not in a crowded attic in the Midlands, but in an area of the upper Lune valley which, though unknown to the Ordnance Survey, was well served by railways. Woe betide the Yardmaster who marshalled traffic for Glasson Dock on the wrong side of the Lancaster stock.

'His dexterity and medical background became obvious when disaster struck and the dreaded words "stop the clock" were uttered. In response to some critical point failure, the beret would go on and he would dive in under the baseboard. After some swift but unerringly accurate diagnosis, a series of medico-military orders would emerge from the depths, and forceps, thread and Spencer Wells surgical grips would be passed to him. The Railway also demonstrated another characteristic of really able people - the recognition of ability in others. Among both young and old members of the operating crew were some truly remarkable talents who were encouraged and developed by the Doctor's thoughtful guidance. Both professionally, and in his hobby, Dr Hendry was a team player.'

Dr Robert Preston Hendry, founder of the Greenlane & Hillside Railway, looks at Hoggsnorton station, which was built in the late 1950s. My father's philosophy was that an attractive and convincing station could be built with operational and scenic potential. The first place where he put this to the test was at Hoggsnorton. The station had enormous operating potential, and recalling the exhibitions and magazine articles of the day, the scenery, although taking little space, was advanced for its day. The high backscene in the central area was then revolutionary, and even today is rare.

As I re-read Philip's remarks, I realised how true they were. We were not in a crowded attic. We faced practical problems familiar to professional railwaymen, and invariably their way to solve them was the right way. My father built his own miniature block instruments as long ago as the 1920s, and most of our system was block-worked. One recent extension was not, and telephone block was in force, until we got round to installing block instruments. One day the regular operator at Hillside No 4 box was away. I was working Hillside No 1, and another talented member of the team was at No 4 box. A coal train arrived to go to the coal yard beyond No 4 box, and I gave a clear and obvious message: 'All Right for a coal through No 6 platform?' The answer 'OK' was equally clear and obvious. But my message meant 'Can I send my inbound train?', and it was translated as 'Is your outbound train ready?'. The reply, which was obvious to me, was equally obvious, but different in meaning, to the operator at No 4 box.

Trains started from each end. This was not a good idea, for on three-rail or stud contact, when power is forward, engines proceed chimney first, and by sheer luck the driver realised that there was another train coming towards him and stopped with the buffers almost touching. A similar misunderstanding of an obvious message led to an accident on the Cornwall Railway in 1873. Two goods trains were standing in the passing loop at Menheniot awaiting orders to proceed. The line was worked on the train order system, and the porter signalman called out to one guard, whom he knew, 'Right away, Dick'. Tragically the guard of the other train was also 'Dick', and assuming the order was for his train, he gave the right away to his enginemen, with the result that two freight trains met head-on in section, with one driver being killed.

In the real world, when you make a mistake like that, people may die. In the model world, at worst it means repairs to rolling-stock, but in our case two experienced operators had made a mistake that led to a head-on collision. Having read L. T. C. Rolt's account of the Menheniot disaster in his classic work *Red for Danger*, I ought to have known better than to give a message that could be mistaken, but it was obvious to me what it meant. The operator at the other end of the section was as familiar with Menheniot as I was, but between us we made the same error. The meaning of the message was equally obvious to all of the participants at Menheniot, and tragically different. If we had a Board of Trade 'Inspecting Officer of Model Railways', his report on the Hillside station collision would not have been complimentary to 'management', who had not installed block working, or the staff, who gave imprecise messages. Block instruments were installed hurriedly to prevent a recurrence.

I believe that what my father accomplished was not just to build an operating model railway, but a living model railway, and it is a railway with which I have lived since I was a child, and which continues to evolve and develop its character. How important is this? I think it is important, for I have often read fascinating articles on exquisite layouts, in which the designer explains that after the previous layout was completed and run for a while, he discarded it. Reading between the lines, one realises that despite the craftsmanship and skill, the layout lacked the character and life to make it enjoyable and permanent. In the end it was boring, or at least it bored its creator, and was cast aside for a new one. Sometimes I have read such articles with sadness, for one sees such magnificent workmanship going into a layout that, one feels, will share the same fate as its predecessor, for it too will become boring.

How does one create a living layout, rather than a boring layout? I would love to say 'Read on, and you will find out'. Modesty forbids that I should, and even if it did not, I am not sure that such a simple answer will suffice. It is easy to create a series of rules and principles, which, if applied correctly, should lead to excellent results, but in life the reverse is often the case. Perhaps the most celebrated example of such pedantry were the rules created in the 17th century by the Meistersingers of Germany, and entitled *The Nuremberg Funnel for Pouring in All the Essence of the Art of German Poetry and Rhyme in Six Lessons*.

It would be possible to produce a book that we could call *The Greenlane & Hillside Funnel for Pouring in All the Essence of the Art of Creating a Living Model Railway in One Volume*. This would be about as useful as the Meistersingers' rules, which stultified musical composition. Instead, I have decided to tell you what we did, why we did it, and why we enjoy it. You may not agree, and may have different ideas, but the important thing is to have ideas. If, at the end of the day, you have as much fun from your model railway as our operating team have had from the layout my father created and guided for over 60 years, then this book will have been well worthwhile, even if you don't do a thing we do!

My first acknowledgment is to my father, who sparked my love of model railways, and created a layout that has given such pleasure to so many people, and continues to do so, after he is no longer with us. Some of his prototype drawings and signalling plans appear in this book. My mother encouraged us in this strange pastime, and as the model railway was supposed to start at the mouth of the River Lune, and actually terminated in our attic, it is said that she was the first to suggest that we were 'Lune-attics'.

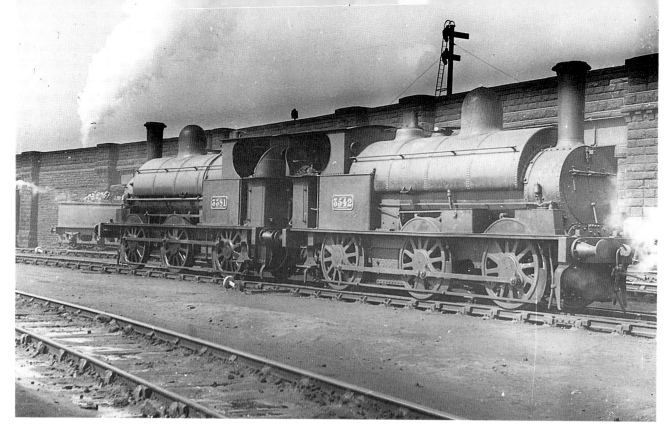

Above What we model is often based on our childhood memories, which may be an idyllic branch-line terminus or the bustle of the inner city. My father was born at Crosby, near Liverpool, and his early memories were of the LNWR, LYR and the forbidding industrial environment of railways on Merseyside. Here a pair of Ramsbottom 'Special Tanks', Nos 3381 and 3542, are caught amongst the smoke and grime of Edge Hill shed in about 1922. The sleepers buried in a cocktail of ash, grease and coal-dust, the pools of water where a tender has overflowed, and the blackened stonework typified any large shed. Because of the romance of steam, modellers often seem to forget the dirt and grime. *Author's Collection*

Below Dad and I wished to give to Hillside (Millbank) shed that character, and both Edge Hill and the CLC shed at Liverpool (Brunswick) provided the inspiration. A grimy and neglected '3F', No 43822, carrying an early BR livery, backs on to the Ransomes & Rapier turntable at Millbank. The tender coal rails are rusted and battered. Sadly Dad did not live to see the scenery developed here, but it followed the concept we had agreed.

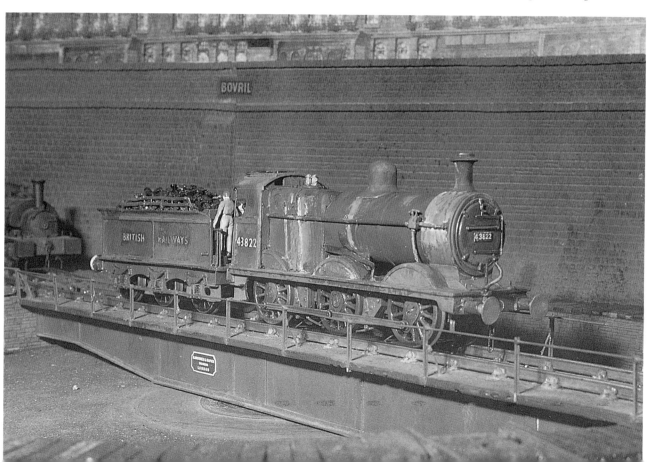

My next tribute is to the Team, but to name names would be invidious, as I could never include all, and their interest, enthusiasm and support has been a feature of my life. When my mother took ill and passed away, they were a wonderful help to Dad. When he passed away, they were an equal help to me. They have included many of my school friends, who have grown into what we must reluctantly admit is middle age, though they are still the lads. They included contemporaries of my father, and today's youngsters. One of the team who was coming in the early 1960s has sometimes brought his young daughter, who has operated a station, and I have heard him point out that he built this wagon or that structure 30 years ago. Another member of the team has brought his son, and he too has been busy offering and accepting trains, pulling off the levers and keeping an eye on the clock.

On the 'book' side, I have had especial help from Blair Ramsay, who has produced some of the plans and guided me through the intricacies of the computer world, and from Robert 'Bill' Cave, who produced a wonderful pen-and-ink cartoon of the GHR for a

Below In the late 1950s and early '60s, the Greenlane & Hillside Railway exhibited at the Benger's 'Doctors' Hobbies Exhibition' in London. Paythorne was the second of four stations built for incorporation into the permanent layout, but initially for exhibition. It was also exhibited elsewhere, and this glimpse of the yard demonstrates many of the techniques that had evolved, including spacing of the yard tracks, the deep backscene and the way in which the 3D road is carried into the 2D backdrop. Although named Paythorne for exhibition purposes, the trackwork became a part of Granton on the permanent layout. The tall signal in the distance is based on a similar signal that existed at Sutton Coldfield. *Dr R. P. Hendry*

Christmas card some years ago. Mike Hodgson and Martin Bloxsom have also made invaluable suggestions.

Below This cartoon drawn by one of the team, Robert 'Bill' Cave, speaks volumes, and enchanted my father. Students of any medical drama will recall the surgeon's staccato 'scalpel', for in an operation, time and precision are vital. The surgeon rarely had to perform his work crouched under a baseboard, with a hand groping out for the necessary tool. Arterial forceps, devised by 'Spencer Wells', were a part of the surgeon's kit, and of the GHR repair kit, too! In Philip Ingram's appreciation of Dr Hendry quoted in the text, the beret received equal mention.

Benger's laboratories were located at Holmes Chapel, and for the next layout, Slaidburn, Dad decided to provide a level crossing and a model of the Benger's building. It was a show stopper, with Benger's research staff saying 'That is my office', etc! The Paythorne control panel was re-used, and shows a classic GHR control console, with up and down controllers, miniature block instruments and lever frame. *Dr R. P. Hendry*

Railway modelling is a hobby in which people are welcome, and their views of interest. I met many outstanding enthusiasts, such as Sir Eric Hutchinson, Sir Philip Wombwell, the Rev Teddy Boston or William Walmsley. It is a hobby that attracts nice people. Sadly some precautions are necessary, for there are a few bad people too, as one friend, who lost much of his collection to burglars, found out. One thing you will not find in this book is any reference to the security system. A highly sophisticated electronic alarm protects the railway today, but that is 'classified information'. I would recommend a good alarm system to any modeller.

The one thing my father never had much patience with was the enthusiast who told you that his way was the *only* way to do something, and that any other approach was rubbish. In 4 mm modelling there is OO, EM and S4/P4. In 7 mm modelling there is coarse scale, fine scale and scale seven. Sadly, a proportion of the devotees of each will denigrate anyone who differs from their approach, and that is wrong, for each approach has its merits and drawbacks, and the wiser modeller respects what someone else does. I believe that firmly, and it has given me some problems in writing this book, for I started out by saying 'This is what we do', and it sounded too dogmatic, so I added 'but you can do it differently', and ended up with a cookery book that says 'take some lamb, or if you prefer pork, or a banana'. The resultant dish can be a trifle unpredictable. When I chatted to Will Adams about this, he said to say what we did, and leave it at that. That was sound advice, so I have taken it. What we have done is *not* the only way to create a model railway you can live with, but it does work. You may have very different ideas, and if this book sparks some thoughts, even if you disagree with what we have done, then if your way gives you pleasure, then that is great. I hope you get as much fun from your model railway as we have from ours.

1.
A VISIT TO HILLSIDE

I decided that the best way to explain what we had done was to take you on a tour of our principal station, Hillside. The town of Hillside, though it is unaccountably absent from the Ordnance survey maps, or most of them, lies in the upper reaches of the Aire valley not far south of Malham Tarn. Two small villages, Kirby and Hanlith, look at one another across the valley, and popular legend has it that when the first section of what was to become the Greenlane & Hillside Railway was built in the 1850s, the promoters did not wish to offend either community, so adopted the neutral name of Hillside. Industry came to the area, and the small villages grew into a thriving northern manufacturing town, with woollen mills, heavy industry, and all that goes with it.

By choosing a geographical location for a fictitious railway, my father produced a degree of realism that ended up by surprising even him. Train services had to connect into the West Coast Main Line at Lancaster and Preston, and through the kindness of the BR Control Office staff at Rugby in the 1950s, passenger and freight Working Timetables for the whole of the LMR Western and Midland Divisions were forthcoming. Trains did not just go 'somewhere', they were for a specific destination, and the Liverpool, London and Greenlane expresses were born. You will have heard of Liverpool, and London, and we will come to Greenlane later on.

Being located on the edge of the West Yorkshire conurbation around Leeds, Bradford, Halifax, etc, trains needed to go in that direction too. This presented a problem, for the line was started before the geography was settled, and we discovered that a route to Skipton was a must, but the only available site was for a short dead-end branch, which had to suffice. Many years later my father found an ingenious way of doubling the length of the dead-end line, but it was still insufficient, and while this book was being prepared we started planning a new extension that will provide direct access to the Great Northern Railway at Bradford.

The previous paragraph reminds us that advance planning is important. The physical element of the railway - baseboard heights, aisles, curves - were worked out meticulously by Dad, but fitting the model railway to the geography came later, and one route that ought to have been there could only be installed in token form. It is a problem that we have wrestled with for 20 years, and had the geography been selected before the first rails were laid, a different approach would have permitted more than a token route from Hillside to the West Riding.

We will start our tour on Hayward Road, named after one of our long-serving operators, Tom Hayward, who first came to the GHR in the 1950s, and last operated trains in 1994 just weeks before his death. Tom's father was a Great Western engineman, and had been fireman on the celebrated Dean Single, *Duke of Connaught*. Although I find it hard to justify a Dean Single in the Pennines (impossible might be a better word), Tom's model of his father's engine is treasured. Tom moved to Rugby in the 1930s, and to a job with the British Thomson-Houston Co, which became a part of AEI and eventually GEC. Tom was a draftsman, a skilled model-maker and an ingenious practical engineer. He was also a member of the BTH fire brigade, and later a part-time fireman in Rugby. One day, when he was at work, he noticed the solitary 120-ton LMS transformer wagon No 300000 in the yard, and decided to measure it up for a model. In due course a shunter came up, and apologetically explained that they had to move the wagon to shunt some other stock, but would return it in a few minutes. Tom did not enlighten them as to the purpose of the measurements! In due course he built a model of No 300000, and as we were thinking of a suitable industrial backdrop to the area, I thought of the transformer

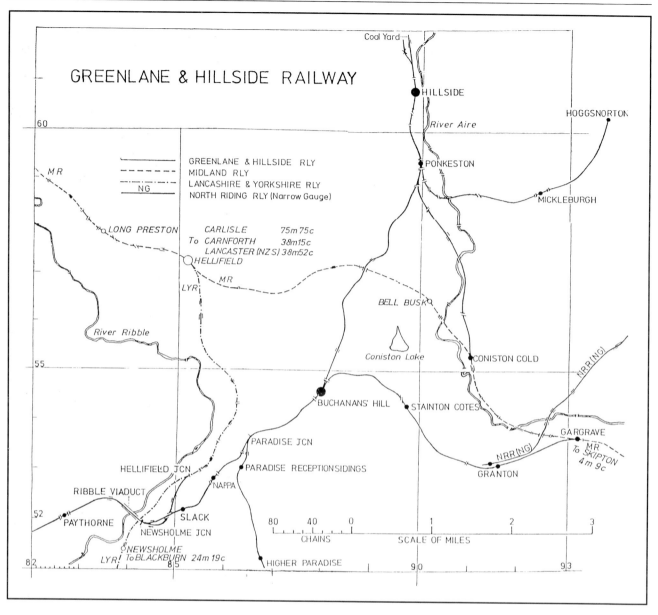

The geography of the GHR was developed at the start of the 1950s, selecting an area where railways could have been built but where fate decreed otherwise. Contours and other features were studied on 1 inch and 6 inch Ordnance Survey maps until an acceptable main line was located with a ruling 1 in 55 grade. The theoretical line runs from Hillside, a few miles north-east of Hellifield, to Glasson Dock, renamed and enlarged as Greenlane on the mouth of the Lune. The section that has been modelled is a 9-mile stretch from Hillside to just west of Paythorne where Middleton loops are located. This map depicts the modelled section, and its connections to the MR and LYR. At the time of writing the Paradise line merely runs to Paradise Reception Sidings, but will be the basis of our next extension, to Bradford.

wagon, and the idea of another BTH plant was born. The name of the road was then obvious.

The BTH building dominates Hayward Road, and the transformer wagon and other suitable stock visits the works yard. As a child I remembered the massive THE BRITISH THOMSON-HOUSTON CO LTD sign on the Rugby plant, and wanted to reproduce this, so I asked Tom if he knew what size the letters were. He replied instantly that they were 8-foot letters on a 14-foot backing, and were red. When the

BTH sign was to be replaced with an AEI sign, no drawing could be found, so volunteers were sought from the drawing office to measure up an object 80 feet or so off the ground. As a fireman, Tom had no qualms, so. . .!

Our building, though large by model railway standards, was less than half the size of the Rugby BTH plant, so in the end we settled for 4-foot letters, which kept their character and were about in proportion to the building. Finding suitable raised 4-foot

Above The Hayward Road works of the British Thomson-Houston Co dominate the skyline as we look up Guild Street, and see an LYR Aspinall 'Pug', No 11217, clatter off the street tramway towards Bray Street yard. The ancient clerestory coach body on the left provides mess and office facilities for the PW gang. The wagons in the elevated siding on the right are part of the Hayward Road coal drops. Similar scenes, with granite setts, industrial premises soaring upwards, and railway tracks in all directions, were found in any industrial town until the 1960s.

Below The British Thomson-Houston works, with its enormous sign, dominated Rugby station, and it was perhaps hardly surprising that a model would appear on the GHR. What may surprise many modellers is the engine in the foreground, LMS Garratt No 7982, arriving on a coal from Leicester in June 1939. These engines were so firmly associated with the Midland Division that many enthusiasts refuse to believe that they ever worked on to the Western Division. *H. J. Stretton Ward*

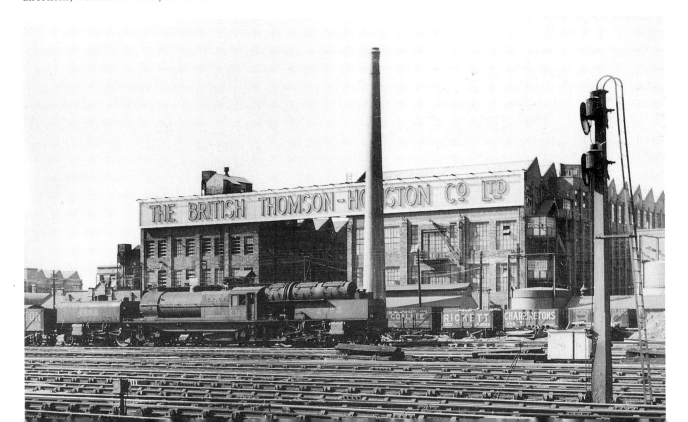

letters was more of a problem; in O gauge this is just over 1 inch. As a small child, I had an alphabet set, so tried some toy shops, but all the letters were peculiar shapes, and would look more at home saying Yogi Bear. I remembered the letters used on cafe menu boards, and tried a variety of stationers, art retailers and sign writers, and got nowhere. After 12 visits and several phone calls, I sat down in disgust with a cup of tea, then went off and had a look in a box of old toys that I had last used many years ago. Five minutes later I emerged clutching a set of 1-inch letters of similar pattern to the BTH sign. The moral is obvious - never throw anything away, for it is surprising

what you can adapt for model railway use. Subsequently I discovered that a firm called Sasco produce letters for cafe fare boards, and that industrial and wholesale stationers stock them; they come in a variety of sizes from about 10 mm upwards. I recall seeing the name of one prototype station done in concrete letters set into a sloping flower bed opposite the platform, which would be an attractive feature on a layout.

Much as I would have liked a full-depth factory, the BTH building had to be low relief. There are two problems that always affect the low-relief building. Sloping roofs are difficult to deal with convincingly, but in this case the original had a false front, hiding the 'ridge and furrow' roof. The second problem was more serious. In the real world buildings have depth, but low-relief buildings do not, and any attempt at perspective modelling may look splendid from the right angle, but looks ghastly if there is a wide angle of view - and in this case there was a very wide angle of view. There was a space in the works yard, however, and I realised that if we could have a structure projecting into that, the real depth there would give an

We are looking across Guild Street PW yard towards the BTH factory. The wagon in the foreground is LMS 300000, the 120-ton transformer wagon that Tom Hayward measured up to make this model. What would be rather nice would be to have a model of Tom, with notebook, speaking to a shunter. The BTH sign on the works tower is photocopied from a BTH catalogue, so is in proportion; catalogues provide a useful source of data for such signs. The high-backdrop idea developed by Dad at Hoggsnorton in the 1950s, so that the eye is not offended by an 'end of the world' effect, was taken to its logical conclusion by the 1990s, reaching to the ceiling.

optical illusion that would mask the lack of depth to the main structure. The ancillary building had to be significantly taller than the main structure if the eye was to be deceived, and relatively modest in depth and width. I remembered that on the English Electric factory in Rugby there was such a tower (which was also the works manager's eyrie!), so the Hillside BTH plant acquired a tower reminiscent of that building, complete with flag staff on top. Two sidings entered the works yard, one terminating short of the buildings, the other continuing into the factory through sliding doors, which just happened to be closed.

Hayward Road sees other rail traffic, for a single track runs up the middle of the road to serve other industrial premises. As exposed crossheads and piston-rods are not permitted on the street section, operation is confined to such engines as an ex-'Lanky' 0-4-0ST 'Pug' or a Sentinel. The principal road access to Hillside coal yard is via Hayward Road. The coal yard follows North Eastern practice, with its coal cells or coal drops. When my father was working on the coal drops, he asked 'What does a 20-ton load of coal look like in O gauge?' and 'What is the angle of repose of coal?'. As we were going to glue the coal, we could have any angle we liked, but the average coal merchant does not pour PVA adhesive over his coal, so this was no help. We didn't know, so I was volunteered to build a dummy 20T bottom-door-discharge wagon, load it with 20 model tons of suitably crushed coal, and hold it over the coal drop and open the door. We soon discovered what 20 tons of coal looked like, and the angle of repose. We found that the angle would increase until it became too steep, then it would slip, widening the base area covered, and start to build up again. Obvious when you think about it, but we didn't know the answer until we experimented. The coal stacks with almost vertical sides in old pictures of engine sheds were hand stacked, like building a dry stone wall, using selected lumps to create a regular pattern. Apart from these stacks, which were to make best use of scarce storage space, coal lay in heaps at its natural angle of repose. Ever since that experiment, one of my foibles on visiting a model railway exhibition has been to look at heaps of coal. It is surprising how often the angle is far too steep. The moral is clear - experiment!

At the south end of the coal yard a narrow lane

Wadman's are obviously expecting a load of coal, but their neighbours at Hillside coal yard still have rather more coal in store. Sunlight slants down between the rails to illuminate the blackened back walls of the individual coal cells.

leads into Guild Street. Back in the 1960s my father decided to name a walkway at our branch terminus of Hoggsnorton 'Railway Walk', but had not got round to producing a street name for it. One day he was telling a visitor that we were going to name it Railway Walk, when the visitor said 'Dr Hendry, it is named Railway Walk'. One of the team, knowing Dad's plans, had produced a suitable sign, and affixed it without telling us. In the 1980s, as Hillside coal yard took shape, Dad decided that the narrow lane would become 'Coalyard Lane'. Jack Ray, the doyen of the Gauge O Guild and producer of the Guild's slide collection, was visiting the railway to take photographs, and Dad explained the plan to him, then looked more

As an NER 40T coal hopper is shunted over the ancient girder bridge spanning Coalyard Lane, a youngster plays catching practice with a ball.

closely and realised that he had been 'had' again. On this occasion I was guilty!

Until natural gas replaced traditional coal gas, every large town and many small ones had their own gas works. Naturally Hillside has a gas works, which is

The retort banks can dimly be seen through the open arches amid the smoke and fumes inside the retort house of the Hillside Gas Light & Coke Co. Note the shallow angle of repose of coal apparent in the adjacent coal yard.

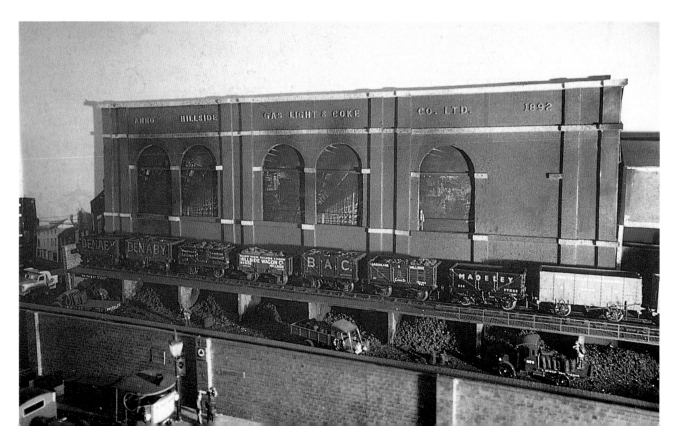

run by the Hillside Gas Light & Coke Co. Gas works often adjoined the railway line, and were in the industrial part of town. That at Hillside backs on to the coal yard, from which it is separated by an iron railing fence with gates where the rail tracks come in. Fumes from the retort house have discoloured the brickwork above the open arches, and remind us of the fumes and dirt associated with the old-style horizontal retort houses. The retort house, reduced to fit our site, was based on the Gas Light & Coke Co retort houses at Beckton and elsewhere.

Further along we see the coke washery and screening plant, which projects over the private sidings into the gas works. The inspiration was the coke screening plant at Dumbrick Pavell, allied to a model of an ideal coal-handling plant for gas works exhibited at the Paris Exhibition in 1900. I carried out the necessary research for these structures, but the idea comes from my father's philosophy of 'find out or experiment'. I knew the constraints of the site we had, and studied technical works on coal handling, gas production and industrial equipment until I found a mix of structures that made reasonable sense in juxtaposition, and fitted the site. Given unlimited space I would have done more, but that was not possible. At the southern end of the gas works site we discover the

scrubbers, purifiers and tar tanks, together with a travelling grab crane. The latter is an accurate model of a single-chain Bleichert grab, of the kind installed in the early 1900s.

The visitor to this part of Hillside will realise that it is the industrial side of town, with the big BTH factory towering up on one hand, and the gas works nearby. Both contribute traffic to the railway, and this emphasises another aspect of Dad's philosophy. We build a model railway because we like trains, and want to recreate them in miniature. Economics, traffic flows, waybills and the presence of Dr Beeching, if there is not enough traffic, does not matter to us. In the real world, people built railways because they thought there was traffic to be carried. In many places the railway runs through open countryside, and wayside stations can be remote from any habitation, but elsewhere the railway is in close contact with the sources of its revenue - coal mines, factories, gas works, breweries and so on.

Fifty years ago the average model railway was largely given over to track, and scenery might comprise a backdrop and railway structures, such as platforms, signal boxes and goods sheds. After the war a new approach developed, in which skilled modellers, such as John Ahearn, placed their railway in an environment. This trend has continued, up to a point at which the scenery often dominates the layout, with little space given over to tracks. This can produce a visually stunning effect, but has its own shortcomings. In the introduction I spoke of accounts of layouts in which the modelling is

A former Caley 'Pug', No 16030, shunts a tar tank at the gasworks. In the background is the travelling crane and the Bleichert grab. The gas works is separated from the coal yard by iron railings and gates.

exquisite, but the owner clearly got bored with the layout, as it had little or no operating potential and, after a few months, became uninteresting.

My father believed that no layout could be convincingly 'scenicked' everywhere if it was to have operating potential, but in the real world you do not see everywhere simultaneously, for even an astronaut circling the earth only sees half the world at any one time. Therefore the answer is to create a convincing *illusion* in the areas you wish to be scenic, and treat other areas as non-scenic. Most modellers do this without realising it, as many layouts run from a scenic branch terminus to a non-scenic fiddle yard. His view was that if a layout was to hold the operator's interest, operating potential had to come first, and the most enchanting scenery, if it compromised operating, would lead to boredom. As some of our team have spent 40 years running the GHR, they do not seem to have become bored up to now, and recently one of our senior operators, who had worked all the main stations, decided he would like to work a minor crossing station on our single-track Hoggsnorton branch, as he had never worked there before.

My father felt that acceptable scenery could be worked into a layout without drastic loss of space or operating potential, and he first put this into effect at our branch terminus, Hoggsnorton, in the 1950s (see the illustration on page 8). The scenery there compared favourably with many of the layouts in the magazines at the time, yet took very little space away from operating potential. There were one or two problems which were not solved, one being the lack of depth in a low-relief building. Occasionally one sees buildings on corner sites that are V-shaped, and looking at the offending building one day I realised that this was the answer, though it has yet to be put into effect.

Returning to Hillside, as we look at the BTH plant, the gas works and coal yard, the industrial landscape explains what the maze of sidings is for. The 0-4-0T that squeals round a tight curve at the gas works is shunting a tar wagon, and until the 1960s we could have visited any large town and seen it for real. Much of the scenery in the industrial area was discussed and planned with Dad. Sadly he did not live to see it, but we followed his concept, and remarks from visitors indicate that they see this as the industrial area, with the railway threading a tortuous course through dismal streets with granite setts, over a level crossing, and with buildings towering up on all sides. As a youngster in Liverpool and Rugby in the 1920s, Dad could remember horse-drawn traffic. As a small child, on visits to Merseyside in the 1950s, I could recall granite setts, and Sentinel steam lorries, which seemed to linger on there long after they had vanished elsewhere. I could also remember the trams and the wonderful Liverpool Overhead Railway, but these were a trifle hard to work into the scene convincingly!

Leaving the coal yard and gas works, we will walk along Guild Street. One of the 1950s team, Joe Brown, became Secretary of the Gauge O Guild, and in recent years, on one visit to the line to operate it, Joe noticed an irate lady complaining to a police officer. Following her outstretched arm, he looked along Guild Street and noticed a couple of young ladies standing on a street corner. We will not enquire too closely into what they are doing, other than to say that this is a large industrial town, nor will we progress that far along Guild Street, as we shall turn to the left and enter the PW Engineer's yard. This is reached off the BTH branch, and provides storage space for sleepers, chairs, and other PW stores. The depot yard is gravel-surfaced, and near the gateway is churned up by road vehicles coming in and out; the vehicle tracks were made by rolling a pair of tyres up and down on the partially set, glued ground cover. An old six-wheel coach body mounted on sleepers to keep it off the ground serves as a PW office. A public footpath adjoins the yard, and there is a sleeper crossing over the Hayward Road branch, before the footpath makes a sudden turn to run alongside Hillside (Ramsay Street) station.

The history books tell us that Ramsay Street was the original Hillside passenger station of the 1850s, and the single platform, with its short timber train shed, bears a close resemblance to Banbury (Merton Street) which opened at the same period. Traffic soon outgrew Ramsay Street, however, and as the valley was narrow at this point, and the area was built up, a

As the photographer takes his life in his hands, dodging the lorries clattering over the granite setts in Guild Street, he hears snatches of the conversation between an indignant housewife and a member of the Constabulary: 'You ought to do something. . .'

new station, Hillside Exchange, was opened a short distance down the line about 20 years later. Ramsay Street, in the heart of the industrial area, and near Hillside Barracks, was retained for troop movements, workmen's trains, and for the Euston and Scottish sleeping car services, as the sleepers could be worked up to that station and away from the bustle of the main passenger station. The name does not mean there is a dedicated *Neighbours* fan in the team, or that we have Australians working the line. One of the team, Blair Ramsay, called in one afternoon as my father was laying the track at the station, and Dad commented about the problems of the single platform face that was then envisaged. Blair suggested an island platform, and about 18 inches of track that had been laid was quickly removed, and the revised suggestion adopted. When we were considering a name for the station, Ramsay Street was the obvious answer!

It must be quite close to train time, as the platform is thronged with people catching one of the evening sleeping car expresses. One of the passengers, with a receding hairline, is wearing the red mess jacket and full dress uniform of the Royal Army Medical Corps. Clearly he must have attended some function, and is now hurrying to catch the train; his batman is carrying a number of cases. It is pure co-incidence that Dad was Medical Officer to the 1st Royal Tank Regiment on the outbreak of war, and my mother used to claim that his hairline receded at a remarkably early age!

Carriage sidings flank Ramsay Street station, but beyond them we see a tall grimy tower of Italianate appearance. It is the campanile hydraulic tower that powers the cranes and lifts of the LNWR&GN Joint goods depot at Hillside (Bray Street). Bray Street is, or will be, a twin-level yard, just as soon as the wagon hoist comes into operation. This will be based on similar hoists at Birmingham (Moor Street) on the GWR, and Broad Street on the North London Railway. Bray Street High Level yard exists, but the low-level sidings are not yet installed, pending construction of the hoist. Operationally this will be cumbersome, but will make an interesting and unusual

Smoke has discoloured the timber cladding of the Ramsay Street train shed, but the structure is otherwise sound, although it sees few passengers. The principal services to use the station are the Glasgow and Aberdeen sleepers.

I was looking at some figures waiting to be painted and realised that one bore a striking resemblance to Dad, and with a few alterations would recall the mess dress he wore when with the 1st Royal Tank Regiment.

Right An LNER 'J39' drifts through Bray Street yard, having brought in a freight from York. The corrugated iron shed houses the yard shunters, but has seen better days, for despite patching there are many holes in the roof sheeting. 'Backdrop' is a part of model railway lore, but 'frontdrop' is a term I shall coin, for the ground dips down at this point and, as at Birmingham Moor Street, Bray Street is a two-level yard. A lorry pokes its nose out of the road entrance.

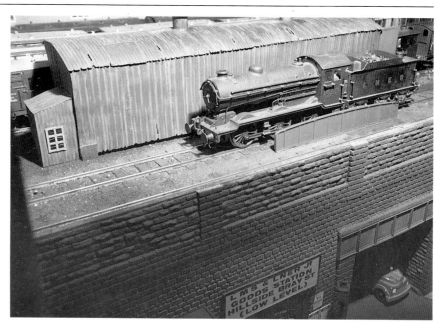

Below right Paperwork litters the counter of the goods office at Bray Street (Low Level). The LMS&LNER Joint sign consists of individual planks secured to battens in the prototype style, with a frame around it. It helps contribute to the industrial character of the neighbourhood.

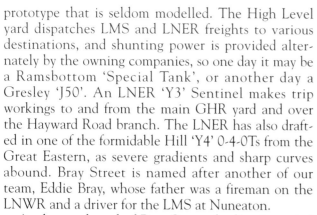

prototype that is seldom modelled. The High Level yard dispatches LMS and LNER freights to various destinations, and shunting power is provided alternately by the owning companies, so one day it may be a Ramsbottom 'Special Tank', or another day a Gresley 'J50'. An LNER 'Y3' Sentinel makes trip workings to and from the main GHR yard and over the Hayward Road branch. The LNER has also drafted in one of the formidable Hill 'Y4' 0-4-0Ts from the Great Eastern, as severe gradients and sharp curves abound. Bray Street is named after another of our team, Eddie Bray, whose father was a fireman on the LNWR and a driver for the LMS at Nuneaton.

At the north end of Bray Street the line is carried high above ground level, and the campanile tower is taller than we first realised. One entrance to the passenger station adjoins the grimy tower, while the goods receiving office and road entrance to the Low Level yard are adjacent.

Bray Street itself is at the far end of the yard, and boasts a level crossing. This was painstakingly built by Dad from measurements of the LNWR crossing at Clifton Mill, just outside Rugby. It was built for an exhibition layout at the start of the 1960s, but did not see use on the layout until the 1990s. The gates close against the road and an LNER 'Y4' 0-4-0T squeals around the tight curve. Something that many visitors comment upon is the prototypical squealing noise on the model, which is in fact the skate, for the GHR is a stud contact system, Dad converting from three-rail in the early 1950s. Instead of adopting the brass screws used by many modellers, Dad opted for panel pins, which are far less obtrusive. Two or three youngsters have accumulated by the crossing gates, as the two-road Hillside (North) MPD of the Greenlane &

Hillside Railway adjoins the crossing. The history books tell us that this was the original GHR shed, but now only handles freight and shunting engines since the new and much larger South shed was opened.

Above As an AA patrolman waits at Bray Street level crossing, an LNER 'Y4' 0-4-0T rumbles by. The wide dumb buffers on these powerful shunting tanks were needed to avoid buffer locking on the sharply curved lines around Bishopsgate, London, for which they were built, and are equally useful at Bray Street. The level crossing was built by Dad after detailed measurements of the LNWR gates at Clifton Mill, near Rugby. In September 1991 my father and I visited the Gauge O Guild convention, and I bought the 'Y4', which was in need of con-siderable work. I started on this and, as usual, Dad was keenly interested in progress, but within days he was seriously ill, and never saw No 7228 operate.

Below A similar set of gates existed at Warrington (Monks Siding), the only significant difference being the taller posts, as these gates are longer than those at Bray Street. The rough granite setts, the signal box by the crossing, and the industrial character recall the model. *Dr R. P. Hendry*

We had better delve into the history books once more to explain the letters 'GHR' seen on some stock, although LMS and LNER equipment is plentiful. They tell us that the first line in the area, the Hillside & Skipton Railway, opened from Gargrave, just west of Skipton on the Midland Railway, to Hillside in the early 1850s. A branch line, which eventually became the main line, was constructed in stages from the 1860s until it made an end-on junction with the LNWR&LYR Preston & Longridge branch. Meanwhile another company was developing a short line in the vicinity of Glasson Dock, which is at the mouth of the River Lune. This line built an extension inland into the hills to serve stone quarries. Eventually a link was proposed between the two companies, but funds ran out and work was abandoned. Thus far the story is typical of a host of railways, and purely imaginary, but, of the lines envisaged, as we researched real railway history, we found that at least two-thirds were either proposed, or even authorised, at various times.

Our story now shifts to the Sudan, where a resourceful Canadian-born Royal Engineers officer, Percy Girouard, has been appointed to take charge of an Egyptian Railway battalion to look after the single-track railway line over which much of the supplies for the Anglo-Egyptian army under General Kitchener must pass. The Sudan is reconquered, but at the turn of the century the Boer War breaks out, and a freshly promoted Girouard becomes Director of Imperial Military Railways in South Africa. On returning to England after the conclusion of the Boer War, Major-General Sir Percy Girouard has an unrivalled experience of military railway working, and is convinced that in any future war an adequate supply of trained railway troops will be vital if the front lines are to be adequately supported. In 1903 Girouard submits a comprehensive report to the War Office, in which he recommends that an existing civilian railway should be acquired and run by Royal Engineers staff. In addition to the training opportunities, the line would continue to handle civilian traffic, so should be self-supporting financially. He recommends the self-contained railways of the Isle of Wight. A second choice is the equally self-contained narrow-gauge lines of the Isle of Man. A third option is the decrepit Manchester & Milford Haven Railway, which meanders southwards from Aberystwyth towards Carmarthen. In the best War Office traditions, a committee is set up to consider the Girouard plans, and the ideas mulled over, altered, pigeon-holed, then largely forgotten. The history books will tell you all this.

What few history books will tell you, other than those we have re-written, is that Girouard's report did not fall on barren ground. Instead, the War Office, still geared to the idea of colonial wars, realises that there are two impecunious lines in the North West, connected by an unfinished road bed. To avoid political pressure and union boycotts from the emergent railway unions, a joint civilian-military structure is worked out, and the Hillside & Skipton and Glasson Dock lines, along with the abandoned link line, become the Greenlane & Hillside Railway. As the army develops in the aftermath of the Boer War, traffic flows into the area and both civilians and military are content. During the First World War, a variety of military establishments and defence industries are established, but as the Railways Act of 1921 wends its way through Parliament, the War Office, chary of losing its training railway, exerts pressure, and the GHR is excluded from the provisions of the Act.

We now realise how it is that when we were near Bray Street station we saw a line of tanks awaiting loading, and the number of military uniforms around becomes clearer. As we join the youngsters looking across to Hillside (South) MPD, we notice that one of the engines carries the drab green livery of the War Department, and 'WD' lettering. It is a Hunslet austerity 0-6-0ST, of the type the LNER, and enthusiasts, will call a 'J94'. Using our track pass, we cross the lines, and see the two-road shed, the grimy shed stores and open-air coal stage. We are glad we don't work there.

Just beyond the coal stage an incline drops at 1 in 28, and to our left the ground falls away, and we see another platform with a passenger canopy. Gilt letters, which have seen much weathering, proclaim that the begrimed stone building, of vaguely classical style, is Hillside (Exchange) station. This was the second station of the 1870s, intended to replace Ramsay Street, but it too is on a constricted site, and has become the parcels depot on the construction of the third station, a quarter of a mile away. The Post Office staff look at us suspiciously as we walk along the platform. PO mail vans are plentiful, and on one of the adjoining tracks we see an LMS TPO. The royal cypher, with its 'ER' letters, on an LMS vehicle surprises us, until we realise that for a few months, until his abdication, Edward VIII reigned after the death of King George V in 1936. The PO staff seem to have the covered area of the platform to themselves, but further on our noses are assailed by a smell that has been growing steadily stronger - fish - for the outer end of the platform is the fish dock. I have to confess that we have not yet invented authentic rail smells, so the visitor, and reader, must imagine the aroma. Maybe that is a good thing, as a cattle dock adjoins one of our signal boxes, and authentic smell might reduce the popularity of that post!

As we walk along Exchange platform, we see a long brick shed on our right. It is the carriage shed, capable of holding 28 coaches on its four roads. It has a flat concrete roof, supported above by reinforced concrete beams. As the roof is obviously more modern than the walls, we realise that the structure must have been re-roofed. The reality is that with a carriage shed that is over 6 feet long and spans four tracks on the model, it is essential to have access to the inside in the event of a derailment (even though these have been officially banished), or a coach becoming uncoupled. The shed butts up to one of the room walls, which has become

Above As a US Transportation Corps 'S160' 2-8-0 makes ready, Royal Tank Regiment personnel check the loading of their 7th Armoured Division Shermans, which bear the 'Desert Rat' 'tac' sign.

Below Hillside Exchange station has long been given over to parcels use, and the pollution of a northern industrial town has blackened the stonework of the station buildings, but the gilt lettering can still be read. On the left the incline rises at 1 in 28 towards Bray Street, while Hillside carriage shed dominates the right of the view. Fish crates by the Bedford lorry direct our attention to the fish train in the far platform. The LMS BG on the right came from Norman Eagles's 'Sherwood Section' many years ago, and is a treasured possession.

a grimy retaining wall, and a pitched roof of any description would have made lifting the roof for access difficult, perhaps impossible. A modern concrete flat roof solved the problem, and many genuine railway structures were modified, although not for that reason!

Working class housing has now replaced factories, and in turn gives way to small shops, then to commercial properties. We glance at some of the shop names - Bloxsom's, Woodcock & Cave - and recall that we know railway staff of the same name! One shop has become the Union office, but not the NUR or ASLEF. One of the problems of operating a sizeable model railway is building up an operating team, and we need a minimum of six people, each capable of doing two jobs simultaneously, to run happily. After one running, when we were unusually short-staffed (and very hot. as it was high summer), exhausted members of staff decided this would not do, and a notice appeared a few days later on the company notice board from the newly formed union, the Organisation of Greenlane & Hillside Railway

An LNWR 'Precursor' tank is on the fish empties at Exchange platform, while a former LYR 2-4-2T, No 10887 in early LMS crimson lake, backs on to a rake of LMS corridors. A 'Jinty', No 7113, completes a trio of engines familiar at many Western and Central Division stations in the late 1920s or early 1930s.

Employees. OGRE shop stewards said that they were willing to continue 'second man' duties, but not third and fourth man duties. For many years OGRE lacked an office, but through the paternal kindness of GHR management, they were given favourable terms on a property. It is a sheer co-incidence that it overlooks the fish dock and gas works.

Resisting the assault on our olfactory organs, we hurry on, and see a large Ransomes & Rapier turntable on our left, its builders proclaimed by a large rectangular maker's plate. The working parts of the turntable were built by Dad, and I was deputed to do the cosmetic work, handrails, girder work and so on. I had a pre-1914 Ransomes & Rapier catalogue, and this included photographs of many of their products. These showed the maker's plates prominently, with the lettering picked out in white on a black ground, and after a few minute's calculation as to size, and with the right reduction on a photocopier, I ended up with a pair of perfect Ransomes & Rapier plates. The turntable, which will handle a Stanier 'Pacific', belongs to the LMS, but by arrangement is also used by visiting LNER engines, and GHR engines at this end of the station.

We now see another platform, which will comfortably handle an 11-coach train, stretching into the distance. This is Hillside (Preston Road) station, the

A Bassett Lowke 'Royal Scot', No 6135 *The East Lancashire Regiment,* poses on Millbank turntable. This engine was detailed by Joe Brown, currently Secretary of the Gauge O Guild, in the 1950s, and received a Stanier tender in 1993. Her 40-year career as first-line motive power equals the life-span of the prototype, which would have been at home in such an environment.

main passenger terminal of the GHR, which replaced the 1870s Exchange station in 1905. The idea of a passenger terminal not at the end of the line came to us following a visit to Altrincham. The original 1849 Manchester, South Junction & Altrincham terminal at the last-named place was south of Moss Lane, and another station, Bowdon, was a short distance away, to the north of Stamford Street. In 1862 a new line, later part of the CLC, was built, diverging from the MSJ&AR between these two stations. In 1881 the old stations were closed, and a new station, which served the terminating line and the CLC, was opened between Stamford Street and Moss Lane. The old 1849 terminal was retained as a carriage shed, later an electric train depot, and the depot fan spread out to within feet of the end of the platforms of the new 1881 station.

The reality on the model was that Hillside originally stopped at the end of the '1905' station, and the extensions 'up the valley' came later, but we built the extensions around the story suggested by events at Altrincham. In creating a model railway we are creating an illusion, but if the illusion is to be convincing, it needs to have a plausible reason. This is often forgotten, and I recall reading that a sinuous curve looks more attractive scenically than a plain straight line. The modeller had worked a beautiful sweeping curve into his layout, but however beautiful it was, it looked wrong. The reason was that the prototype railway engineers did not create curves because they looked pretty, but because they had to. High ground, buildings which were too expensive or too politically sensitive to demolish were reasons, but the aesthetics of a sweeping curve was not. The modeller had the curve, but no reason for it, and it looked unrealistic. Had he put a ruin of a medieval monastery or an ancient ring of stones in the field, the curve would have been necessary, for there might have been parliamentary opposition to destroying such venerable ruins, however much of a nuisance to the engineer. We are building the model because we enjoy railways, but railway promoters and engineers built railways for a practical purpose. Hillside developed as it did because the room in which the industrial area developed was not available when work began in 1947, but only became free later.

If we were to make use of the space, Hillside had to grow beyond the '1905' station, and a convincing reason was necessary. The growth of the town and the rising traffic, making the 1850 and 1870 stations inadequate, thus grew from that Altrincham visit.

We are now on No 6 platform at Hillside (Preston Road) station, and the way in which the passenger accommodation has been progressively moved down the valley is apparent, for on our left is a further locomotive depot, which, we see, is LMS property. It is Hillside (Millbank) shed, 11F, in the Carnforth district. Readers with shed code books that unaccountably omit 11F will now be able to correct them to allow for this important facility. The 'coal hole' that adjoins No 6 platform, not to the liking of some passengers, tells us that this was an LNWR shed, but with the Grouping, 'Compounds', '3Fs', '4Fs' and

'Jinties' have become common. There will probably be two or three 'Compounds' on shed, and perhaps a couple of '4Fs'. The severe grades between Preston and Hillside, over which the LMS expresses operate, mean that Millbank shed sees premier league motive power too, in the shape of 'Royal Scot' Class 4-6-0s, and even Stanier 'Pacifics', the latter usually on running-in duties from Crewe (North).

Millbank shed, which, like Cambridge, adjoins the platform, and is visible by looking over the boundary wall, recalls another aspect of Dad's philosophy, rare even in 4 mm gauge, let alone 7 mm modelling. At any sizeable prototype shed one would expect to see various different classes, but usually several of any common class. It was rare to visit a GWR depot and see just one 'Hall' or one 'Castle'; likewise one 'Scot', 'Compound' or '4F' was unusual. If the classes were to be found at the shed, one was more likely to see a couple of engines of the same class than otherwise. Many modellers build up as diverse a loco stud as possible; once they have a '4F', why bother with another? A '2F' or '3F' or 'Austin 7' are more interesting, as they are different. My father liked diversity, but felt that a nucleus of common classes added to authenticity. As a result our fleet included three Fowler '4Fs', four 'Scots' and five 'Compounds'. As this chapter

We look past the coal hole at Millbank towards a grimy '3F', No 43822, and an equally neglected 'Lanky' 2-4-2T, No 10823. This woebegone machine is a sorry contrast to the gleaming crimson lake 2-4-2T in an earlier scene. As the shed foreman gives instructions to one of his staff by the coal hole, he receives a friendly greeting from a visiting enthusiast whose clerical garb recalls the close association of the church and steam power, with figures such Bishop Eric Treacy and the Rev Teddy Boston.

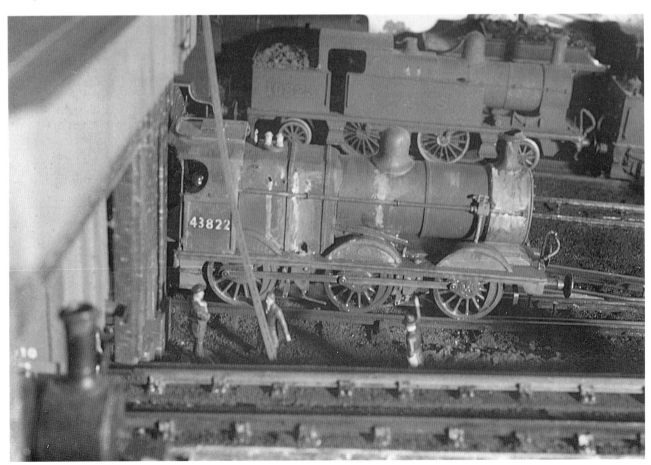

was being written, the latest engine to enter service was a fourth '4F', and another two 'Scots' will enter service in due course, giving us almost 9 per cent of the Class !

Apart from the coal hole, scenery at Millbank is rudimentary at the time of writing. If I was not writing this book, the scenery might make better progress, but it is fun to do both. As we walk along No 6 platform, the main passenger station comes into view. Three of the six platforms can handle eight-coach expresses, and do so regularly. Another can handle six- or seven-coach trains, and two are used for motor trains for a variety of destinations. Had Hillside actually existed, there might well have been a Preston Road, and one of our routes provides a direct express service to Preston and the West Coast Main Line, but the name was my idea, as it has been a tradition in the Hendry family for generations that the middle name comes from the girl's side. Grandmother's maiden name was Preston, and Dad's middle name was accordingly Preston. If one's middle name is Jeremiah, that might seem a trifle doleful for a station name, but that's another matter!

At the end of the passenger station we see a 'scissors' crossover with three double slips, an incredible piece of trackwork, built by Dad for the pre-war GHR in his parent's home in Rugby, and re-used on the present layout when construction began in 1947. The scissors and the station throat, which is at a slight

As GHR 4-6-0 No 301 drifts forwards out of No 6 platform, we see that she has a special headboard and floral decorations for a Special Excursion. The bracket signals above and to the right of her control movements to and from the platforms. The elevated signal box on the left is Hillside No 2, which controls Preston Road goods depot. Above No 2 box is the Hillside driving position, installed in the days when we could afford a separate driver at Hillside station. The scenery was produced before Dad had evolved the high backdrop approach. For a while the cinema, at the far end of the station, changed programme weekly, depending on what was showing at the local cinema in Rugby!

angle, provide the most space-efficient entrance to the station, and maximise the platform length. I had long realised that the scissors was a space-saver, but it was only a casual comment by Dad not long before he passed away that made me realise the value of the angled approach, visible in some of the photographs. Without that, the platforms would have been at least a foot shorter.

Hillside (Preston Road) goods station is on our right, controlled from Hillside No 2 signal box. It can accommodate well over 100 wagons, but yard masters still claim that they are short of space. As it handles numerous trains, it has three reception arrival/departure roads, A, B and C, and without that facility it would be hard to operate. A common fault on layouts is that goods yards have inadequate or non-existent reception roads or headshunts, which would strangle operation. From experience with the pre-war layouts, Dad realised this was a failing, and while the yard master would wel-

A Stanier '8F' shunts fish stock for the Hoggsnorton service in 1963, as an LMS local set is pulled out of the carriage sidings for the morning rush-hour. The station is fully signalled, and a separate driver is able to carry out most shunt moves merely by watching the signals, without a word from the signalman, which is as it should be on the prototype. The existence of an LMS engine in GHR livery is explained by the existence of a joint line in the Longridge area. Like the S&DJR or M&GN, 'standard' types of the day are provided by the parent companies.

come more facilities, they are adequate. Another fault is that 'the goods yard' is often a fan or four or five parallel sidings with no room for loading or unloading wagons. Paradoxically this seems to be as prevalent on the most scenic layouts as non-scenic ones. Parallel sidings with no intermediate spaces did exist, as at the massive Edge Hill grid-iron, but these were for marshalling, and not for public freight handling. The space given over to road access at the LNW&GN Joint depot at Bray Street, and at the GHR depot, are not as generous as we would like, but represent what was to be found. Indeed, parts of the massive GER yard at Bishopsgate were even more cramped.

Our pass gives us entry to Hillside No 1 signal box. We are confronted with an 85-lever frame, controlling movements to and from the passenger station, to Hillside (South) MPD, to the carriage and railcar depot off No 1 platform, to No 2 box, which controls Preston Road yard, and to No 4 box, which controls the facilities further up the valley in the vicinity of Millbank and Exchange. The signalling system was devised by Dad in the 1930s for the pre-war clockwork layout, and although in this day and age of electronics it may sound archaic, it is a genuine mechanical system. Instead of using point rodding and signal wires, Dad used a stout waxed twine, the return force coming from counterweights on the signals, or springs, weights or elastic bands for the points. It has worked for more than half a century, and our first power-operated point was not installed until 1991, and then only because it was to be operated from two places, and we could see no mechanical method of doing so. One tribute to the mechanical system was that a visitor from a club layout, who had watched Hillside during a running, asked what point motors we used, as they were so reliable and so quiet!

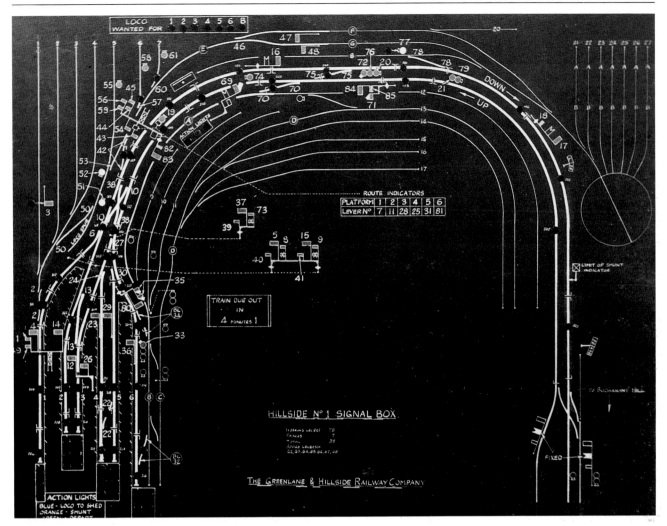

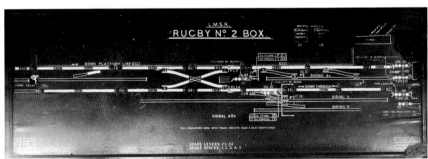

Comprehensive signalling is installed at Hillside No 1, with all routes fully signalled. Once the operator learns the frame, lever frame operation is far quicker and easier than banks of switches, switches on a geographical console, or wander-leads to trigger point solenoids. It also permits the signalman to see at a glance what route has been set up. Where conflicting routes could be set up, all that is needed is a simple twine loop from one lever to the conflicting lever, then only one of the two can be pulled. On the pre-war clockwork layout, this was all that was attempted. On the post-war electric layout, opportunity was

Above Prior to the extensions to Bray Street and beyond, Hillside was a large station, even by prototype standards. This signal box diagram was produced in the 1950s, and as Dad was familiar with early LMS white-on-black track circuit diagrams, he followed that company's practice. All points and signals are shown on the diagram, and the passenger lines are fully track circuited. The frame is brilliantly laid out, and complex moves, although fully signalled, require surprisingly few signals or points. To depart from platform 1 (extreme left-hand side) requires signals 4 and 5, points 6, and signals 16 and 17. To arrive in platform 5 requires points 30, route indicator 31, and signals 83 and 84. At large stations Platform Inspectors often had 'action lights' to the signal box to indicate 'Train ready ex platform 3', etc, so such lights were installed between the driving panel at Hillside and No 1 box, and between Nos 1 and 2 boxes. *Dr R. P. Hendry*

Above left Rugby No 2 box had fewer levers than Hillside No 1, but the family resemblance is striking, even down to the 'feathering' on the platform edges. No 2 box controlled the scissors crossover between the platform and through lines on the down side of the station, as well as adjacent sidings. The direction of travel on both passenger lines is right to left. *Dr R. P. Hendry*

taken to feed power via signals and points; each lever carries an insulated sleeve so that a short cannot develop from one lever, via the metal pull-plate, to another. A metal contact band is fitted over the insulating sleeve and, when the lever is pulled, contact arms fixed to the frame, two or three at a time, are joined by the bridge. On complex circuits there may be separate upper and lower bridges on the lever, joining up to four contact arms in two pairs. For a train to proceed on any route, the appropriate signals and points must be pulled; unless they are, the pulled position bridges do not complete the contacts, and power is not fed into the line.

This method might provide power where it is required, but it might also provide power to where it was not wanted, and protection from conflicting moves would be solely dependent upon the twine locking. Dad's answer was ingenious, for similar contact arms exist when levers are in the normal position. If a train is routed over a crossover, when the point lever is pulled the appropriate power sections are connected up, but the normal contacts on that lever are broken; as power to the conflicting tracks is routed via that point lever in the normal position, power cannot be put on to a conflicting route.

Hillside No 1 frame was built as a straight mechanical frame in the 1930s, and rebuilt with electric power contacts after the war. In its electro-mechanical guise it has given almost half a century of service, which would not be a bad by prototype standards. Some contact arms are becoming worn, as they required a special grade of spring phosphor-bronze, which was not easy to obtain. Spot replacement of a

few arms has been needed, and in the long term one pre-war frame may be rebuilt using modern micro-switch technology which did not exist when Dad designed the system almost half a century ago.

As this chapter is being written, six points in the Hillside No 4/5 box area are power-worked. Three required to be worked from two positions, while the rest were part of an experiment to assess the maintenance levels on point motors compared to the mechanical system. The biggest drawback with the mechanical system is when points are remote from the frame - 15 feet or more. This is a scale 200 yards, and is not far off the distance at which mechanical pulls on prototype points started to get tough! In the long term we envisage following prototype practice by converting long pulls to power operation, to reduce maintenance needs.

Having spent a good deal of my life working miniature lever frames set out in the prototype fashion, and having tried other control systems, none of which give the same realism, I would wholeheartedly recommend the GHR locking frame system developed by Dad from the late 1920s. One of the team started work at Paythorne, which is the only large station where power sectioning is not through the frame but via switch banks - it was left that way as a training post. Since he moved to full lever frame stations, his

Nowadays Hillside (South) shed houses GHR motive power, but when this view was taken LMS engines were still to be seen, including a 'Watford' tank, a 'Prince of Wales' 4-6-0, and a Johnson '2F', the latter scratch-built by the author. The two carriages were built by Tom Hayward in the 1950s, from drawings he made of the Rugby breakdown crane.

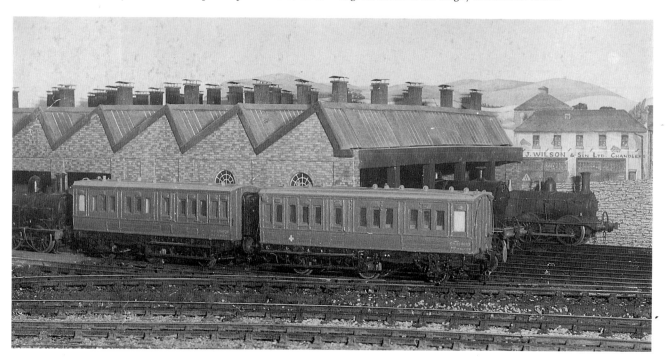

The originals were two of the pioneer WCJS six-wheel sleeping cars of 1874, which we see here in Rugby steam shed at the time Tom was making the models. *T. W. J. Hayward*

ambition has been to rebuild Paythorne with a standard lever frame, but using microswitch and other modern components.

We have almost completed our visit to Hillside station, but we should visit Hillside (South) shed, which provides most of the motive power for trains originating in the No 1 and 2 box areas (Millbank or North Sheds providing power for workings from Nos 4 and 5 boxes). The shed possesses an entry road, at which engines can drop ash, take on coal and water, then turn before going on shed or to the exit road. A fault on model railway sheds is inadequate access and exit facilities, for however spacious the shed yard may be, if the access or exit is cramped, operation is handicapped.

In making this tour of Hillside station I have pointed out a variety of scenic, operational and other features that reveal how we have blended scenery and operation, geography and the constraints of the space we actually have, historical fact and fiction, to end up with a believable composite picture. With unlimited space, time and funds, Dad would have done some things differently, and so would I, but a model railway is a compromise, and what we are doing is to re-create a world we find fascinating in a way that is plausible and will hold our interest over the years. The scissors crossover at Hillside dates from the 1930s, as do some of our lever frames, and while the last of the early 1950s operators, Tom Hayward, passed away in 1994, team members from the 1960s still seem to find as much fascination and joy in the railway as they did 30 years ago. Some stations have been enlarged in that time, but others have scarcely altered in all that time.

HILLSIDE
(PRESTON RD)

2.
A LAYOUT *YOU* CAN LIVE WITH

In the previous chapter we visited Hillside station to see how my father's concept of a 'living' model railway worked out in practice. My father was born in Crosby, Liverpool, in 1912, and his formative years were on the Lancashire & Yorkshire Liverpool-Southport line, and at Liverpool Exchange station. In 1925 the family moved to Rugby, where he soon got to know some of the staff at what had been the LNWR station until two years previously. LYR, LNWR and LMS working practices, a busy terminus station and important through stations were a part of his life. In the 1930s he went up to Queen's College, Cambridge, where he gained a familiarity with the Great Eastern. These early memories had a strong influence upon the kind of railway he most enjoyed, and the sort of model railway he wanted to create.

My childhood was spent in Rugby, and 'Royal Scots', 'Duchesses' and 'Black Fives' became a part of my life, both in model form on the layout, and in prototype form, half a mile away. As we had a model of No 6115 *Scots Guardsman*, it was a particular thrill to see the BR version of our engine for the first time! One of the finest models we had was of a 'Jubilee', No 45723 *Fearless*. Several of the team had seen her, but I always missed out. One day Dad and I were at Rugby shed, and he wanted to take some detail photos of the push-pull gear on a Ivatt 2-6-2T. As I was standing there while he was up on the engine with the camera, I glanced at the adjacent engine - 4. . .5. . .7. . .2. . . and there was the important 3. Within minutes we had found out from the Shed Master when she would be going off shed, and photographed her leaving shed, and taking a train from Rugby to Peterborough.

The 'Jubilee' model had been built by William Walmsley. His father had been a prosperous coal merchant in Stockport and, in common with many Mancunian businessmen, the family lived at Southport. The young Bill Walmsley was not encouraged to be idle, and on occasion was put to painting some of the firm's 'private owner' coal wagons. In the early 1920s he built a sleek side-car for his motorbike, working in the garage, a far cry from the crude side-cars then available. Friends were impressed, and asked if he could make one for them. The neighbours' son, William Lyons, realised that there was a business here, and with Walmsley providing the design and technical flair, and Lyons the showmanship, SS Side-cars was formed, later to become Jaguar Cars. Like many inventors Walmsley was a perfectionist, and eventually the pressure of production as opposed to innovation prompted his retirement, but it was his skill that created one of Britain's classic car companies.

Dad got to know Bill Walmsley, and we often visited his railway. He never found it a chore to make a small child welcome, and when he decided to sell his railway collection Dad bought ten engines, one of which was No 45723. One of Walmsley's friends told the story that he would say 'I think I'll build a "Jubilee" - could you get some plans?'. Plans of locos were not so easy to come by then, and in ten days or so he would arrive with plans, and Walmsley would point to an engine on the layout. It was rumoured that he would go to Rugby, Leamington or Warwick shed, and if the Shed Master did not have one available, they would order one for him to measure up!

One of our operators, Blair Ramsay, spent his childhood in Chelmsford. His earliest memories are of 'B1s', 'B17s' and 'Britannias'. To him, a 'B1' or a 'B17' is far more exciting than a 'Royal Scot', and his opinion of my plan to add more 'Scots' to the fleet, when we do not have a single 'B17', is not flattering! Tom Hayward, a friend of Dad's for 40 years, was a Great Western devotee, not surprisingly as his father was a GW engineman. Eddie Bray, another member of the team, is an LNWR disciple, for although Eddie was born long after the LNWR ceased to exist, and his early memories are of the Stanier LMS, his father had started as a North Western cleaner, and worked his

As a dingy '4F' waits for a path off the down slow at Slack, No 45723 *Fearless* roars through on the 2.10 pm Euston express. The colliery was built by two of our team, Bill Cave and Rodney Woodcock, in the 1960s, using the plans of Arley Colliery near Nuneaton.

Having admired the Walmsley model of No 45723 *Fearless*, I wanted to see the prototype, but while most of our team had, I always missed her, until a visit to Rugby shed on 3 July 1964, when she came off shed to take an afternoon service to Peterborough. She was an accurate copy of the model!

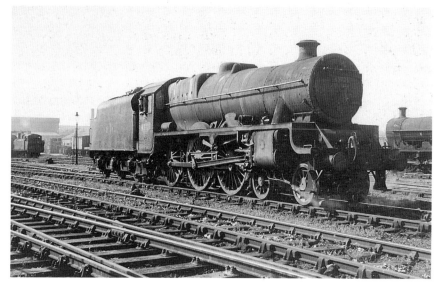

Now that the express has gone, we can give more attention to the empty coal on the down slow. The first wagon is one of the Walmsley private owner fleet, and as Bill Walmsley had to paint his father's wagons as a youngster, ought to be accurate! Apart from the Arley pit near Nuneaton, there was an Arley pit on the Severn Valley, and an Arley coal seam in the North of England. We added yet another Arley pit at Slack, so the second wagon is heading for its home colliery.

Left While my childhood was spent within sound of the West Coast Main Line, an abiding memory is of a trip on the Hythe-Southampton ferry in 1958. At Southampton, as we approached the Quay, we could see a quaint 0-4-0T with safety valves peeping out of the dome. Dad and I went to see if we could have a look at it, but it was the wrong side of the gate, and the gateman was adamant. I must have looked decidedly woebegone, for suddenly he relented, and 'If you're quick' we could go and look at the engine. It was one of the Drummond 'C14' tanks, No 77s in the service stock, and had been at Redbridge sleeper depot, until the withdrawal of its sisters in 1957 led to its transfer to Southampton to shunt the Town Quay. It lasted until 1959.

Below Some years ago Connoisseur Models produced a starter kit for a small 0-4-0T. Although an inside-cylindered engine, it was so closely based upon the 'C14' that with the provision of outside cylinders, motion, and a revised cab cut-out, it made a convincing replica of No 77s. She is used on Engineer's duties on the GHR, and is a reminder of a treasured moment from my childhood.

Above Blair Ramsay tells me there is not enough 'Great Eastern' influence in the book, so to keep him quiet I have included this portrait of an 'N7' at Liverpool Street in 1927. No 970 carries a Hertford destination board, and is on the 'Jazz' service. In fact, the illustration serves several purposes; it reminds us of the need for watering facilities at stations, the inner urban environment with the buildings towering above the lines, retaining walls, bridges, point rodding and so on. Although Liverpool Street would be larger than most modellers could cope with, some of the East London termini of the GER, such as North Greenwich, North Woolwich, Beckton or Palace Gates, offer possibilities of a modest-sized station, usually with an intensive service. *H. J. Stretton Ward*

I pull Blair's leg for his GE affinities, while he complains about my LMS Western Division desires. I bought a 'J69' kit to augment our LNER stock, and after it had been in store for some months, Blair said that if he didn't build it, no one else would, so he did! He did a marvellous job, but far more than a delightful engine, it indicates the spirit of this marvellous hobby, and the contribution made by the GHR team to the layout over the years.

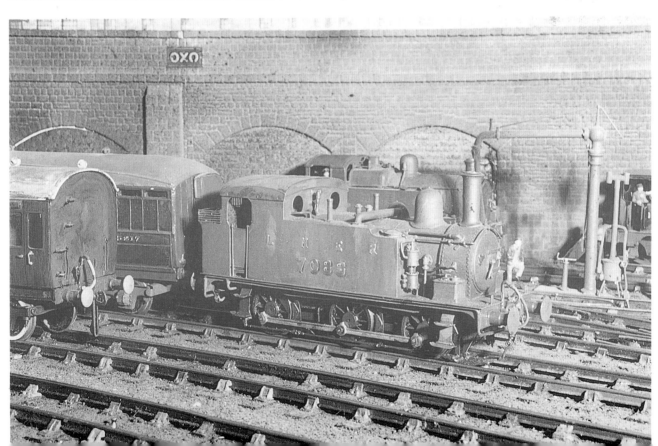

way up to driving, and was a staunch North Western man.

Five people, all with different preferences, and if you took a hundred enthusiasts they, too, would have their favourites. I have called this chapter 'A layout *you* can live with', for your preferences will decide the kind of layout you actually want. A psychologist, if he or she were not of the 'railway enthusiasts are retarded' ilk - and such people should be ignored as not being with it - might say that my father's preferences or mine were based on childhood associations. For Tom Hayward there was family tradition, as well as personal association. Eddie Bray admits an affection for the post-war LMS and early BR period in which he grew up, but in his case the family association with the Premier Line is such that he prefers that era. Our experiences or family associations are often a significant factor in shaping our interests, likes and dislikes, and I suspect that as today's youngsters become the modellers of the 21st century, they will look back with affection on HSTs, 'Sprinters' or even 'Pacers'! But these are not the only factors to shape our likes, for if they were it would be impossible to explain the exquisite models of 1830s, 1840s and 1850s engines

Below Tom Hayward came of railway stock, and his father had been fireman on No 3065 *Duke of Connaught*. When *City of Truro* made her legendary 100 mph run in 1904, it was No 3065 that took over for the second half of the journey to Paddington. Appropriately this photograph was taken on 9 May 1994, the 90th anniversary of that celebrated run. I am sure that Tom would have been thrilled to have a photo of his father's engine, taken on such an anniversary, appearing in this book.

Right Tom's own railway was in a small loft, and I have never seen so much railway crammed into so little space. One of the GHR team, on seeing the layout plan for the first time and without knowing its source, concluded it was of a large 4 mm club layout, and not a one-man layout in a small loft. Tom's principal station included scissors crossovers, double slips and other complexities.

Below right Tom spent his formative years in Newport, and had a great affection for the 'Valleys' engines. One of his most attractive models was of GWR No 39, a Hurry Riches Class 'R' 0-6-2T of the Rhymney Railway, and in the background are some of Tom's GWR clerestory stock. I cannot produce a convincing reason for a Dean Single or a 'Valleys' 0-6-2T in Yorkshire, other than that they were built by a valued friend whose memory lives on, as his engines roll back and forth over our metals. It is not a convincing explanation, but perhaps the best reason of all. I suppose No 77s falls in a similar category, a happy day with my father long ago.

built by Mike Sharman! Similarly, no one would model the broad gauge, and the number of modellers of American steam railroading who saw US roads in the days of steam must be limited.

In deciding what to model, we need to understand ourselves, and ask what aspects of railways appeal to us. The Great Western branch terminus, with '48xx' auto tank, Prairie and 'Dean Goods', has been modelled time and again, often to the highest standards, but I wonder if some of the layouts are not in fact a model of someone else's layout, because a GW branch at an exhibition looked good. If you are genuinely attracted to the GWR branch-line atmosphere, and inspired by a layout in a magazine or at an exhibition, this can work out, but if your real interest is in Gresley 'Pacifics' and the East Coast Main Line, and you opt for a GW branch because it is pretty, in the end it is unlikely to give satisfaction.

The first question to ask is 'What do I like, and what do I want to re-create in miniature?'. You may

be an LMS man, or LNER or Network SouthEast. On the other hand, it may be Colonel Stephens, narrow gauge or overseas railways that interest you. Once you know the answer, you have made a start. If it is Colonel Stephens, his lines were remote, rural railways with infrequent services with a variety of antiquated, and quaint, stock, much of it scattered about the principal stations often in an advanced state of decay - thus the kind of railway you *can* model is determined. A multi-track main-line Colonel Stephens layout is about as likely as a pink GWR 'King'.

Although the Colonel Stephen's enthusiast may have answered most of the other questions in his first answer, for the LMS man, or GW, Southern or LNER, it is not so easy. Are you a North Western, Midland, Lanky or Caley devotee? Is your preference for multi-track main lines, perhaps with an inner urban environment, or a sleepy single-track branch line? Does shunting bore you, or do you enjoy it?

Modellers sometimes stretch credulity, but Colonel H. F. Stephens strained reality beyond what even the most hardened modeller would essay. It was with the Criggion branch train that the Colonel scaled the heights of fantasy, for what modeller would dare to invent an 0-4-2WT, which had started life as a 2-2-2WT, for private trips on the M&GN and GER, pulling a pensioned off ex-LCC horse-tram body as a coach?

This fantastic combination is seen here sitting in the sidings at Kinnerley in 1931. If that were not sufficient, the other two vehicles comprise a Ford Model T lorry converted to run on rails, and the body from one of the Colonels' Ford rail-cars. The services on the Shropshire & Montgomeryshire were sparse, but the bizarre mixture of stock would go far to making up for such deficiencies. *H. J. Stretton Ward*

If you like constant activity, lots of shunting, 4-6-0s arriving and departing on expresses, and the general bustle of a major railway station, then the sleepy branch line with an occasional auto-train and a once-daily goods is not for you. Because the single-track branch terminus is so popular in the magazines, and on the exhibition circuit, many modellers think that it is the key to happiness, and act accordingly. It is rather like choosing your girlfriend because your friend likes blondes; his 'ideal' girl may not be right for you.

What are the options, and what do they signify? Apart from the obvious company and period definitions, we can divide layouts into the type of railway they are, such as the country branch line, a wayside station on a main line, an important main-line through station or a medium or large terminus. Each has its own characteristics and operating potential, and unless we realise this we may discover that even if company and period are right, the layout is 'wrong' for us.

The small branch terminus

For space reasons, the branch terminus, reached off a single-track line, is popular, and is the most common layout on the exhibition circuit. Moreover, its popu-larity breeds a host of imitations, often without thought as to the implications. Often the branch terminus leads directly on to a fiddle yard, and the layout can be operated by one person. This can be a blessing, as it means that the modeller can relax and operate whenever he wants, without the need to assemble a team of operators, but on the other hand it lacks the camaraderie of team operation of a different layout.

The service on many of these country branch lines was limited, perhaps three or four trains a day, rarely more than a dozen. On many branches, services were worked by an auto-train or push-pull, so that there is not even the interest of running round the passenger service. The freight service might be a single daily goods in and out. In the steam age there might be the odd horsebox worked in on the push-pull, or milk traffic to shunt on or off the passenger service. However, to some modellers an infrequent service with minimal shunting *is* the answer. That is what

One of the most popular layouts is the GW branch terminus, with a single platform and a '14xx' 0-4-2T. No 1447 at Wallingford in 1953 typifies such lines, about which thousands of words have been written and from which hundreds of layouts have been created. Picturesque though they were, their limited traffic means that they offer limited operating potential. *H. J. Stretton Ward*

Likewise, the Watlington branch shows the rural setting of many branches, but it was this tranquillity that sealed the fate of so many of them under Beeching. In 1948 Watlington dispatched five passenger trains and two freights each day, with similar arrivals. Although enchanting to model, such a layout carries the seeds of boredom. *H. J. Stretton Ward*

they like. If so, the quiet country branch terminus is right for *them*. Only *you* can tell what will suit you.

On quite a few occasions I have heard country branch terminus modellers say 'Of course the service would only be a few auto-trains each day, and a single goods, but that would be boring, so we do it differently'. Their single-track branch line unaccountably carries a fantastic service, and may play host to highly improbable motive power on through expresses from the City. It gets over the boredom, but is unconvincing. Sooner or later the modeller realises that he either operates a station that is boring if it carries a realistic service, or he operates it unrealistically, which he may find equally frustrating. If that happens, then he has built the wrong layout; with a different choice it could have worked out right.

The busy small terminus

Before tens of thousands of modellers cast forth their ideas of the single-track terminus, let me say that we do not need to throw out the baby with the bath

water. If you want a terminus with plenty of traffic, but which will remain convincing, you have to be selective. Sometimes the passenger service might not be intensive, but freight might make up for the deficiencies. Banbury (Merton Street) served two single track-branches and a cattle market.

There were plenty of small single- or double-track termini that carried an intensive or fluctuating traffic. At seaside resorts there was a limited service to meet local needs in winter, but in summer the local population was swollen by the visitors, most of whom travelled by rail. This necessitated a frequent passenger service throughout the week, but as holidays were usually 'Saturday to Saturday', there would be numerous Summer Saturday extras. Day-trip traffic also reached a peak on Saturdays, and could result in unusual locomotive and stock movements, and in 'foreign' engines straying to places they would rarely get to. For the modeller who wants a single-track terminus, but who hankers for a busy service and a variety of motive power and stock, the seaside resort is well worth considering.

Warrenpoint, on the Great Northern Railway (Ireland), was a typical branch terminus in winter, with some trains even worked by a primitive four-wheeled railbus, but in summer it had to cope with a variety of excursions, hauled by 0-6-0s or 4-4-0s. As loco and carriage stabling was minimal, the station

Banbury (Merton Street) with an island platform and two routes, from Bletchley and Verney Junction on the LNWR, and Towcester on the S&MJR, offers more potential, yet is still quite modest. A Stanier 2-6-4T, No 2591, is ready to depart with a local on 18 September 1948. Despite the two routes, passenger business was light, with about five trains on the LNWR and two or three on the S&MJR. However, freight made up for it, with a substantial cattle trade to the nearby market; the cattle dock is on the extreme right of the view. The timber train shed was used as the prototype for Hillside (Bray Street) station. *R. E. Tustin*

could become congested quite easily. The limited additional facilities make it an attractive prototype for the modeller who is cramped for space.

The Midland & Great Northern Joint Railway offers a classic example of a system that carried an immense summer traffic on predominantly single-track line, although the final approaches to both Cromer Beach and Yarmouth Beach stations were doubled. They were two- or four-platform stations, with considerable facilities, and would make attractive and interesting models. Selective curtailment would be feasible.

The list could be multiplied endlessly, for the seaside resort terminus has immense possibilities. However, there were also a few inland resorts, one of the best known being the LNWR station at Windermere. Today this survives as a basic railway with a single platform, but in its heyday boasted four platforms, a

turntable and a modest loco depot, with an adjacent gunpowder store! 'Black Fives' were common on excursions and through London services from the Lakes.

Small termini with an intensive service existed elsewhere. Until the 1950s the War Department was an intensive user of rail services, with camps scattered throughout the British Isles. Many were served by quite modest stations, which had to cope with sudden flows of traffic, as troops moved in or out of camp. This could involve hundreds or thousands of men in a few days, and at such times a modest terminus could become hectic. As the pre-war army included officer's chargers, ample horse unloading facilities were needed, and movements of ammunition limbers, guns and supply wagons called for side- and end-loading facilities. When my father qualified in medicine before the war, he was posted to Tidworth, on Salisbury Plain, in the Army's 'Southern Command'. This was a major depot, but the station was on the end of a single-track branch of the Midland & South Western Junction Railway, which had been absorbed into the GWR in 1923. The civilian population was heavily outnumbered by military personnel, and freight traffic was heavier than would be expected for a small country branch. By co-incidence, my parents' flat was less than 200 yards from the railway station, and Dad confirmed that it was a very busy station at times.

Above Warrenpoint, on the Great Northern Railway (Ireland), served a popular seaside resort and carried a substantial seasonal excursion traffic. It would make a delightful model, whether as an Irish broad gauge line, or as the inspiration for a British standard gauge line. The station was particularly attractive for its short, brick, timber and slate train shed.

Below At Yarmouth Beach on the M&GN, the loco depot and goods shed adjoined the platform, with residential property nearby. Despite heavy summer traffic, the M&GN never progressed beyond 4-4-0s - to the left is a 'Peacock', which came from Beyer Peacock & Co of Manchester, and to the right a pure Johnson 4-4-0 in M&GN 'golden gorse' livery. *H. J. Stretton Ward*

Above Windermere would make an interesting model and, unlike the typical country branch line, carried a heavy service.

Below Tidworth Camp came into being during the massive expansion of the army at the time of the Boer War, and construction of the Tidworth Camp Railway commenced in 1900.

Worked by the Midland & South Western Junction Railway, and later the GWR, regular public services ended in 1955, but the line survived for several years for military traffic, and as late as April 1962 presented a neat appearance. The substantial side- and end-loading facilities and long loops were typical of military needs. *Dr R. P. Hendry*

A small double-track terminus will not take up much more space than a single-track station. Bath (Green Park) was the joint terminus of the MR and Somerset & Dorset, but despite its legendary status it was compact, and the variety of motive power would make for a fascinating layout. Another small, but exceptionally busy, station was Birmingham (Moor Street). The GW Birmingham main line in the vicinity of Moor Street is carried on arches, but the ground rises up steeply, and the line plunges into a tunnel *en route* to Snow Hill. The new BR Moor Street station is on the re-opened line into Snow Hill, but the old station, which still survived in 1994, out of use, diverged away from the main lines, to terminate shortly before the rising ground. It possessed three platforms, but the GWR was faced with the same problem as modellers, inadequate space, and instead of the customary escape crossovers a traverser was provided. Limited freight facilities existed alongside the station, but given high land values and the viaduct location, wagon lifts were used to give access to the principal goods depot, which was beneath the station. A model of Moor Street would permit an intensive suburban service, freight trains, and a busy main line passing one side of the station, handling everything up to and including GWR 'Kings'.

When Eddie Bray invited Dad to design a layout for him, he said he wanted a three- or four-platform terminus with a carriage road on one platform, and loco and freight facilities. It was quite a job to envisage a station that would justify such facilities, but after much thought we came up with an LNWR version of Moor Street, but as there was no space for the main lines to continue onwards, it did not have that complication. The theory went that the LNWR found enlargement of Birmingham (New Street) impossible (which they would have done), and opted for a new terminus to relieve congestion by handling some of the suburban traffic from the north-east side of the city, much as the GWR had done with Moor Street for the south-west of Birmingham. It is to be regretted that the LNWR did not have our foresight and build Birmingham (City), as it would have been a most interesting station!

Below A former Somerset & Dorset Joint Railway '2P' is seen as LMS No 326 on a Templecombe train at Bath on 22 September 1948. *R. E. Tustin*

Above right Birmingham (Moor Street) with its three platforms was not much bigger than many branch termini, but as a city terminus it carried a heavy traffic, and would offer enormous potential to the modeller with or without the adjacent main lines. The lamp above the station entrance illuminates the sign as well as the entry itself; positioning of lamps is something we often neglect, and there is a good deal we need yet to do on the GHR.

The secondary line wayside station

Like the branch terminus, the wayside station on a single-track cross-country route can be enchanting, and recall all the rural charm of yesteryear, but as the service could be no more than four of five trains each way, which might or might not cross, the operating potential is again frequently limited. After a few weeks of operation, the station could become boring and lead to the scrap-and-replace approach, often

No 5515 leaves Stow-on-the-Wold on 18 September 1948, in a scene that epitomises the charm of the Great Western cross-country routes. The station, in the beautiful Cotswolds, is on the long GW branch from Banbury to Kingham and Cheltenham. Regrettably, the passenger service was in keeping with the rural setting - four trains each way daily. The engine carries a 'light engine' headcode (one lamp at the centre of the bufferbeam) rather than the proper local passenger code. *R. E. Tustin*

Above I suspect that most modellers will have been enchanted by the late Ivo Peters's stunning photography of the Somerset & Dorset Joint Railway. Dad and I got to know the S&DJR at the end of its existence, and photographed Shepton Mallet station in 1966 after the most violent hailstorm we had ever encountered.

Below I intended to include only one view of Shepton Mallet, but the signal box was so delightful that I had to share it with you.

with an equally boring replacement, as the question 'Why was it boring?' was never asked.

One way to avoid this is to chose a line that carried heavy traffic for some reason, or, if shunting appeals to you, where there was a substantial freight traffic to be handled. We have mentioned the heavy Summer Saturday traffic on the single-track M&GN, and the Joint line wayside stations, although small, saw a procession of heavy excursions to and from the North Norfolk resorts. The Somerset & Dorset, which has been made legendary by the books and films of the late Ivo Peters, was similar, with an astonishing variety of motive power as a bonus. The Stratford upon Avon & Midland Junction Railway fell into the LMS camp in 1923, and although passenger traffic was limited, it became a link between the Midland main line and the Bristol-Birmingham route, gaining new importance as a result of the Grouping. The growth of ironstone mining in the South Midlands in the Second World War added to its strategic role, as did the establishment of a major armaments depot at Burton Dassett in 1942. A model of the SMJ would recapture a traditional cross-country line, but with a heavy freight service. For a brief period, the LMS experimented with the Karrier 'road-railer' omnibus to provide a competitive service with the GWR into Stratford.

The secondary junction

A junction of two minor routes has potential, with trains crossing, combining and splitting. Towcester, on the S&MJ, as well as being a junction had a racecourse. Horseboxes would arrive from stables all over the country, and have to be unloaded promptly. Race specials would bring the crowds, and take them back. Towcester would be within the realms of many modellers, whereas Doncaster or Aintree would demand a rather ambitious layout. Stratford-upon-Avon would make another interesting prototype, for

A grimy '3F', No 43520, drifts past the old signal box at Stratford-upon-Avon in May 1951. Although passenger workings were few, locos moving on and off shed and shunting provided plenty of activity. In BR days the great majority of engines were dirty, especially freight and shunting classes, and a weathered engine of this period looks far more convincing than a glossy black machine. One of the greatest modellers of all time, John Allen, did not even paint his engines black. He reasoned that the weathering they pick up is a mixture of red brown rust and various hues of grey, and even white, so he used a dark grey base, adding highlights. Many of our engines are similarly painted. Even in pre-Grouping days, when engines were kept clean, the interior of coal spaces and tender tops were *not* varnished glossy black, and it is surprising how many superb models scream 'model' for this very reason. I have even seen an engine with varnished coal! *H. J. Stretton Ward*

Seaton Junction, on the LNWR cross-country line from Rugby to Peterborough, handled 'main-line' and two branch services, and was quite busy. It saw a variety of stock from MR 0-4-4Ts on the Luffenham motor train, to 'Claughtons' and 'Black Fives' on the through services. It would make a delightful model, and even on the last day, 4 June 1966, retained its period character. There are many details to help the modeller, such as the smoke shields under the footbridge, the LNWR 'pointing hand' CROSS THE LINE BY THE BRIDGE notices, the timbered level crossing, or the cut-out in the left-hand platform for the point and signal rodding from the ground frame that controlled the gates and adjacent signals.

while the junction is merely a freight curve on to the GWR, it was the headquarters of the S&MJ in independent days and retained its loco depot into the 1950s.

Seaton Junction, on the LNWR Rugby-Peterborough line, is another station with a double junction, comprising the original route to Peterborough, via Luffenham and the Midland Railway, the subsequent LNWR cut-off, and the 1890s Uppingham branch. Such junctions, even though on minor routes, can offer plenty of interest, and if additional traffic can be worked in, that is all to the good. The Rugby-Peterborough line saw the passage of the Continental boat trains from the Midlands to Harwich, the most important workings of the day.

The main-line wayside station

A main-line wayside station will carry a frequent passenger and freight service, and for the modeller who wants to run a variety of 'Castles' and 'Halls', 'Duchesses' and 'Scots', 'A3s' and 'A4s' and so on, such a station offers potential. The local service was often sparse, and at Brinklow, on the Trent Valley main line, there were just four down and three up stopping passenger trains, largely because of the intensity of traffic on the main line. Wayside stations possessed small goods yards, served at most by one or two freights a day, and a station of this sort is excellent for the modeller who wants to see trains racing through, but not for the man who enjoys shunting.

For the 'shunter', a station with more freight is essential, and an obvious example is Charwelton on the GCR. While this did not carry the same intensity of service as the Trent Valley, a substantial passenger and freight traffic existed, while private owner 0-4-0STs trundled back and forth bringing in rakes of ironstone wagons from the nearby workings. Main-line freights arrived and departed with this traffic.

We can even dispense with a station altogether, for many large industrial plants, such as collieries, joined

Above No 6200 *The Princess Royal* shatters the afternoon tranquillity at Brinklow as she races south with a featherweight six-coach load in the mid-1930s. To the enthusiast whose idea of heaven is to see big engines roaring by, Brinklow would be ideal. There is an additional up road, traditionally called 'The Third Line', behind the opposite platform. For the modeller who is also short of space, the station buildings carried across the tracks are useful, and have been adopted on the GHR. *H. J. Stretton Ward*

Below Charwelton, on the GC London Extension between Rugby and Woodford Halse, combined main-line services with plenty of shunting, for the Parkgate Iron & Steel Co's iron-stone workings, which came into production in 1917, were served off a connection into the goods yard. Here Parkgate No 8 brings in a rake of loaded iron ore tipplers from the quarries in 1956.

A LAYOUT *YOU* CAN LIVE WITH

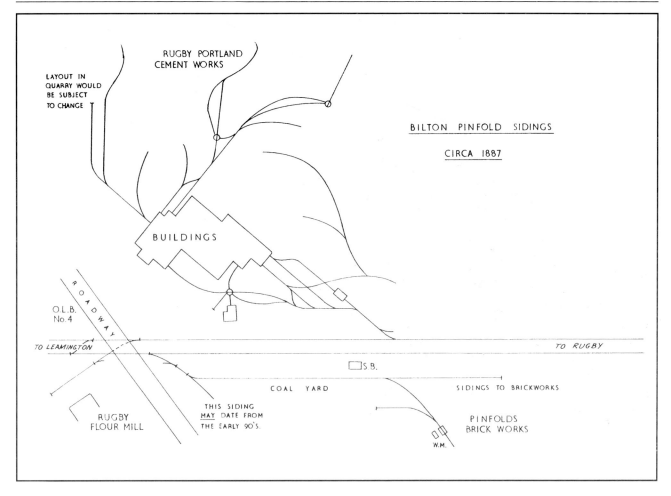

Above left A closer look at Parkgate No 8, which was built by the Yorkshire Engine Co in 1905, and transferred to Charwelton in 1952. She was finished in black with yellow lining, with a brass numeral on the front of the chimney.

Left Private owner engines, such as Rugby Portland Cement No 5, make attractive models. No 5 was built by Robert Stephenson & Hawthorn in 1948, and was painted a medium green, lined in black edged in orange, with a red bufferbeam and side rods. The large dumb buffers were to shunt the antiquated tipper wagons used in the quarry itself.

the main lines away from passenger stations, and while the main-line traffic was just the same, there was the bonus of colliery, chemical works or other activity. The LNWR used to produce meticulously drawn 'Private Siding Books', and we have reproduced selected plans later in the book, for they provide an interesting prototype that is seldom modelled, perhaps because little has appeared in print.

Above For the shunter, Bilton Sidings, on the LNWR Rugby-Leamington branch, would make a fascinating prototype. There was a public coal yard, a flour mill, a brickworks and the Rugby Portland Cement Co sidings, and enough scope to keep the shunter happy for years. As a bonus, the Leamington line was sometimes used as a diversion route, so could see a succession of heavy expresses hauled by 'Scots' and 'Patriots'.

The main-line junction

Main-line junctions can be quite small, and need not even be at a station. At their simplest they are no more than a divergence of routes, in other words a couple of points and perhaps a trailing crossover, but can become increasingly complex until one reaches stations such as Rugby, Crewe or Preston. At the plain junction without any station facilities there will be a plethora of trains, but little station work or shunting. As one moves up the scale, to junctions such as Radley, south of Oxford on the GWR, where the Abingdon branch came in, there are branch trains arriving and departing. Aylesbury on the GCR or Blisworth on the LNWR are larger still, but would be feasible in the smaller gauges. Rugby or Crewe would present problems to the modeller, unless he happens to own a spare RAF hanger.

Left Inverkeithing, on the north bank of the Forth, shows how small a junction station can be, as BR Standard Class '5' No 73106 heads for the Forth Bridge with a fully fitted freight in 1958. The headlights, one above the left-hand buffer and one above the coupling, tell the signalman that the train is composed of piped or vacuum-fitted stock, with the brake operative on at least a third of the stock, so can run faster than the ordinary unfitted freight, because of its better braking power. *Dr R. P. Hendry*

Below left Looking towards Inverkeithing South box, the main line, to the Forth Bridge and Edinburgh, is to the right, while the line to the left is the original route to the ferry port on the north bank of the Forth. This also served the important Admiralty base of Rosyth, which with Scapa Floe was the main fleet base in both World Wars. The goods yard is in a restricted site in the divergence of the two routes, and with both lines curving to the right, would make an ideal model. The running lines are protected by means of the trap points at the exit from the yard. *Dr R. P. Hendry*

Above 'For the modeller with a spare RAF hanger.' After the compact layout at Inverkeithing I could not resist this panorama of Rugby, looking from the gas works by No 7 box towards the passenger station and London, with 'Duchess' 'Pacific' No 46241 *City of Edinburgh* on the down 'Royal Scot' on Sunday 14 September 1958. With over 25 parallel tracks, there are four passenger running lines, several goods loops or through sidings in each direction, and various dead-end roads. Note the ash and cinder ballast on the freight tracks. This is a scene that few modellers can hope to emulate, but even on a reduced scale could make an absorbing model.

Below Few British modellers have portrayed the inner urban railway, with the backs of buildings towering above the station. It has been done brilliantly on a number of American layouts, and perhaps the classic British location is Birmingham (New Street), where the old station was below road level, and overshadowed by buildings soaring skywards. Lighting is required in station areas generally, and not just on platforms, hence the gas lamp by the walkway on the extreme right. Stanier 'Jubilee' No 45681 *Aboukir* departs with empty coaching stock from platform 4.

At Paythorne we tried to re-create that character, and while a good deal of work still requires to be done, the area that has been completed captures the claustrophobic nature of the inner urban environment. Footsteps lead down from an 'over-the tracks' station building, and shadows from a tall building block out the sun. Even the peeling paint at the top of the valance tells a story. What I particularly like in this photograph is the broken shadow cast by the ornamental fretwork upon the side of the building.

The large terminus

Large termini either served sizeable towns or cities, or major resorts such as Blackpool or Llandudno. The facilities would depend upon the traffic handled and the space available, for land values might be too high in the centre of the town. Goods depots were commonly separate from the passenger terminal at the largest stations, and MPDs were often some distance out on cheaper land. Birkenhead (Woodside) demonstrated the problems railway engineers had to face, with a tunnel at the station throat, a bridge across the site near the mid-point, and high retaining walls encompassing much of the site.

If passenger and freight facilities are not separated, they will usually be 'in balance'. In other words, a massive passenger station implies a large community, which demands extensive freight facilities. At seaside resorts this neat linkage often broke down, for while the visitors would swell the local population, they were only resident for a short period, so freight traffic, though heavier due to the tourists, remained light

compared to a city terminal of comparable size. Given the vast influx of visitors, and of specials to carry them, carriage stabling was often generous. At Llandudno, there was significant carriage stabling, but the site, close to the waterfront and bounded by swampy ground further out, precluded all facilities from being concentrated there, and additional loco and carriage stabling was provided at Llandudno Junction. For the modeller who wants a busy branch line but does not have the space for the requisite loco and carriage stabling, this is an answer.

These two stations take us into the realms of the large terminus, and some modellers may throw up their hands in horror, and say it takes up too much space, or would be impossible to operate. The Gainsborough Model Railway Society has produced an evocative representation of the East Coast Main Line, including King's Cross, in O gauge, which repays a visit. There is selective compression, but the layout captures the atmosphere of 'The Cross' in

Above right Birkenhead (Woodside), with joint LNWR and GWR workings into a cramped terminus on a curved site, a tunnel mouth at the station throat, and an overbridge crossing the station just short of the train shed, was a fascinating station. While an ex-LNWR 0-6-2T with an LMS set simmers quietly in the background, a GWR '36xx' is more exuberant in the foreground. *H. J. Stretton Ward*

Right A North Western 4-6-2T, unusually carrying a smoke-box numberplate, receives attention in the centre road at Woodside in 1929. Note the check-rail in the platform. *H. J. Stretton Ward*

Above Llandudno Town was a sizeable station, especially after its 1890s rebuilding, by which time it had five platforms and a wide cab road - modellers may need to trim the facilities considerably. One of the GHR team took one look at this view and enthused over the roof trusses, longitudinal lattice girders and columns, and said 'Modellers, please note'. *Dr R. P. Hendry*

Below An impressive signal gantry spanned the end of platforms 1 and 2 at Llandudno. In common with most seaside resorts, carriage sidings abounded, to hold excursions sets, particularly on a Saturday. As siding space was inadequate at the station, additional accommodation was sited at Llandudno Junction. The gantry reveals the construction of a lattice span. It is divided into equal sections, with the diagonal reversing direction at the mid-point of the span. If there is an uneven number of sections, the centre section has an 'X' bracing, rather than an 'N' or reversed 'N'. In this case there are an even number, but the two middle sections are 'X' for added strength. Smoke deflectors are provided below the span. *Dr R. P. Hendry*

Above A Fairburn 2-6-4T makes a spirited departure from platform 9 at Southport (Chapel Street) on 22 July 1964, threading her way through a maze of tracks and signals. It was stations such as Woodside, Southport and Liverpool (Exchange) that Dad came to know as a youngster, and which shaped his approach to model railways. At a station throat such as this there would be a profusion of single and double slips.

Below A GHR Class 'U' 4-4-0 approaches Hillside (Preston Road) with an up express, as an LMS 'Compound' shunts out of No 2 platform. As with the previous scene, this view was taken in 1964, and although it is a model railway, the mass of tracks and signals reminds us of stations such as Southport. When I first drafted the caption to this view, I wrote that the 'Compound' was 'departing' from platform 2, but on looking at the signal gantry in the distance, I realised that it was signalled into the loco spurs, so is on a shunt move.

steam days. Our own Hillside terminus is a six-platform station, which is worked from No 1 box and can be controlled by one man. It is desirable to have a second operator, looking after No 2 box and the main GHR goods yard, but often we are short-staffed, and the No 1 operator must handle the additional work. This means that freight traffic is not shunted as thoroughly as we would like, but it is still workable. Another operator is required in the Hillside 4/5 areas, but on occasion we have had to dispense with him too. That makes life very hectic, and is the kind of thing that OGRE was formed to combat!

It is hard to say which main-line termini could be modelled, and where to draw the line. Waterloo would present problems, both on account of the number of platforms and the intensity of the service. King's Cross, St Pancras or Marylebone all offer possibilities, but Euston or Liverpool Street would be somewhat daunting. Liverpool (Exchange) or Southport fall in between.

A different approach

So far we have concentrated on stations, but this is not the only approach. Many railway enthusiasts are, in fact, locomotive enthusiasts. As many MPDs for the larger city stations were some distance away from the station, due to high land values, a model of a steam shed, with an adjoining main line and perhaps a small halt, would be attractive. The MPD layout would see numerous loco movements on and off shed, and if the servicing sequence were followed, with coaling, watering, dropping ash, turning, and going on shed or awaiting the next duty,

there would be continuous activity. Loco coal wagons would arrive for the coal plant, and ash wagons would be required. There would be periodic stores vans, and perhaps movements by the breakdown crane.

We have already discussed eliminating the station in favour of private siding connections to a major factory or colliery. A much smaller 'shunting layout' at the docks or a pure industrial railway would also offer scope. Such a layout might not appeal to the man who worships 'Pacifics', but a procession of 'A4s' might not appeal to someone else.

Narrow gauge is a specialist field, but can be modelled on its own or at a tranship station with the standard gauge. Minffordd or Dinas Junction in Wales are examples, as is Barnstaple Town. Halesworth in Suffolk is another source of ideas, while the plethora of 3-foot gauge lines in Ireland offers a variety of junctions, such as Strabane, Ballymena or Ballymoney.

This list does not claim to be exhaustive. The objective has been to ask you, the modeller, what you like in railways, what are the things you want to recapture, and what are the implications. If you love the atmosphere of a sleepy GW branch line, but want the excitement of a main line, a minor branch

For the modeller whose interests focus on motive power, the MPD has possibilities. Perth shed, built by the Scottish Central Railway in the 1850s, was an important Caledonian depot, but by the early 1930s LMS influence was in the ascendant, with a pair of 'Compounds', Nos 921 and 1144, and a Hughes-Fowler 'Crab' still carrying its original number 13183. The number of broken windows at a working shed long before the Age of the Vandal is remarkable. Some of the smoke stacks have lost their rain cowls. *H. J. Stretton Ward*

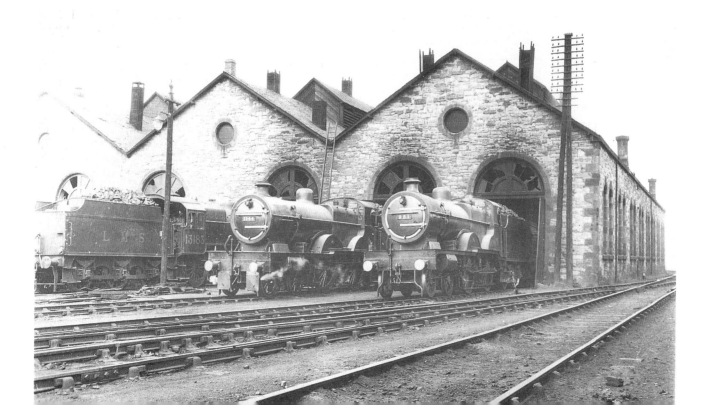

terminus is probably *not* the best for you, nor is a model of Manchester (Victoria). What will probably suit you best is a small GW junction on a route that carried a reasonable variety of traffic, but can be sleepy or busy as you prefer. Radley, Gobowen or Hatton spring to mind, but that is merely because I happen to know those stations, and there are dozens of other possibilities. If this chapter has a moral, it would be 'Think what you want to end up with before you build it'.

Above Coventry shed, depicted here in 1911, was on a compact site, with the 'coal hole' butting on to the steam shed itself, an unusual arrangement. Note the drop from the coal hole towards the loco yard throat, and the 'illiterate' diamonds on the wagons. The wagons have a single brake block, worked from one side only, hence the apparent absence of brakes on several of them. *H. J. Stretton Ward*

Below Although it is 4 October 1964, and Great Western steam has but months to run, this portrait of the cluttered shed yard at Banbury recalls how congested sheds could become. Engines include Nos 4989 *Cherwell Hall*, 6129 and 6813 *Eastbury Grange*.

I could not resist this delightful view of Westbury on 20 September 1964, for in addition to No 4697, we have the GWR coal stage, the shed crane, a liberal helping of ash and clinker, and the fire-dropping pit. Modellers sometimes forget that the steam engine was a dirty machine, producing vast quantities of ash and clinker that collected in heaps between the tracks on all but the most mechanised sheds.

At Southampton or Newport, where there were numerous small 0-4-0Ts, the shunters had their own shed convenient for their work. At Hillside (Bray Street) a dilapidated corrugated iron structure is 'home' for the 0-4-0Ts that work the sharply curved lines. The shed is based on a pre-1914 Hill & Smith design, a firm that made corrugated iron structures to order, ranging from bicycle sheds to churches and tea factories. The gap between the cladding and the ground is not bad modelling, but intentional, as a space was often left to avoid corrosion of the sheeting in the earth. The heap of cinders and ash in the foreground is genuine sieved loco ash.

On the GHR we have two formidable banks and, unusually for a model railway, banking engines are stationed at Buchanans Hill to assist heavy trains to Ponkeston. It requires skilful driving and strict attention, but the same applied on the prototype. Here Nos 47305 and 47502 bank a ten-coach express out of Bromsgrove on to the start of the gruelling 1 in 37 Lickey Incline in 1956. The rear banker should have a tail lamp, but the leading banker is also lamped!

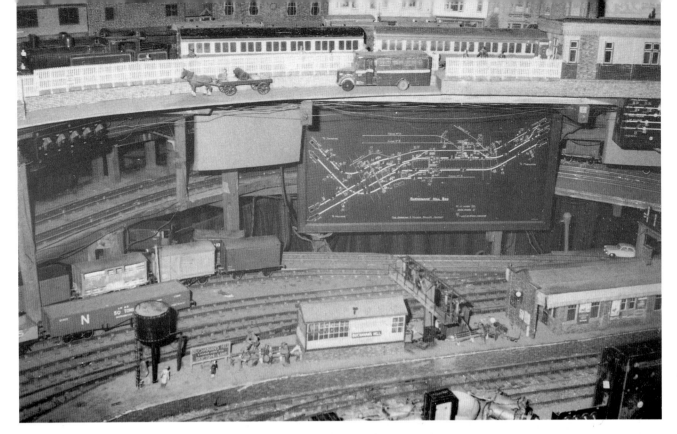

Above This view of Buchanans Hill reveals just why bankers are called for, as the line sweeping round the back of the signal box diagram is the bank that up trains must tackle. A special banking engine bell code, 2-2, is given after the 'Train Entering Section' block message, so the signalman at the far end of the section knows to expect the banker. The top level is Hoggsnorton, reached by a fearsome 1 in 28 grade, but on a branch line that is acceptable. Although the present layout has been under construction since 1947, and has inherited significant sections of the early 1930s layouts, there is much still to do, including scenery at Buchanans Hill. It will probably end up looking like Birmingham (New Street).

Below left Because of the spread of standard gauge metals in Great Britain, narrow gauge was a rarity, but where narrow gauge and standard gauge met there was plenty to hold the interest. In this 1929 scene, taken at Halesworth a few days before the 3-foot gauge Southwold Railway closed, a lady passenger on the Great Eastern station takes a look at No 4 *Wenhaston* as she shunts wagons. *H. J. Stretton Ward*

Below right On the GHR a narrow-gauge feeder strikes north-east from Granton to run up the remote valley of the River Wharfe. The area abounds in limestone and, with rail communication, has become industrialised. A 200-ton coal elevator/hopper provides coal to feed the hungry lime kilns up the valley, while an elevated tip siding offers convenient transfer from narrow to standard gauge for limestone.

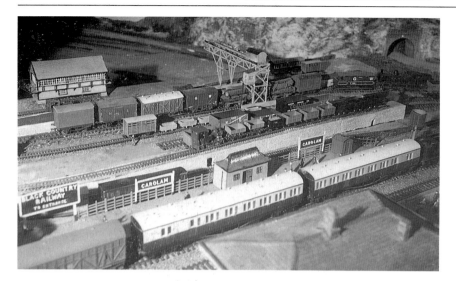

Left One of our friends, Tony Walker, asked Dad to design a layout for his loft, with the standard gauge in the main loft, and a narrow-gauge section in an annex. The main-line station was decidedly GWR in character, with the narrow-gauge section drawing on the Welsh lines for inspiration, though with rather more extensive interchange facilities than was common. The standard gauge van in the right distance came from the late Edward Beal, whose writings inspired a generation of modellers.

Below left Tony is a guide at the Black Country Museum, and has made exquisite models of many of the museum buildings, including the rolling mill; naturally this became rail connected. Today it is only the largest factories that are rail connected, but once upon a time it was very different, and quite small works could be rail-served.

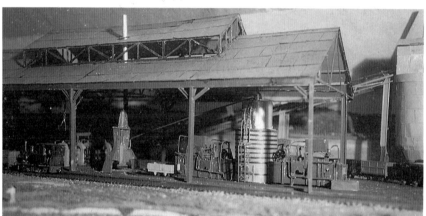

Below Dad's partner at the start of the 1950s was an elderly lady doctor of Scots background, and her husband retained plans of an engineering works with which he had been associated. Dad drew out the works, hoping we might be able to use it on the GHR; the narrow-gauge bogie line, jib crane, travelling crane and varied roof line would make an attractive model. If we do manage to incorporate St Mungo Works, then it will become C. R. Norrie & Co in memory of a delightful and kind-hearted lady whose heart lay in the glens of Scotland.

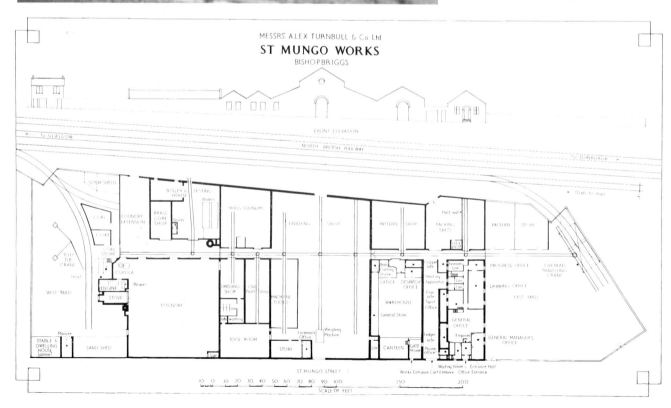

Narrow gauge interchange facilities were required for company purposes, as well as for ordinary traffic, and LMS NCC 2-4-2T No 43 is coaling at Ballymoney on 12 June 1948. The 3-foot narrow gauge line ran to the coast at Ballycastle, while the main line, to the Irish 5 ft 3 in broad gauge, ran between Belfast and Londonderry. *R. E. Tustin*

Mixed-gauge track adds a further dimension, and one of the most complex mixed gauge layouts in the British Isles was on the LMS NCC at Larne Harbour. In June 1948 both systems were still extant, but the narrow-gauge track was destined to vanish, although the broad gauge tracks remained substantially unaltered until the 1960s. Some tracks are pure broad gauge, other pure narrow gauge, and we see a mixed-gauge point in the foreground, a broad gauge point near the signal box with a narrow-gauge through line on one track, and a divergence to the left of the box where broad and narrow split; this requires a single-bladed point. *R. E. Tustin*

The TSS *Princess Margaret* of 1931 is alongside the quay at Larne Harbour. A ribbon of rails for the travelling crane and broad and narrow gauge wagons snake along the jetty. A model with a working crane and all the clutter of a port would be fascinating. *R. E. Tustin*

Above With 124 route miles, five termini and three junctions, the County Donegal Railways were the largest narrow-gauge system in the British Isles. A Class '5' tank, No 20 *Raphoe*, is ready to depart from Londonderry (Victoria Road) station in 1931. She became No 8 *Foyle* in 1937, and was broken up in 1955. The exceptionally ornate valance to the canopy repays study. With the ambitious plans of the South Donegal Railway Restoration Society to re-lay a section of the CDRJC, interest in the line is increasing, and a number of kits are available. *H. J. Stretton Ward*

Below With sparse population, cost-cutting was vital if the CDRJC was to survive, and the Donegal pioneered diesel railcars between the wars. Railcar 14, built by the Great Northern Railway (Ireland) and Walker Bros in 1935, enters Castlefinn station on 17 June 1948. *R. E. Tustin*

Inventing your own line

In Chapter 1 I explained how my father established a geographical location for the GHR, so that it was not 'somewhere' but in a specific location. This enabled us to envisage the kind of place it was, what sort of traffic would exist, and how it would connect into existing railways. This is a theme we will develop in the timetable and freight and passenger service chapters later on, but how *do* you invent your own line?

One option is to look at lines that were proposed but never built, and they can offer a fruitful source of ideas. The GHR narrow-gauge division postulates a line through Upper Wharfedale. The Skipton & Kettlewell Railway was genuinely formed in 1879 to build a line from Gargrave on the MR, via Flasby, Hetton, Threshfield and Conistone. An extension to Aysgarth was proposed in 1881. Some of the evidence given in the Parliamentary hearings spoke of the millions of tons of limestone lying unworked due to the cost of transport. Lead mines were also lying idle. However, neither scheme laid a yard of track. The Grassington branch, built in 1902, served the lower end of the valley, but proposals continued over Upper Wharfedale. The North Yorkshire Dales proposal of 1903 was for a main line from Hellifield to Kettlewell, Buckden and on to the NER Wensleydale and Richmond lines.

The valley section would have opened up immense deposits of limestone, and one of our operators, Mike Christensen, who read geography at university, did a detailed geographical survey of the GHR and the narrow-gauge Wharfedale division. The narrow-gauge data was never correlated, and when I did so I found that we had a line with 1 in 21 gradients, and 1 million tons of minerals a year. This was far busier than the normal British narrow-gauge line, where 30,000 tons of freight was 'good going'. The narrow-gauge division started out with 2-4-0Ts or 0-6-0Ts, but in light of the Christensen Report, larger motive power had to be ordered, as typical British narrow-gauge engines would have been incapable of handling such loads. As we opted for a construction date of circa 1900, as a result of the Light Railways Act of 1896 our line would be opening when the motive power famine hit Britain, with the UK loco builders quoting long delivery times. The Midland, GN and GC all acquired American locomotives, as did the Lynton & Barnstaple. After a brief dalliance with the traditional British narrow-gauge loco and four-wheeled wagon, the North Riding Railway followed suit, adding a pair of Baldwin 'light Pacifics'.

As traffic rose on the narrow-gauge division, and as more limestone quarries opened up, even these were

Rising traffic and the pressure on the British loco builders at the turn of the century led to some exotic motive power appearing. The Lynton & Barnstaple Railway was one of the lines affected, and had to go to Baldwin for an additional locomotive in 1900. She became SR No E762, and survived until the closure of the line in 1935. *R. E. Tustin Collection*

A Baldwin-built 'Pacific', No 153, of the GHR 'North Riding Division', heads an empty mineral train up the valley of the Wharfe towards Ratts Sidings. The narrow-gauge division engines are numbered in the parent company loco list to avoid confusion with standard-gauge motive power, as was done by the LMS NCC with its narrow-gauge power. It is postulated that the narrow-gauge division acquired an American chief officer in the 1930s, hence the US styling of the livery.

inadequate for the heaviest trains, and NBL articulateds and rigid 2-8-2s, and even a 2-10-2, appeared. In this case the motive power was 'driven' by geographical and traffic factors, as is the case in reality. Had any of the British narrow-gauge lines faced the combination of fearsome gradients and 1 million tons-plus of freight a year, this would have been the logical outcome. In this instance we followed an authorised but unbuilt route, so we (a) knew it was feasible, and (b) could follow its course on proposal maps.

You may wish to design your own route, rather than adopt somebody's 'cast-off', and the starting point is the 1 inch Ordnance Survey map, or its modern metric equivalent; the former shows contours at 50 feet intervals. The key to surveying your own railway is to determine your start and finish points. If the line is to connect a harbour 20-30 feet above sea level with a nearby main line 220 feet above sea level, can you do this? To climb 200 feet at a continuous 1 in 60 takes 2.25 miles. If you can trace in a route on the map that

could be built at a continuous 1 in 60 climb from harbour to junction station without prohibitive earthworks, then you have a plausible railway. If, on the other hand, the harbour is ringed by 200-foot-high cliffs, then you may be able to build a cliff-top terminus, but not a harbour branch. If you are determined to have a harbour branch, you must find another port.

How do you know if a route can be built at a steady 1 in 60? You must study the contour lines, which are marked lightly on the map. They swing all over the place, and are hard to follow. You will find little knolls, with 'passes' between them, and areas where contour lines almost meet! The contour heights are marked at intervals, and if you have never studied contour lines before, the first thing is to familiarise yourself with them. Once you have done so, you can work out the start and finish heights of your proposed line, and the trick is to find a route that does not require 300 foot embankments or cuttings, or 5-mile-long tunnels, or 1 in 5 gradients!

If you opt for a ruling gradient of 1 in 60, you can gain or lose 50 feet in every 1,000 yards of route, or a little over half a mile. The Lickey Incline, at 1 in 37, permits you to gain 50 feet in just over 600 yards. On average, therefore, you can cross a fresh contour line every 1,000 yards at 1 in 60, or every 600 yards at 1 in 37. Of course you may cross contour lines more frequently, but the penalty is in embankments, cuttings,

Above No 168, an NBL 2-10-2, shunts at Granton (Crosby Road) station, with the interchange sidings with the GHR in the background. This engine, at just over 70 feet in length, is a scaled-down version of SAR Class '21' experimental 2-10-4 No 2551 of 1937. She is larger than most of the standard-gauge division engines, but would be invaluable on the heavy coal drags to the limeworks in Upper Wharfedale.

Below The largest narrow-gauge engine of all is No 170, a 4-6-4+4-6-4 Beyer Garratt, which closely follows Rhodesia Railways practice, although on 2 ft 6 in gauge. Beyer Peacock provided side elevations of Garratts, but were chary of providing detailed working drawings, as this might help their com-

petitors. In building No 170, I wanted to get the pivot points, cradle and steam pipes correct, and it was only when I found an elevated photo in an erecting shop that some of the secrets of the boiler cradle were revealed. Although it is not possible to see on the finished model, the cradle on No 170 is built and braced as per the prototype. 'Freelance' modelling is sometimes seen as an excuse for short-cuts and a casual approach, but can be very rewarding *if* done correctly. The smokebox door must be able to clear the front platform *and* the front tank unit. The engine is named *R. A. Hendry*, after Dad's father, who although not a railway enthusiast, encouraged Dad's interest and started him on a lifetime's wonderful hobby.

viaducts or tunnels. Cuttings or embankments that exceed 50 feet in depth are costly, and you should start to think of viaducts or tunnels, but these are very costly and will soon make a line uneconomic. If you look at any route in difficult terrain, you will find that it does not follow an arrow-straight path, but meanders around, because the engineer is following the contours, gaining or losing height gradually, but keeping earthworks to a minimum.

For younger readers unfortunate enough to have been brought up on the metric system, a metre is approx 3 inches longer than a yard, ie 39 inches instead of 36 inches. A 1 in 50 gradient, ie 1 m in 50 m, would allow one to climb 20 metre per kilometre.

The GN&GH Bradford Extension Railway has gone through these preliminaries, and Blair Ramsey, Consulting Engineer to the project, prepared a cross-section between Salterforth Junction on the Barnoldswick line and Denholme Clough on the GNR, reproduced here. This is a cross-section taken off the contour lines, with the formation superimposed. Even with a ruling gradient of 1 in 53/54, the earthworks are formidable, but this applied to most of the GNR lines in the West Riding. The most costly works will be the embankment and viaduct at Shaw Gate, to the east of Foulridge, and the 1,184-yard Cobling Farm Tunnel near Oxenhope. I have to admit that we have not gone so far, but the Civil Engineer would estimate the quantities of material to be removed from the cuttings, and required for the embankments, and aim to balance the two. With steeper gradients it may be possible to reduce the earthworks around Shaw Gate, but we have the prob-

lems that every railway surveyor from the days of George Stephenson has faced. Is there a better or a cheaper route, and what is the price, in increased length, or higher operating costs?

A civil engineer will know that I have simplified enormously, for cuttings through rock or soft material differ greatly in cost, while boulder clay offers a slippery and treacherous material that will give trouble for ever more, but there is a point at which it is sensible to say 'enough is enough'.

Finally, one story from the GHR archives. In the 1960s the GHR Operating Department asked for continuous triple track from Middleton to Slack, but as Dad was working on the baseboards the Consulting Civil Engineer (Mike Christensen) pointed out that the line crossed the Ribble valley on a tall viaduct between Paythorne and Slack, and that killed the triple track in that area. The model formation had been commenced, and lay abandoned until it was revamped as the Power House branch, handling coal traffic to a small pre-grid electricity power station.

What period do you wish to model? Like most questions connected with model railways, this generates plenty of heat. I recall one modeller pontificating about 'period modelling' and the need to stick to rigid rules. I asked what period he modelled. It was pre-Grouping, 1890-1914. I forget which railway he modelled, but if it had been the LNWR, he would have had Trevithick 2-4-0Ts, 'Lady of the Lake' singles and Webb compounds at the start of the period, and

Cross-section of the proposed GN&GH Bradford Extension Railway.

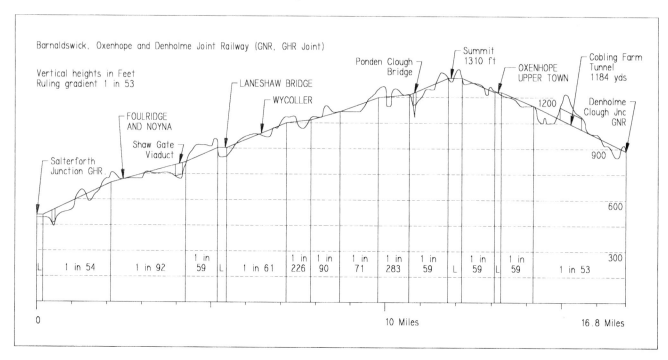

Preserved lines can offer an intensive service, impressive motive power on quite small trains, and a legitimate time-warp, with BR diesels alongside pre-Grouping liveries. A favourite childhood route could be 'added' to the ranks of the preserved lines, and we could run virtually any of the 400 or so classes of steam loco to survive into BR ownership. Here No 34105 *Swanage* arrives at Ropley on the Mid Hants Railway in July 1993. Other than for the steam and diesel locos in the distance, the scene is remarkably 'prototypical' for a preserved line.

'Claughtons' at the end, but those classes did not overlap in service. His period was too broad, and taking a similar period, of 24 years, from 1944 to 1968, one could justify streamlined 'Duchesses' operating alongside 25kV AC electrics! Had I suggested that by his guide-lines we could run such engines side by side, he might have thought I was taking the mickey, and that is perhaps the moral of this story. Your choice may seem logical to you, but before you tell others that your way is the only way, ask whether it is. If you decide that 1911, or 1937 or 1970 is what *you* want, then that is right for you. If you decide that 1890-1914 is right, then it is, and don't let anyone tell you that it isn't, but in turn don't tell them that yours is the only answer.

Dad started out to model the late 1930s, but as it happened most of our Exley carriages carried LMS 1946 lettering, which, although widely used by Exley, was little used by the LMS! As collectors items, we could hardly repaint and reletter them, so our coaching stock is predominantly 1946, though it is only an expert on LMS carriage liveries who could tell! Most of the LMS engines were in the 1930s livery, but when we bought Bill Walmsley's 'Jubilee', it was so beautifully painted, in early 1950s BR green, that it would have been a sin to repaint it. Then Dad had the chance of acquiring a Bassett Lowke LNWR 'Precursor' tank, in perfect Bassett LNWR black. We then had a pre-Grouping engine and a BR-liveried engine, and our purist with the 1890-1914 time-span might criticise, but whereas a Trevithick 2-4-0T and a 'Claughton' could not be seen together, a 'Precursor' tank and a 'Jubilee' could have co-existed, as the last of the former survived until 1940. The liveries were incompatible, but at least the engines could have co-existed.

The purist, though I do not count the 25-year purist in that category, creates a more authentic picture than the more flexible approach, and if that is what gives him pleasure, then it is right for him. I do not have the heart to repaint our LNWR tank or our BR-liveried 'Jubilee'. If I did, I know I would regret it, and as we are having fun, that is how I intend to leave it.

With Sectorisation, the drab 'Rail Blue' of the 1970s and 1980s has succumbed to a bewildering variety of new names and liveries. No 60032 *William Booth* heads a rake of coal empties from Fiddlers Ferry power station into Warrington (Arpley) in 1992. This is a prototype for the multi-level layout, as the lines pass beneath Warrington (Bank Quay) station, then through the Lever works in the background.

No 50002 *Superb* prepares to leave Salisbury with a Waterloo express in July 1991. The LSWR buildings that saw the engines of Adams and Drummond have outlived the Class '50s'. 'Modern image' modelling can blend traditional and new in an enjoyable manner. *Dr R. P. Hendry*

Another example of the traditional alongside the modern - as an HST makes ready to leave St Pancras in 1992.

3.
I HAVEN'T GOT ROOM

One of the remarks one encounters is 'I haven't got room for a model railway'. My father and I were fortunate in having a good deal of space, though not as much as we would have liked, but I look back with wonder on the railway 'room' of a friend, the late Sir Philip Wombwell, Bart. Sir Philip had practical experience of railway operation in the Army in the Second World War, and was appointed by the late Marquess of Ailsa to manage the Isle of Man Railway, when it re-opened under the Marquess's auspices in 1967. Philip was, in every sense, larger than life, full of enthusiasm, zest and ideas. He moved to the lovely Baldwin valley just outside Douglas, and behind the house a railway room was built. It was like no ordinary railway room, for it was an industrial unit, about 120 feet long by 30 feet wide, with a workshop annex at one side. The ground sloped upwards, and the entry was 4 feet below the concrete floor level. Sunken walkways led to a central viewing area, with a passage to the workshop and control position. The latter was a cross between a church pulpit and the conning tower of a U-boat.

In the early 1970s a party from the American 'National Model Railroaders Association' visited the Island, and their itinerary included a visit to the layout. Philip would make fantastic progress, then decide on a drastic revision, and at the time of the visit such a revision was in hand, so the line was not as advanced as had been expected. He invited Dad and I, plus two of our team who were visiting the Island, to demonstrate the line. Philip would be with the party, explaining the layout, and I ended up in the conning tower. Out on the line, automatic signalling took over, but at the extremities the control system was a simple button that I could push to apply power when the train was ready to go. A system of hand signalling was agreed between myself and the rest of the team, so we did not have to shout. On a trial run I found it useful to see what was going on at the far ends of the site (which you will remember was 120 feet long); if I knew what

As the daughters of one of our 1960s team look after Granton station on the left, Ted Boocock, who has made a 50-mile journey to be present, operates Middleton lever frame during the 1987 reunion running. Subsequent to this view, the bare brick wall received a backdrop. This is a narrow loft, yet shows what can be accomplished by careful planning, even in O gauge.

was happening I could prepare for the hand signals. On the day, I brought Dad's field glasses with me, and they were very useful. I was looking through them and had just put them down, when an American voice called out, 'Hey, son, would you do that again? I've never seen a Pike [American for model railway] where you needed field glasses to see it'. I did so, and there was the click of a camera. The rest of the party felt that this was too good to miss, so there must be a good number of photos of me in the States using field glasses to operate a model railroad. I wish I had one of them!

Of course, few modellers will have the zest or financial resources to build a layout large enough to need field glasses, but I could not resist that story in introducing this chapter. For those who do not own an unwanted portal frame industrial unit, or an RAF hanger, space is often at a premium.

Choosing the location

The best place for a railway is a spare room, as a fair amount of dust, dirt, noise and even smell is generated when one is making baseboards, sawing wood, laying track, soldering or painting. Computers and other delicate electric apparatus are not renowned for tolerance to high levels of sawdust in the atmosphere, and wives and girlfriends are not renowned for their tolerance to glue, paint and sawdust in the carpet. If your wife does have a high tolerance to these things, please arrange to have lots of daughters, all brought up in the same way, as this will be good for the railway modellers of the 21st century.

If a spare room exists, that is the logical answer. If not, then part of another room must suffice. A perimeter shelf around two or three walls will provide a sufficient site, in the smaller gauges, provided that you do not want to model Manchester (Victoria). A leaf can be taken from the purveyors of fitted kitchens by boxing in the underside of the layout, so it becomes a furniture unit, with a moving visual diorama above. I have seen plans of layouts that are suspended by cables from the ceiling, and raised out of the way when not in use. I am sure that Damocles did not find the idea of a sword suspended above his person too enjoyable, and unless a ceiling-suspended layout has been built with the advice of a professional builder, I would not recommend it, as the Laws of Gravity apply to model railways as forcefully as to swords.

The loft is a possibility, but again you must take the advice of a builder, who will advise you as to what is safe, and also on building and planning regulations. In old houses the joists were often far stronger than necessary, and would support almost

any weight. In our house, the principal joists are comparable to the solebars of a 12-ton coal wagon, but in modern houses structural timbers are often inferior to what Dad used for baseboard legs! One friend's loft had a weight restriction of not more than three people at any time. Traditional roofing left the loft space empty except for the water tank and any chimney stacks. Today an 'A-frame' is often used, due to the matchstick timbers, and not even a dedicated hurdler would care to operate a model railway if he had to vault over a waist-high cross-member every few feet. I have seen an A-frame roof rebuilt by a builder to eliminate the cross-members, but this is costly, and is *not* work an amateur should tackle, as you may contravene building regulations. Also the roof might collapse. A dormer or gable window can make the loft more pleasant to work in, but these are subject to planning and building regulations too.

While many of these tasks are best left to the professional builder, you may be able to save money by flooring the loft yourself, for the average space is not boarded over. Care is still required, for house wiring is commonly run over the tops of the beams that will be supporting your new flooring, and may need to be re-routed or protected in other ways. In old houses, where timbers were far more generous, and cables were often in iron conduiting, and the beams were often drilled or slotted. When fitting new cables or central heating pipes in lower floors, electricians and plumbers will often drill or slot the beams, but before you start chopping bits away from structural members, *take advice*. Whatever you do, do *not* rest a plank directly on top of mains wiring or water pipes.

You should sheet the inner slopes of the roof, for cleanliness and brightness as well as insulation, as you will probably be standing above all the nice insulation that stops heat going to waste, but which makes the loft darn cold! Having done all this, and added electric light and power points, you can then start to worry about a railway. A loft will commonly slope downwards in two, three or four directions, so the highest point is in the centre, which is likely to be the only area where there will be sufficient room to stand upright; this will determine where your operating aisle is. The lower your layout, the greater the space, but if the layout is too low it is unpleasant to bend down all the time to operate it, and as you will need to crawl under the baseboard for maintenance work, anything lower than 20 inches offers additional problems.

The loft has other pitfalls, one of which can literally involve a fall. Access to most lofts is via a loft ladder and trap door. When you are in the loft, your attention will be directed to the trains, not where you put your feet, and if you should put your foot where the trap is, you will discover the force of gravity in a

In the previous chapter I showed a view of Tony Walker's rolling mill. In this scene we reveal the narrow loft into which this part of the layout must be squeezed.

The coal mine is further indication of how much can be accomplished in a limited space, for that available for Tony's narrow-gauge section is limited. The combination of scenic backdrop, rising ground, and the tracks partially obscured by buildings in the foreground helps to create an illusion of space. The Newcomen engine on the right is based on a replica at the Black Country Museum, while the pit-head is from another Museum structure.

painful manner. The trap must either be barriered off, or have a door that you can lower from the loft. As we all suffer from good intentions, a hinged door is a wise precaution. It would be sensible once again to consult your builder. The size of wood that you can manoeuvre into the loft will be determined by the dimensions of the hatch, and also the height above the hatch. While most modellers can manoeuvre the traditional 8 ft x 4 ft sheet of ply in the house, few loft hatches can take a 4-foot sheet of wood, even on the diagonal, and many will not have 8-foot headroom. It may be therefore that you are very limited in the size of sheet that you can manoeuvre into the loft. If so, you may have to build up the baseboard from a num-

ber of smaller pieces of wood. Lofts commonly contain a water tank. These last for many years, but can need replacing, and it is important that the builder can get a new tank into your loft.

If going up is not possible, in older houses it is sometimes possible to go down into the cellar or basement, but cellars are rarely suited to model railways as they are often damp, so this option should not to be tackled lightly.

If a railway room is unavailable, perimeter layouts or the Damocles idea are unwelcome, and the loft unsuitable, there is the garage or a garden shed. A railway is a more sensible use for a garage than its intended purpose, as you will probably be changing the car in two or three years and it is only intermittently in the garage, while the layout will be there 24 hours a day, 7 days a week. The average garden shed is far smaller than most rooms, but it is possible to build an enjoyable layout even in O gauge.

Some of my happiest memories are of visits to a line built by a friend of my father. Arthur Forsythe was a Scot and a dedicated Caley man, so his layout was based on the Callander & Oban line, of which he had first-hand memories in Edwardian days. It was coarse scale O gauge layout, using a mixture of ancient tin-plate and litho stock, together with models built by Arthur himself. The early models were crude, but he became a fine model-maker and built exquisite Caley locos in later years. It was clockwork, and when the Connel Ferry bridge was in place we were ready to run. Highlight of the day was the passage of the Pullman car 'Maid of Morven'. It was not fine-scale, meticulous modelling as is understood today, but Arthur breathed character into rudimentary scenery, trackwork and a mix of beautiful and nondescript models. It was *fun*. Many years after he passed away, I chanced to purchase the body and tender of a Pickersgill '300' Class 0-6-0 that he had dismantled to provide the mechanism for a better engine, intending to obtain a new clockwork mech for the discarded engine later. As our own line was electric, I fitted a new electric mechanism, and repaired and rebuilt the engine much as I think Arthur Forsythe would have done. When I see that engine run today on the GHR,

it reminds me of happy visits to an enjoyable railway that was contained in a modest garden hut. If Arthur could do that in O gauge, it can be done in 00 or N gauge.

There is always the garden, with or without garden sheds, and many modellers prefer that anyway. Garden railways can be fun, and I have had enormous enjoyment from working on a friend's line. His railway commences from a garden hut, goes down one side of the garden and comes back up the other side, with a number of wayside stations *en route*.

So before saying 'I haven't got room', go through

Below The scenery and much of the stock on Arthur Forsythe's 'Callander & Oban' railway was crude by modern standards, but when the door was closed and the Connel Ferry bridge put in place, the Caley came to life for an hour or two. Removable bridges such as this provide a convenient way of coping with the problems of access doors to sheds or rooms.

Right In case you wonder how much space Arthur had on each side of the door, this is the answer: not a lot. Yet in such cramped confines there was a layout that gave pleasure to its owner for many years, and to those who visited it.

Below right When I rescued Arthur's Caley Pickersgill '300' she was a sorry sight, but she has been restored and detailed as I feel Arthur Forsythe would have done, and is a link with happy visits of long ago. Here she is shunting in Hayward Road coal yard, with the long window-less coke washery and screening plant in the background. One of the team asked who did the transfers for the Caley coat of arms. It was a nice question to be asked, as they were hand-painted.

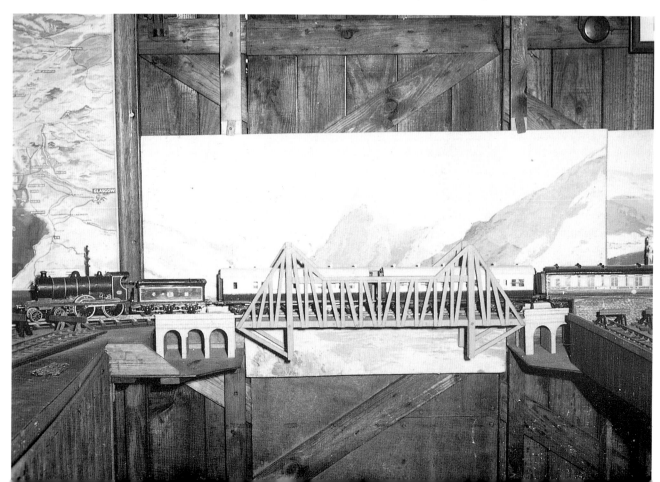

As a regular operator on Martin Bloxsom's garden layout, I can vouch for the enjoyment of this side of the hobby. As with most outdoor layouts, the garden shed provides covered accommodation for the principal terminus, Holt Central. Martin welcomes guest locos, and one of the 'J50s' in the yard is a visitor from the GHR. When members of the Manchester Model Railway Society visited in 1991, Martin discovered the Machiavellian side of the railway modeller, for *all* guest engines were Derby 4-4-0s, 14 of them! Two years later Martin was inundated with TPOs! I admit a hand in these dastardly deeds.

A 'Princess Elizabeth' approaches Holt Central. Outdoors the line is carried on substantial brick pillars or well-creosoted timber uprights. Even so there is occasional subsidence, and regular treatment of all wood with preservative is essential. The tunnel mouth to the right of the shed accommodates the Quay branch, which Martin plans to extend. My father suggested a complete model of the Birkenhead docks, and as these extended for a distance of 2 miles, they could be modelled in a space of less than 250 feet, and there is a field next to the house! Sadly Martin has not yet adopted this interesting idea.

The weather is not always kind to the garden railway fraternity, and agricultural plastic sacks are used to protect the baseboard between runnings, and are kept handy under the baseboard in case 'rain stops play'. If the weather is threatening, buildings are not put out, so the only structures visible at New Woodford are the platforms and the loco shed.

the list, and unless you cannot find space equal to the average garden shed, you can have your own model railway. If you can't, then there may be a local model railway club, and you may prefer that anyway. If that is not possible, if I were you I would drown my sorrows with wine, women and song.

Planning

Having discussed possible sites for a layout, the next thing is to measure up the chosen site, making allowance for doors, which need to be opened, for chimney breasts, mantelpieces, water tanks in lofts, and the other obstructions that the builders of houses thoughtlessly strew in our paths. The measurements should be taken precisely and checked, as it is not very easy to fit a 12 ft 2 in baseboard into a 12-foot space. Dad was meticulous over this. After he passed away I measured up the site for a new baseboard, and when it came it would not fit by half an inch. I had over-estimated the space by a quarter of an inch, and the timber merchant had trimmed the wood on the generous side. I had the pleasure of having to retrim it, when it was already nicely trimmed and squared up.

Once you have the measurements, they should be put on to a scale diagram, unless you are adept at Computer Aided Design (CAD). If you are a pencil-and-paper man, draw out the room on a large sheet of paper, to at least 1 inch to the foot (ie 1:12), putting in all obstructions. If you are metricised you may prefer 1:10.

Once you have the outline plan, take some photocopies, for you will make many changes as you develop the scheme, and if these are on the master plan, it will soon get tatty. You may also want to try a change, and if you do not have to scrap everything you have already drawn, you can compare the two plans, and even add further variants. When we began planning our next extension, I looked out Dad's plans file, and found nine different plans for the site we are looking at. Because of subsequent work at a different level, several were of no help, but others, dating back to 1950, have been very useful during our planning round. The current planning session has a dozen alternatives so far, each of which was drafted, discussed and its shortcomings analysed. One plan offered excellent passenger-handling facilities, but freight working was awkward. A revision improved the freight operation, but made loco-handling less convenient. The ultimate plan must balance all these factors.

A pencil and compass are essential in setting out curves on a drawing, but drawing templates are also invaluable; some manufacturers produce templates for their proprietary trackwork. Even if no template is available, one can be constructed, using card (which suffers wear with prolonged use) or opaque or translucent plastic. The template should have a straight edge, and a curve; the latter should be a bit over 180 degrees (ie a little over half a circle). On the other side, mark out the dimensions of a crossover, as you will use this a lot, and it saves a vast amount of time and promotes accuracy if they can be template-drawn. Once you have your template, to the same scale as the site plan, you can start to plan the tracks.

At this stage there is a conflict. Human beings come in a variety of shapes and sizes, but possess many anatomical features in common. One of these is that arms are not infinitely telescopic; in fact, they have little telescopic capacity at all, which is a remiss feature in the design of the human being, and should be corrected. Until it is, the modeller has to accept it. The First Law of Cussedness says that if a vehicle can derail at the most inaccessible spot, it will do so. Your track plan needs therefore to bear this in mind, and you must be able to get at all tracks for maintenance and derailments. Earlier on I mentioned that we had banished derailments on the GHR, but we do have wheel-to-rail disorientations, and operators will confirm that all parts of the GHR are accessible. It may be necessary to lie on one's back with one's arm groping about above the baseboard which you are beneath, or to assume some other interesting and relaxing position, such as having the head at right angles to the body, but this merely adds to the feeling of triumph when the errant vehicle is recovered. In one location, some 20 years after the line had been started, we discovered a blind spot when a vehicle derailed there (before derailments were banished), and prior to the next running Dad had to saw an access hole to extricate it, and avoid future problems! It would have been far easier to make the access when the layout was designed.

The moral is simple - study what your maximum reach is, deduct a bit to be on the safe side, then make sure that there is an access aisle or hole within that range. The higher the baseboard is, the less your reach, so 3 feet is the maximum convenient distance, unless the baseboard is accessible from both sides, or from on top. I recall reading of one American railroad that had 20 or more parallel tracks, and an overhead travelling platform for maintenance and derailments. On the GHR, Hillside station throat is significantly wider than 3 feet, and the baseboard has been constructed to bear the weight of an operator walking on it. This is not ideal, and one has to be careful to avoid damage to signals and other infrastructure, but it was the only option open.

Apart from non-telescopic arms, the human being

has other drawbacks. He prefers to stand upright or to sit down, and the aisles for operators need to be wide enough to allow for these idiosyncrasies. Even if your layout is intended for one-man operation, it is likely that you will want to show it to someone, so it is a good idea if any self-contained aisles that have to be reached via duck-unders are large enough to hold two people. Passing places are also useful, for if there are two operators in a narrow aisle, you can guarantee that A will wish to get to the far side of B. As the average operator is incapable of levitation, passing must be on the same level. This is another fault in the design of the human being, and should also be corrected.

By this stage you should have a site plan, a template, and some ideas of how you wish to develop baseboards and aisles. It is a mistake to fix this firmly at the beginning, for you may change your plans dramatically as they develop. Taking the ordinary room, one option is a perimeter layout around the walls, with a bridge if you wish to span the door opening. When you come to the electrics, the bridge should be protected so that trains do not race over the open draw, as Americans term it. A perimeter layout can have a depth of 3 feet around all walls with a single centre operating area; this is a convenient operating pattern.

An alternative is to have the layout in the centre of the room, with perimeter access. Using our 3-foot rule, this permits a 6-foot square layout. We can put an access in the middle of a central layout, and this will require a duck-under. The average operator does not mind ducking under a few times in a running, but it is not wise, unless one wants time off work with a bad back, to do so incessantly. If the line is to be run by two or more people, the second area can be 'home'

to the other operator, who, hopefully, will go there when the running starts and emerge afterwards. A perimeter layout with a tongue projecting into the centre of the room is a further possibility, so that we have a U-shaped access area, which avoids a duck-under. In the original railway room on the GHR, we have an L-shaped aisle for operating the Hillside area, and a crawl-under to a separate operating area to work some of the outstations. Operators claim that you can squeeze three operators into this area, but it was designed to hold five. Dad was familiar with the army principle 'Hommes 40, Chevaux 8', and, as MO to the 1st Royal Tank Regiment, with the space allowed to tank crews. He pointed out that the space allowed to GHR operators was much greater than to tank crews, with the added advantages of no engine noise, vibration as the tank rolled along, cordite fumes, or the possibility of shells from other people disrupting the process. Designers of layouts anxious to ascertain the minimum space into which the human body can be crammed could visit the Royal Armoured Corps Museum at Bovington.

For access aisles, a minimum width of 18 inches is necessary, with passing places; a wider aisle is all to the good, but the space may be needed for trackwork or scenic effects. A couple of tables put at the appropriate distance apart will give you an idea of what such aisles are like, and you can widen or reduce them to taste, as the cookery books tell us. Once the baseboard is in place, it is not a good idea to decide you need a wider aisle, so err on the side of generosity, unless you have experience of tanks.

Some modellers say 'Plan your baseboards first, then plan the tracks'. Other will tell you to plan the tracks and then the baseboards and aisles. The right answer is to think what sort of shape will suit you

'Designed for five, but will comfortably hold three': Ponkeston, Buchanans Hill and Hoggsnorton stations are worked from an operating area in the centre of the room. Operators say it will comfortably hold three people, but five people can be accommodated in much greater comfort than in a tank. Lighting is important on a model railway, and many layouts are spoiled by inadequate illumination, which leaves exquisite work in shadow or backlit.

The main access aisle at Hillside is 18 inches wide, and is adequate for an operator or guest to move up and down. However, 'passing loops' are needed for operators. When the scenery for Hillside was produced in the 1950s, Dad had not developed the deep scenery concept, but even so the backdrop was higher than was usual. A new backdrop is planned, and one of the team visited Dad in hospital less than eight hours before he passed away, and showed him some preliminary work on the backdrop, which delighted him. The elevated signal cabin is in the only possible location, but is exposed to knocks; having suffered severe damage, it was undergoing major re-inforcing work when photographed, hence all the structural timbers being visible prior to the cladding being added. Embarrassingly, the repair took some 15 years to carry out, due to other tasks cropping up!

best, draw the baseboard lines in, then try the track pattern and scenic effects you need, bearing in mind that you can revise the baseboard at this stage, as it only needs an eraser. You may try a variety of different baseboard patterns before arriving at the right one. There is no point in my saying that it should be X, Y or Z, because room sizes differ, our ideal plans differ and there are different gauges. That leads me to another point. Plans sometimes appear in magazines and are said to be suitable for various gauges. The track plan may be sufficient, but if the aisle is right for O gauge, it will be a bit tight for 4 mm, and will require operators to go on a starvation diet in 2 mm. If the aisle is OK for 2 mm, a vast amount of space is wasted in 7 mm, unless your operators are all 20-stone giants.

As you develop the plan, you will find that unless you have something like Sir Philip Wombwell's railway 'room', you may not be able to get in all you want. It may be that if you rearrange things, you can do so. On the first of our Bradford Extension plans, I had five loops. I looked at Dad's plans, and found that he had seven loops, which were longer than mine, merely by slightly altering their start and end posi-

tions. If I had said 'Five is all we can do', I would have under-utilised the space. Merely because it does not fit on the first attempt, do not assume that it is impossible. It may be, but with a slight change it might be feasible.

If you are modelling a prototype station, it will probably be too long and will need shortening. As model railway curves are much sharper than on the prototype, there is a margin. It may be necessary to reduce the width of roadways and sidings, or even omit sidings altogether, provided this does not destroy the character of what we are creating. If, for example, the prototype had an eight-road loco shed, and we reduce it to six, our model is not strictly accurate, but the character is not destroyed. If we reduce it to a two-road shed, then the gap between the model and the prototype is too vast, and we must think of something else.

If we create our own station, as many of us do, then we are not chained to the prototype in the same way, *but* if our layout is to make sense, the stations should reflect prototype practice. A weakness of many layouts is that while modellers take immense pains to get locomotives and carriages exactly right, and would

not dream of building a loco without drawings and photos, they will design a station without considering how station layouts evolved in practice. On layouts of the highest workmanship I have seen features that would never have been tolerated by the Board of Trade Inspecting Officers, or a professional railwayman. In chapter 4 we will look at how stations evolved, and some of the dos and don'ts.

Once you have a track plan it is useful to try out in your mind how each move will be accomplished. For example, how does a passenger train arrive in the station? How does it depart? Have you forgotten a crossover, so that trains cannot depart from some platforms? What about loco movements to and from the shed? How awkward are they, and do incoming moves conflict with outgoing moves? Can freight trains arrive and depart? A problem with one of the Bradford Extension plans was that the passenger and loco side were excellent, but freight handling was awkward. It is easy to change at the planning stage, but difficult when the track is in situ. Layout design is a compromise, and you may have to accept some restrictions, or move to a bigger house. On the other hand, if the compromise is a fundamental flaw that makes operation difficult, then the plan is wrong, and needs replacing.

An example of the skill that went into the design of the Hillside station area by my father was that

when the line was being built in the early 1950s, it was in one room, had some 30 engines, and a couple of hundred vehicles in total. It has expanded to a second room and two attics, and there are 150 engines in the fleet and 1,200 vehicles. The extensions beyond the old part of Hillside provide new carriage sheds, loco facilities, a coal yard and goods depot, but in the main station area the only change necessary in over 40 years has been one additional crossover in the goods yard to facilitate shunting. It is useful, but was not essential. Hillside can handle far more traffic today than was dreamed of when the line was built, yet the design has the flexibility to cope without significant alterations.

Some modellers say that on the prototype the scenery was there first, so you should plan your scenery and then your tracks. Others will say the exact opposite. Again, I believe the right answer is to consider both, and as a part of our scenery will be a low-relief backdrop or scenic sheets, it is a good idea to take the track plan, photocopy it, then forget about the room confines and sketch in the scenery that lies beyond. If we only take our planning up to the wall, then we are creating a three-dimensional image in two dimensions. If we expand the scenery beyond the room, although we cannot put it there, we can see if it makes sense or not. If it does not, then we will have avoided making a glaring mistake. If it does make

Dunstall Park station served the industrial quarter of Wolverhampton, and from the platforms passengers had a superb panoramic view of the gas works. These two adjoining views offer a vast amount of detail to the modeller. In this case we see low structures in the foreground, with the gas holders and taller buildings in the distance. This would have made a wonderful panorama for Hillside, but for space reasons I had to reverse the order, with the tall buildings in the foreground.

sense, then we will probably have a better idea of how to convert that three-dimensional ground plan into a two-dimensional vertical backscene.

When designing Hillside gas works, I collected plans and photos of gas works and sketched out our trackplan and the walls and chimney breast we were stuck with. I then said 'What happens here?'. Coal has to be unloaded, using bottom-door wagons. Is it taken by a conveyor to a coal store to provide a strategic reserve, or to the retort house for immediate use? The hot coke is discharged from the retort house, quenched, screened, sorted, and some used for internal purposes in a water gas plant, while some is sold locally for road delivery, and some goes out by rail. What happens to the gas? You may say 'Who cares?', as it goes along pipes to the consumers. It does matter, for the gas that comes from the retort house is hot and impure. It passes through coolers, purifiers and scrubbers, and then into gas holders. In the cooling and purification process, tar and ammoniacal liquor

are produced, and will be shipped out by rail. The volume of these products, compared to the coal and coke, is small, so the siding space to handle them is limited. A short siding had been provided for this purpose, and it was an obvious site to locate the appropriate part of the plant. My gas works is not perfect, but given the constraints it was the best we could do and, I believe, is workable. It would have been nice to have modelled a gas holder, but we had to be content with two-dimensional examples on the backdrop.

One of the substances used in purification is iron ore, and occasional shipments of iron ore are needed; this is one reason for the Bleichert grab. The spent iron ore is an unpleasant substance with a high sulphur content, and is called bog ore. It has splendid weed-killing properties, and was tried out on railways as ballast. It killed weeds, but the sulphur meant that in wet conditions it produced an acid solution which was not beneficial to the rails, let alone timber sleepers. Its volatile content meant that it was also combustible, and combustible ballast is not a good idea. Quenching the ballast with water did not put out the flames, but produced some excellent acid gas clouds. Thankfully our model gas works does not produce any bog ore, so we are relieved of the need to dispose of it, though we should work a wagon in every so often to take the stuff away!

I have outlined the development of Hillside gas

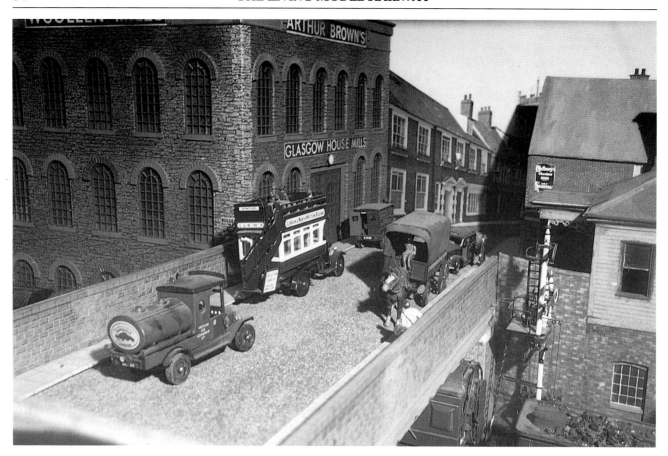

Above The scenic treatment at Ponkeston characterises the 'beyond the walls' scenic approach. The station building on the right is a 3D model of the LNWR's Kilsby & Crick station, and the shop behind it is a 3D model. Arthur Brown's Glasgow House woollen mill is a low-relief model masking the chimney breast, while the bridge in the foreground begins to angle, then merges into the backdrop of an angled street scene.

Left This photograph was actually taken to show the English Electric experimental 'Deltic' entering Carlisle, but the scenic treatment is of particular interest. See how the prototype follows the Ponkeston plan, with an overbridge at one end of the station, and Little & Ballantyne's premises rising up above road level. The only thing missing is the chimney breast!

works beyond the confines of the room to illustrate the benefits to be derived from the 'expanded' approach. Road and building patterns can be worked out, and a tiered scenic backdrop developed that will make sense. Once the track plan makes sense, the aisles and access work out, and the expanded scenic plan is plausible, we can start to cut wood for baseboards. It sounds a formidable exercise, and one is tempted to take short-cuts, but time expended at this stage is often repaid amply later on.

4.
HOW *NOT* TO DESIGN YOUR STATION

I have decided to open this chapter on station design with a drawing of a locomotive! It is a pre-1914 Bassett Lowke plan of a 'Precursor' 4-4-0, or what Bassett Lowke was pleased to call a 'Precursor'! Bassett Lowke was one of the leading model-makers of its day, yet a manufacturer producing such a model now, and submitting it for review, could expect scathing comments; today we expect high standards of accuracy from the most humble ready-to-run model. The model railway industry has come a long way in the last 90 years, and had it not been for pioneers such as W. J. Bassett Lowke, or R. F. Stedman, the modellers of yesterday would not have had the basic equipment to make a start and to inspire the modellers of today.

Rolling-stock and scenery have made comparable advances, yet there is one area in which we have made little progress in the past nine decades. If one looks at photographs and plans of the very early layouts, stations were often peculiar. Sadly, some of the layouts in magazines or on the exhibition circuit today show little improvement on the pioneers, and

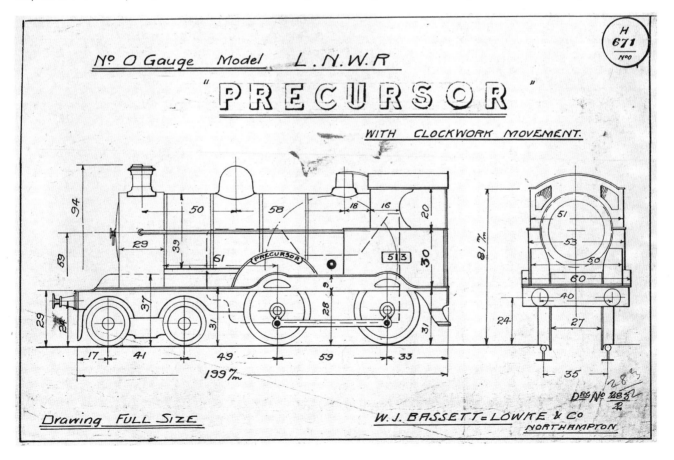

track plans that would have given the BOT Inspecting Officers a heart attack are encountered. This is a pity, for it detracts from realism, and layouts that are badly designed are often difficult to operate properly and necessitate unrealistic working methods, and this can lead to boredom.

I have often wondered how some model railway stations bear so little resemblance to the real thing. I suspect that there are a number of reasons. If we are building a GWR 'King', we obtain drawings and photographs, and few modellers would dare to build a loco 'from memory'; I know what a 'Hall' is like, but I would not care to vouch for the accuracy of a model I built using memory as my sole guide. When designing a station, I suspect that some modellers say 'I know what a station is like', and do not consult a single plan in devising their layout.

I also believe that many modellers are inspired by layouts seen at exhibitions or in magazines. If one man's creativity inspires someone else to have a go at this wonderful hobby, that is good, but what sometimes happens is that a modeller has built a layout, and although the scenery may be magnificent, the track plan may be good or bad; another modeller is inspired to follow suit, but instead of making a model of a railway station, he makes a model of the other model. Even if it is a slavish imitation, it will contain the compromises of the first model, and if it is not, compromise and error may be heaped upon compromise and error. If the first chap exhibits his layout, and the second is inspired to follow suit. . .!

The advice given to a modeller when building an engine is to obtain drawing and photos of the prototype. The pundit who suggested that you borrow Fred Smith's model, and work from that, would be regarded as eccentric, for any error in Fred's model will be reproduced in yours. If that is then loaned out again. . .! This principle is as valid for stations as for locomotives. It does not mean that we should not seek inspiration from others - far from it. I have seen brilliant ideas on other layouts, some of which we have adopted, but if we are to build a convincing model let us remember that the answer is to model the real thing, not someone else's impression of that reality.

Basics of a station layout

How, then, do we devise a sensible station layout? The principle is the same as for any railway equipment. First of all, what do we want? Is it a large terminal, a major junction, a wayside station or a small branch terminus? Until we know that, we are in the position of the man who does not know whether he is building an 'A4' 'Pacific' or a 'Y4' 0-4-0T. Once we know what engine we want to build, we obtain plans.

Once we know what sort of station we want, it is sensible also to look at plans. At first sight this is difficult, for while BR inherited some 400 classes of engine, it inherited thousands of stations, so how do we select the track plan we need?

In fact, it is not so daunting. Of the thousands of stations and depots, many hundreds were similar, and we do not need to confine ourselves to a specific railway, for the problems confronting a GWR civil engineer in designing a station mirrored those before a Caley man. While plans of a CR 'Cardean' 4-6-0 would be of little use in building even a different Caley 4-6-0, let alone a GWR 'Hall', a trackplan of a Caley station may give us ideas for a GW layout, and vice versa. We cannot carry this too far, for the stations on the Highland 'Farther North' line would naturally be of little use to anyone modelling the LSWR suburban network.

We will therefore look at several stations and discuss various features, but before we do so, what factors influenced station layouts? A station, whether passenger, or goods, was a place where the railway made contact with the public. With few exceptions, road access was mandatory. Except at the smallest halts, there was a booking office, waiting rooms, toilets and platforms. In the earliest days passengers crossed the lines using barrow-ways, but on busy lines footbridges appeared, and became a BOT requirement for new lines or major rebuilding work. However, stations on minor lines, or where there had been little change in many years, might never boast a footbridge. As existing roads had to be crossed by level crossing or bridge, the station was often located where this occurred, as it saved building long access roads. While many stations do not possess either feature, a substantial proportion do.

Above right There is no such thing as a 'typical' railway station, as every station possessed its own character, but Byfield, on the S&MJ, is a classic example of the minor wayside station on a single-track branch. The main building is on one side and a modest shelter suffices on the other platform. The yard connections trail in from the left. There are two sidings, with a crane in the divergence, and the sidings are well separated. The signal box is on the platform, near the yard connections but sufficiently central to work the points at each end of the passing loop. A road overbridge spans the tracks at one end of the station.

Right Slack station, in its exhibition guise prior to industrialisation, displayed these common features as well. In this case there is an island platform, where the signal box is situated. On the right is a trailing refuge siding. There is an overbridge in the distance, and road access to the goods yard on the right. The sidings are well separated, and a lorry has driven from the goods shed and paused by the weighbridge hut. Slack has changed so dramatically in its permanent location, with the addition of a colliery and chemical works, that one member of the team with 25 years experience of the line only recognised the station after careful study of the track layout. *Dr R. P. Hendry*

Some stations only offered passenger facilities, and this included the smallest and largest. There were separate goods stations as well, but most stations handled both goods and passengers. The goods yard was under the supervision of the station master or a goods agent. For effective supervision, and to simplify shunting, goods facilities were commonly grouped together. There was provision for unloading wagons, in other words space between the tracks for road vehicles. Some commodities would be damaged by exposure to rain, or might need storage until collection, and all but the smallest stations had a goods shed, which would also often house the agent's office. Cattle and sheep were moved by rail, and required livestock pens for loading and unloading. Other than at the smallest stations, a crane was usual. This might be inside the goods shed or outdoors, and would usually vary from 1.5 to 5 tons. At many stations coal was handled at the general yard, with ground rented out to merchants for stacking. The local coal merchant's 'office' might be a hut in the goods yard. In some places a separate coal yard was provided. In the North East, primarily on the NER but also at some GCR and LNWR stations, elevated tracks were carried over coal drops or coal cells, and bottom-door

Above left No 2835 heads west through Warwick in 1955 on an iron ore train from the Oxfordshire ironfields to the Black Country, as a short freight shunts in the yard. The coal stack is supported on the left by large stacked lumps, but has its natural angle of repose to the right. The wide separation of the yard tracks on the right is often overlooked by the modeller. The '6-foot way' between running lines is increased to about 10 feet between running lines and sidings for safety reasons, something often overlooked in layout design. *H. J. Stretton Ward*

Left The signalman at Hatton South box has set a clear road for No 5634 on a humble 'pick-up' goods in 1947, and Hatton North has cleared his distant, telling us that the train is routed for the Birmingham line. When I selected this view it was to illustrate a typical 'end of the platform' location for the horse and carriage landing (on the far side); there is even a horsebox there. However, there is much else to interest the modeller. The upper or starting arms on the bracket on the left are omitted, but the distant signals are visible. The arm on the left is the main-line distant for Hatton North, and is giving a typical GWR 'off' indication. The arm on the right is for the Stratford line, and as this was on a tight curve with speed restrictions, the distant is fixed at danger; it does not have the usual spectacle plate or pivot point. The bracket signal is secured by various stay wires, one going to the post on the right, the tensioning turnbuckle being visible by the post. The diamond plate below the wooden platform of the right-hand signal indicates that the signal is 'Rule 55 exempt'; in other words, it is track circuited, so the fireman does not have to go to the box to remind the signalman of the train if it is held for a few minutes. This right-hand bracket controls movements out of the near platform, and in this case both Distants are fixed. The dark blue paving bricks in the platform and point rodding runs also merit study. *H. J. Stretton Ward*

wagons used. Discharge was rapid, and it is astonishing that such methods did not become universal, but they did not. Coal cells would be appropriate for a layout in the North East, but unlikely in Cornwall or the Home Counties. This is one instance where plans for a station on a particular railway may not suit another.

Horse and carriage traffic was heavy, but was rated as passenger traffic and was often conveyed on passenger trains rather than freight services. A horse and carriage dock would often trail in at one end of the passenger station; often it was at the same end as the yard.

When railways appeared in the 1820s and 1830s they were a novelty, and engineers and operators discovered by trial, error and catastrophe what was sensible. Early accounts speak of pilot engines helping trains out of Euston, uncoupling then running ahead of the train and into a facing siding, the point being returned as soon as the tender was clear to route the express on to the main line! This was *not* safe, and by the 1850s a fear of facing points had developed. The BOT Inspecting Officers, who examined every new line or alteration prior to passing it for traffic, were adamant in their opposition to facing points, except where unavoidable at, for example, junctions or where there were several platforms. But facing connections into non-passenger lines were abhorred. Until facing point locks were developed, this fear was justified, though inconvenient. Slow-moving freight trains would hold up expresses unless they could be shunted clear of the running lines, but rather than provide facing connections into goods loops, trailing refuge sidings were used, involving a time-consuming reversal. It was only in the 20th century that the fear of facing connections weakened, and finally vanished.

At first points were worked by 'pointsmen' or 'policemen', who gave the appropriate hand signals to drivers. Later a signal on a post was found to be more conspicuous and could show a steady indication. Gathering point and signal levers together permitted more efficient operation, and reduced manpower, and in due course the levers controlling conflicting moves were locked against one another in these new signal boxes; this became mandatory after 1889.

The signal box had a marked effect on the shape of stations, for BOT requirements laid down a maximum distance at which facing points could be worked from a box. On a single line the box was usually located at the centre of the station, to permit the maximum length of loop. On railways such as the Highland, where long trains needed to be operated in season, this was insufficient, so the alternative was a box at each end of the loop; usually one box was small, controlling just the loop points, as all goods facilities were at the other end of the station.

On double-track lines it was usual to have the box at one end of the platforms, with the goods facilities grouped together on one side of the line beyond the platforms. If the yard was fairly long, the box might be some distance from the platforms, at about the mid-point of the yard.

At a terminus the box would have a good view of the station throat. This minimised the length of point pulls and simplified shunting. At large stations it was impossible to bring all connections within range of a single box, and two of more boxes were used; the LNWR provided no fewer than *seven* boxes to control the Rugby station area. Individual signals might be worked from two or more boxes, by a process called 'slotting'. Similarly, points might be worked by one box, but with a lock lever in another box that had to be pulled first.

Level crossings required protection, and the box was often by the gates, which were worked manually by the signalman, or opened by a geared gate wheel in the box located by the window overlooking the road. At Seaton Junction, on the LNWR Rugby-Peterborough line, there was a level crossing at the west end of the station, and a double junction at the east end. As the points were mostly at the east end, that was the logical site for the box, so the level crossing was worked by the station staff and controlled from a ground frame, the levers of which were interlocked from the signal box.

Until we understand something of the steam locomotive, it is difficult to see why a designer adopted specific features. Why were the driving wheels on express engines bigger than on freight locos? Why were shunting tanks rarely superheated? Once we know the background, we can appreciate the ideas in the designer's mind. With stations it is similar, and

Oxford (Rewley Road) signal box was perfectly located at the station throat of this two-platform LNWR terminus. The signalman had an excellent view and point runs were kept to a minimum, both to comply with BOT rules and to make for easier working. Rewley Road was an important depot for Anglo-American Oil and other companies, with two long sidings on the north side of the station. The Great Western main line is to the left, and beyond that the GWR timber-built loco sheds. The roof of the two-road LNWR 'northlight' MPD is to the left of the far rake of tank wagons. *H. J. Stretton Ward*

A small ground frame handled the gate locks and signals protecting the level crossing at Seaton Junction on the LNWR, as the signal box was at the far end of the station where the lines diverged. The 'stirrups' on the front of the levers were an LNWR peculiarity, instead of the usual catch handle at the rear.

once we discover the constraints that faced the civil engineer, we can see why a station evolved in a particular way. The Board of Trade rules set out the important issues:

Catch points to be provided at junctions of passenger tracks with goods lines or sidings.

Junctions at stations to be formed so as to avoid standing passenger trains on them if possible. [Instances exist where this was not the case.]

Junctions between a double and a single line to be formed as a double line ordinarily, combining as single track after the divergence.

At termini, double track lines shall not become single track.

Platforms to be not less than 6 feet wide at minor stations, and preferably 12 feet at larger stations. Ends to be ramped. Pillars, buildings and other fixed objects to be not less than 6 feet from the platform edge. [Fenny Compton on the S&MJ did not comply when the line was built or during the rest of its 80-year passenger history!]

Minimum acceptable platform height [by 1908] is 2 ft 6 in, and preferably 3 ft 0 in. Platform ramps, subways, etc, to be not steeper than 1 in 8. Landings on any steps over 10 feet.

Footbridges or subways at any new station unless on a very minor line/light railway.

No stations on gradients steeper than 1 in 260 if avoidable. Where steep grades exist, runaway catch points/sidings to be provided.

Turntables at termini and junctions unless there is an undertaking to use tank engines or stop trains at all intermediate stations.

Check rails on all curves of 10 chains or less.

Interval between adjacent tracks not less than 6 feet, increasing to 9 ft 6 in for additional running lines, sidings, etc, if possible.

Facing points to be not more than 200 yards from the lever or 250 yards if the bolt lock can be detected as well as the points. Trailing points and traps on goods lines 300 yards.

Level crossings over public roads to close across road or railway. Gates must not open outwards towards the road, but towards the railway. A red disc or target to be fixed on the gates with lamp for night-time.

On occupation crossings the gates to open outwards, ie away from railway line [as these crossings were unstaffed].

Distant, home and starting signals for passenger lines. Extra signals into and out of bay, etc, passenger lines. Crossovers and all connections to be protected by signals.

Sample locations

Perhaps we could design convincing stations without further reference to the prototype, but to emphasise the message, and to provide a nucleus of ideas, let us now look at photographs and plans of a number of actual locations.

A Johnson '2F' blows off at the head of a Stratford-bound local at Ettington, on the Stratford-upon-Avon & Midland Junction Railway, in 1929. This is a classic single-track station, with the box located part-way along the loop, and the yard at one end of the site. The road overbridge provides a fine vantage point for the photographer but, more importantly, reminds us that wayside stations were often located by overbridges or level crossings. The large station nameboard at the approach end of the platform, or 'running-in board', was once common, and were far easier to read than the modern 'designer' signs. The goods yard on the left is spacious, allowing ample access for road vehicles. The goods shed platform is on the near side of the building, permitting the station forecourt to double up for passenger and goods vehicles. *H. J. Stretton Ward*

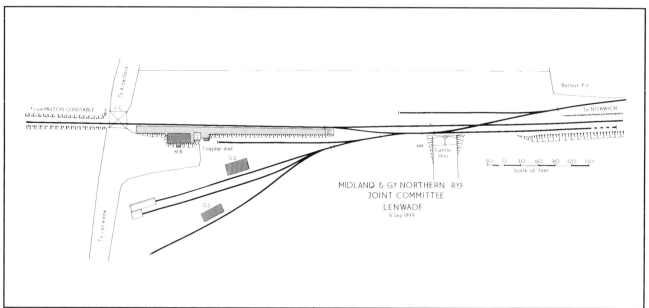

Lenwade, on the M&GN line from Melton Constable to Norwich, follows a classic pattern, with the signal box adjacent to the level crossing and a starting signal at the end of the platform to protect the gates. The gates are wide enough for double track, although the route is single. On many single lines the formation, bridges, etc, were built with doubling in mind; at a level crossing the road may require the wider gates even if this was not the case.

Lenwade is not a passing loop, but the plan shows that it still has much of interest. First of all we have a level crossing. Secondly the goods yard has a single access, and is only conveniently shunted by a train from Melton. Finally the connection into the ballast pit is taken off the goods headshunt, and through the running line by a diamond crossing to avoid another pair of facing points. Today, facing points are accepted without qualm, and diamonds frowned upon!

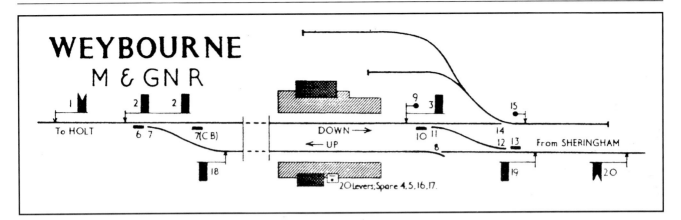

Weybourne station, also on the M&GN, is framed in the bridge arch in the first photograph. The station facilities are grouped on one platform with a modest shelter on the other side. The ornamental ridge tiles, chimney stacks and date carved into plinths above the windows add charm to the road frontage.

Weybourne is a typical single-track crossing station, and the diagram shows the full signalling. Note that there is a distant signal in each direction; on single lines, some companies had working distants, as with the M&GN, but other favoured fixed distants, on the basis that the train *had* to approach under caution, given the points in and out of the loop. The yard is reached off a head shunt at one end of the station.

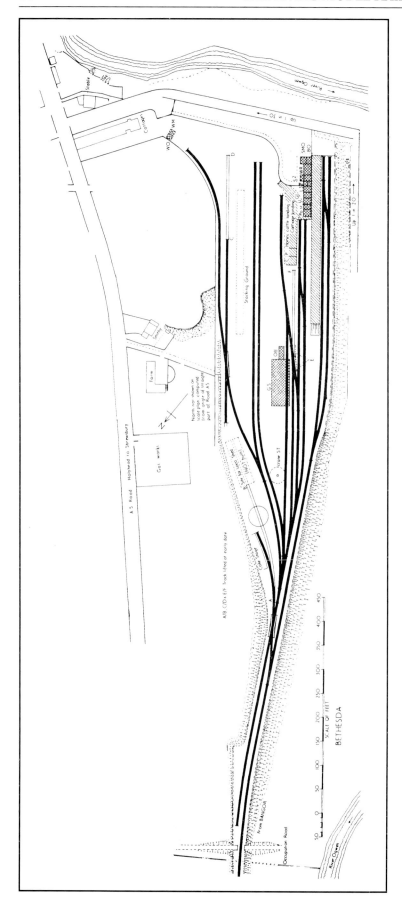

Above Bethesda was the terminus of a steeply graded but short North Western branch that left the Chester & Holyhead line east of Bangor. The accompanying layout is taken from the construction plan, and depicts a typical single-track branch terminus. The station has a single platform with run-round loop, the latter 'trapped' at the country end. The tracks near the passenger station are for arrival, run-round and shunting purposes, while the connection into the goods yard is further out. The headshunt permits shunting to continue even while a passenger train is arriving or departing, and also 'traps' the yard connections against runaways on to the passenger line. There is a crane at the divergence of the yard, a location that allows it to serve two tracks and road vehicles as well. The coal yard is slightly removed from the rest of the yard. Note the way in which the two long sidings are paired; there is road access from the east side to one line, and from the west to the other, which was the most efficient use of space in a railway goods yard. The turntable and site for the shed, which were not built, are tucked away at the north of the station.

Below Plodder Lane, on the LNWR line from Manchester to Bolton, reveals many typical features. The coal yard is south of the passenger station (left-hand end of upper plan) and is controlled from a small ground frame released from Plodder Lane No 1 signal box (right-hand end). The passenger station is in a cutting with the booking office at road level and footsteps down to the platforms. As the goods yard (lower part of plan) is too long to be worked from one box, the connections at the south end are worked by No 1 box, immediately beyond Plodder Lane roadbridge. The connections at the north end are worked by No 2 box. Although the yard is on one side of the line, and is only reached by trailing connections, once in the yard the sidings face both north and south. This is unusual, but is explained by the site and the traffic to be handled. The 'stop blocks' on each side of the goods shed are movable devices and protect men working on wagons in the goods shed. There is a weighing machine and office by the yard entrance, and a stable block for the delivery horses. Finally, we have Plodder Lane MPD on the opposite side of the line. As usual, access is via a trailing connection, and locos will set back, and water and coal at the coal hole, then run via the tail shunt to the disposal pit by the coal hole, where they will clean their fires. They will then go on shed or wait their next duty. The pits in each road outside the shed are the preparation pits, where engines going into traffic stand for examination and oiling. On model railways we often lack space for these facilities, but we should do our best to replicate them.

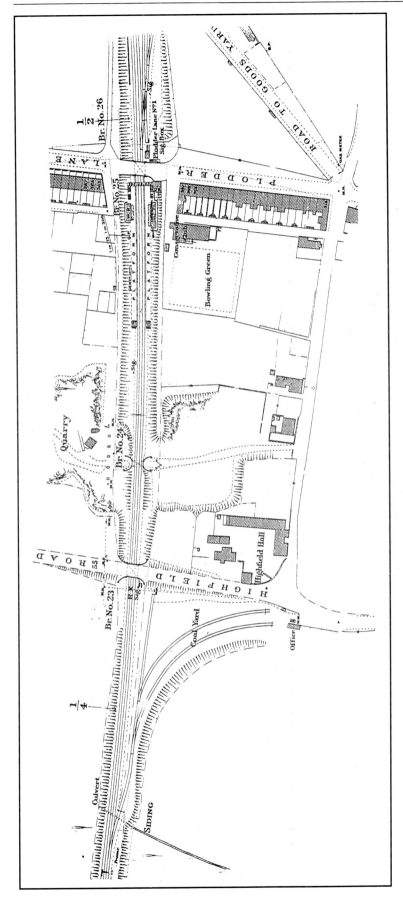

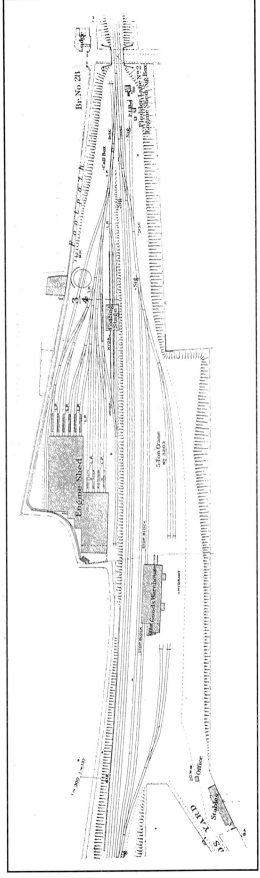

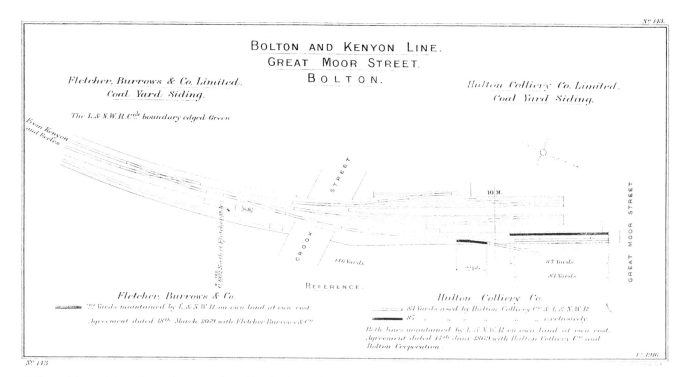

Bolton (Great Moor Street), coincidentally the basis for Trevor Booth's 'Platt Lane' O gauge layout dealt with in other books in the Silver Link Library of Railway Modelling, is a modest double track terminus. A horse and carriage landing exists on one side of the line, but the provision of coal facilities adjacent to the passenger platforms on the other side of the station (the dark-coloured tracks) is unusual. It is included as an example from the 'prototype for everything' department. Few modellers would have space to cover the entire goods facilities at Moor Street, so we have depicted only the throat, with connections into the Fletcher Street coal yard, the Astley & Tyldesley coal yard and the cattle landing. There is a double junction into a yard of this size, but all the tracks are trapped on to the third road, which runs under Fletcher Street bridge, and which serves other private sidings.

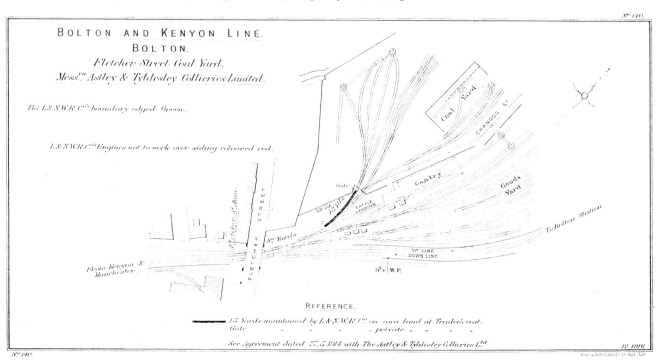

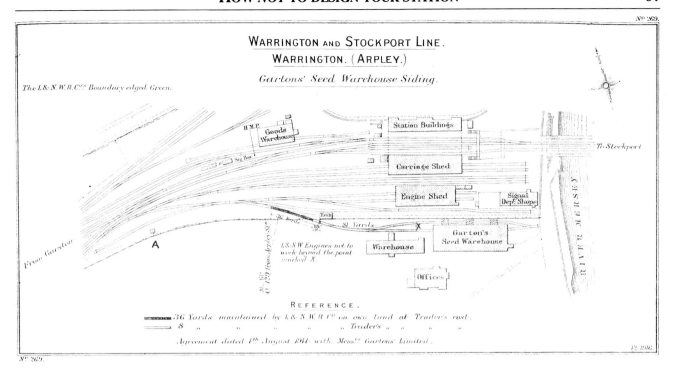

No 269.

WARRINGTON AND STOCKPORT LINE.
WARRINGTON. (ARPLEY.)

Gartons' Seed Warehouse Siding.

The L&N.W.R.C?.S Boundary edged Green.

REFERENCE.

36 Yards maintained by L&N.W.R C? on own land at Traders cost.
8 " " " " " Traders'

Agreement dated 4th August 1911 with Mess?.s Gartons' Limited.

N° 269.

Above At Warrington (Arpley) the goods yard is north of the line, reached off trailing connections at the station; there were also trailing connections at the far end. The signal box is near the divergence of the Liverpool and Walton Old Junction lines. On the south platform the station buildings and carriage shed adjoin one another; the latter was removed prior to 1940. There is a separate two-road engine shed, but no turntable is shown, although one existed by the small building marked A on the plan. A connection runs from the loco yard to Garton's seed warehouse. In the smaller gauges this layout would provide enormous operating potential.

Below Although the LNWR signal box survives, as does the junction, Arpley station has been swept away and diesel locomotives now congregate where steam engines once stood. The diamond crossing at the junction is a movable or switch diamond, to provide better running than the traditional type of crossing, but the 'dog-leg' in the track is not too impressive.

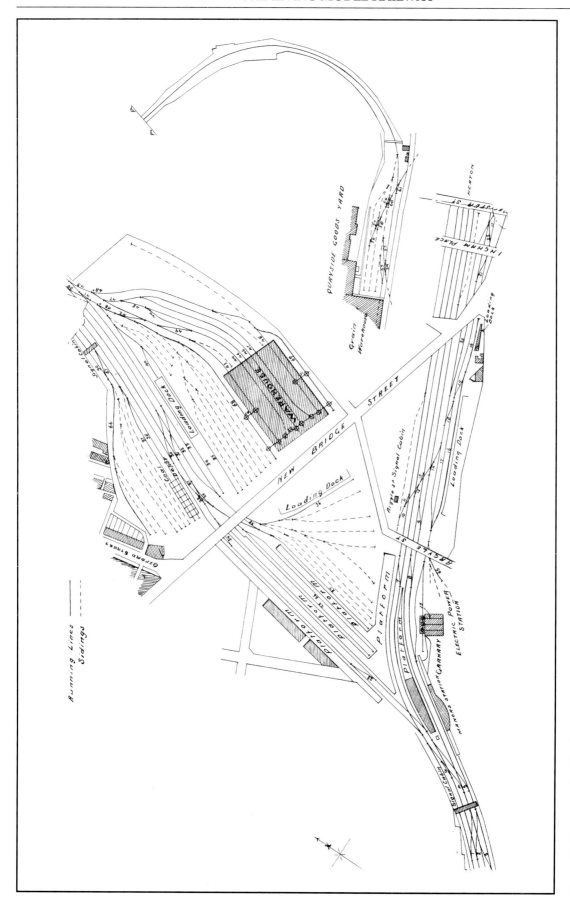

Running Lines ———————
Sidings — — — — — —

To avoid allegations of a North Western bias, and to cater for the modeller who has an RAF hanger vacant, I have selected Newcastle (Manors) station, the divergence of the Jesmond and Heaton lines, and the Quayside goods branch. We see a multi-track passenger station, extensive goods facilities, coal cells, signal boxes all over the place, including elevated examples spanning the tracks, and the steeply graded Quayside branch, which was worked by electric Bo-Bo locomotives due to horrendous footplate conditions for steam traction in its three restricted tunnels. This selection is perhaps tongue-in-cheek, but while few modellers may have the space for such a layout, the double junctions, trailing crossovers and other features typify any busy railway centre: at Argyle Street on the Heaton line there is a series of trailing single slips; the granary by Manors station is reached off wagon turntables; and the goods warehouse shows the internal arrangements in such a large facility, with its various wagon turntables. The diagram is schematic, not to scale, so not all the track spacings are shown as they should be, but that should be clear from what has been said previously.

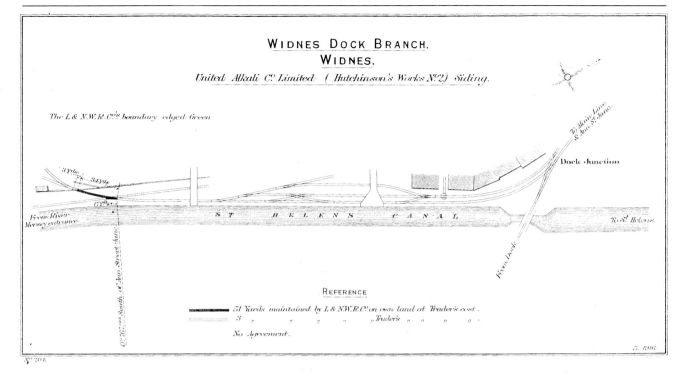

WIDNES DOCK BRANCH.
WIDNES.
United Alkali C.º Limited (Hutchinson's Works Nº2) Siding.

The L & N.W.R.C.ºˢ boundary edged Green

Dock Junction

*From River
Mersey entrance*

St. Helens Canal

To St. Helens

REFERENCE

51 Yards maintained by L & N.W.R.Cº on own land at Trader's cost.
3   "   "   "   "   "   Trader's   "   "   "   " .
No Agreement.

Shunting layouts can offer operating potential in a small space. I have therefore included a plan of part of the Widnes Dock branch, serving the St Helens Canal.

One could illustrate dozens of stations and only scratch the surface. Where is the modeller to begin? Hundreds of authors have written thousands of books and articles on locomotives, but station layouts were neglected for many years. The doyen in this field was the late Ralph Clark, who produced three small booklets of photos and one of track plans in the late 1940s, but found little support. In the 1970s Ralph produced the first volume of a series on Great Western Railway stations for Oxford Publishing Co. My father and I followed suit with two volumes on LMS stations. Similar books have appeared from other authors, and many line histories contain station track plans. As I have said, if one is a GWR modeller, it is not necessary to stick to GWR track plans for inspiration, so any of the books on station layouts can provide the necessary background, and more importantly, the dos and don'ts.

Dos and don'ts

I have concentrated on the prototype, for the moral has been 'model the real thing, not the model'. This is fine up to a point, but the prototype civil engineers seldom committed the errors that some modellers make, so I will now undertake a 'How not to design a station' exercise, and an alternative version of how a layout could look on the same piece of baseboard. Some features look ridiculous in the 'how not to' version, but I

have seen virtually all of them on occasions. The letters refer to the diagrams overleaf.

Signal box
On the 'how not to' plan the box (A) is at one end of the station, and would not be able to work connections at the other end. If it was located at the other end of the platform at B, it might be possible to control all pointwork. However, the single-track branch will be worked on the train staff system; customarily the staff, whether a wooden baton or electric token, was managed from the signal box, and if the box was on the up side the signalman would have to cross the main lines to hand the staff to the driver of the branch train. This is dangerous, and we owe a 'duty of care' to our 2 mm, 4 mm or 7 mm staff, even if they are plastic or white metal. If, however, the box was positioned at C on the 'how to' plan, this is closer to the far connections, and safer. Depending on the length of the layout, a second box may be required at D on either plan.

Goods yard
The facing lead into the goods shed road off the up main at E contravenes the facing point rule. There are no traps at either end of the yard at F1 or F2, and there is no headshunt at F2, so a freight cannot work the yard without obstructing the up main line.

The goods shed is surrounded by tracks, so road access is impossible, and the three sidings at G have little or no road access, so cannot be used for loading or unloading.

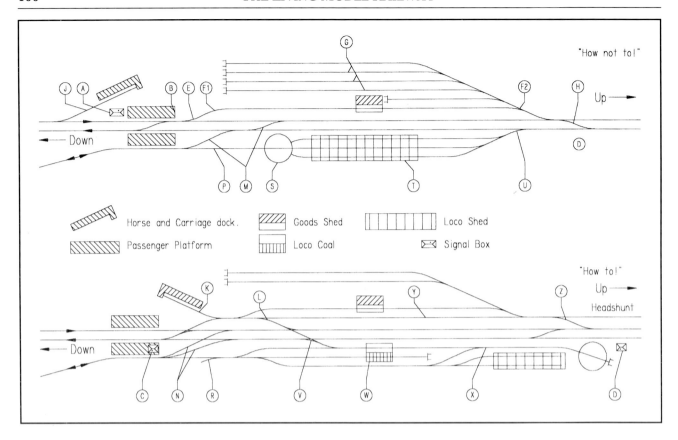

'How not to design a station' (above), and the alternative, more satisfactory and more realistic version occupying the same baseboard area (below). The plan is of a through station on a double-track line, with a single-track branch leaving from the rear of the down island platform (left-hand end); there is a goods yard on the up side of the main line and a loco shed opposite.

Although the facing crossover at H allows direct access to the yard from the down direction, this is merely to dead-end sidings or to the goods shed, and engines should not run through a goods shed, so it is of little use. Also a facing connection on a passenger lines would be frowned upon.

The facing lead into the horse and carriage landing at J would give the BOT hysterics. An H&C dock at K on the revised plan is better, and the trailing crossover at L permits access without going all the way to the far end of the yard.

Branch line
The ladder connections off the branch at M on the 'how not to' would be fine today, but in steam days would not have met with approval. The traditional approach is set out at N on the second plan.

Loco shed
The lead from the loco depot at P is untrapped, even though it runs on to a passenger line; this would not be permitted, and it should be trapped as at R. In a

few places straight steam sheds were served off a turntable, as at S, but it is unusual. We often do this on model railways to save space or points, and I have to admit that we have two such sheds. One prototype example was Lancaster (Green Ayre) on the Midland Railway. If it can be avoided, do so. If not, quote Lancaster! Roundhouses, of the round or square variety, were directly accessed, so are more plausible.

Virtually the whole of the MPD (T) is given over to the shed, with no facilities for watering, coaling, ash disposal, etc. This is improbable. The plan of Plodder Lane shows a real shed, and its approach and ancillary tracks. The facing lead into the shed at U, and lack of a trap would not be permitted. On the 'how to' layout the shed exit is trapped at R, and a second trailing approach is provided at V. A further connection, between L and V, adds flexibility, and reminds us of the series of single slips at Newcastle (Manors). Note that the two slips are trailing as far as the running lines are concerned. A coal hole is provided at W, with a road for loco coals. This should extend beyond the coal hole for fulls, and would usually be on an incline, so that empties are run out and full wagons run in by gravity as required. We have such a coal hole at Hillside (Millbank) shed, and it can accommodate two wagons in the coal hole and approximately two on each side. I would prefer longer head and tail space, but it was not available. After engines have coaled and watered, they proceed via X to the outward track, and can go on shed or await their next turn. The shed will house fewer engines than in the 'how not to' version, but offers prototypical working, including loco coal movements. The turntable has been sited at the tail of X road.

Another track that has no counterpart on the 'how not to' plan is Y in the goods yard. An up freight can arrive, set back into Y road, then shunt without the engine needing to enter the goods shed. The headshunt permits shunting to go on while up trains are running. When it is ready to leave the train can depart via the crossover at Z. A down freight, meanwhile, can stop in the platform and set back over the trailing connections into Y road. The train engine can run round via the crossover at Z to shunt the yard, or a yard shunter can do the necessary work.

The two layouts take up the same space, and while the second version uses more points, 28 as against 18, it is laid out realistically, and has far more operating potential. If I were judging layouts at an exhibition, I would conclude that the man who designed 'HOWNOTTO' might be a brilliant modeller, but knew little about railways, and I would mark it accordingly. On the other hand, the designer of 'HOWTO' has made a serious effort to design a station that could have existed. I would award one the gold cup, and make the other operate a fleet of pink 'Kings' for the entire exhibition.

Having laid down a set of rules to follow, it is as well to remember that the prototype could create bizarre stations on occasion. One of the most eccentric was Ventnor in the Isle of Wight. A single-bore tunnel debouched on the station throat, so that any shunting moves required the engine to shunt in and out of the tunnel. The station was surrounded by cliffs, and the local coal merchants were quite literally cavemen, conducting their business from the caves! *R. E. Tustin*

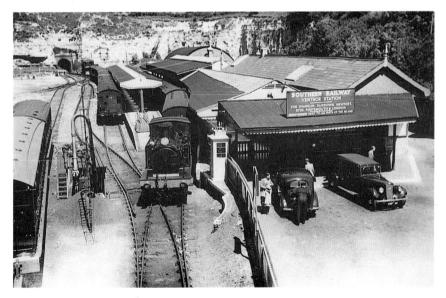

The other end of the station was equally freakish, for the left-hand island platform could only be reached via a train standing at the right-hand face, or via a 'ship's gangway'. When a train was in the platform the gangway had to be moved clear, and it can be seen on the island just to the left of the 'O2' locomotive. Had such a fantastic station not existed, a modeller creating such a layout would have courted derision. *R. E. Tustin*

5.
THE REST OF THE WORLD

This is not a chapter on an England v Rest of the World sporting fixture, or how to model the railways of the USA, Germany or Outer Mongolia. Writing a book about modelling English railways is hard enough without added complications! Instead it raises a few more questions in order to spread alarm and despondency, and provides some answers to complete the process. Hopefully by now you will have decided what you want to model, found out what space you have, which probably means you can't model it anyway, then thought about what the station should look like. On the prototype the tracks stretch out into the distance, and somewhere out there is another station or, rather, hundreds of them. As we do not have the space to model the whole of British Railways, we cannot do this, and while we may add a second or third station, there is a time at which we have to represent 'the Rest of the World'.

Sometimes one sees self-contained layouts, running from station A to B, but except for narrow-gauge lines and a few exceptional systems, railways are *not* self-contained, and not all trains will run from A to B and nowhere else. Even if you have two splendid termini,

The 1960s 'Doctors' Hobbies Exhibitions' culminated in Stephen Moor station, at 28 feet overall the largest-ever GHR exhibition layout, which won the class prize. Dad measured the LNWR buildings at Kilsby & Crick on the Northampton line, but when he built the model he found that while the overall dimensions of one half of the staircase agreed with the individual window he had measured up, the other half did not by 9 inches. He went back and found that while both sections looked identical, each window was an inch narrower on one half, making up the discrepancy. Here No 45723 *Fearless* bursts into sight from 'the Rest of the World' at the head of a long express. The scenery was painted by one of Benger's staff artists. Dad explained it was a moorland area in the Pennines, and the artist was somewhat exuberant, with a backdrop of Alpine proportions, which included a fairytale castle more suited to the Wicked Queen in Snow White. *Dr R. P. Hendry*

Going from the scenic section to 'the Rest of the World' is always a problem. For the Stephen Moor layout Dad solved it in grand style, borrowing the south portal of Kilsby tunnel. When he studied the tunnel mouth he discovered that the strata was clearly visible in the stone, and used individual blocks of fine veneer, with the grain running in the right direction as per the original. Sadly time ran out, and the ornamental coping to the tunnel could not be modelled. One problem that is apparent in most model railway tunnels is that the entire inside of the hill has been hollowed out, and to obviate this effect a tunnel profile went some distance into the hill. Another mistake that some modellers make is to have the ground bulge up and the railway head straight for it. A tunnel was invariably in a cutting, and the ground would rise well above the portal, otherwise the engineer would have settled for a cutting. *Dr R. P. Hendry*

Sutton Coldfield offers a wonderful prototype for the modeller, with a sharply curved tunnel at the very end of the platforms. The signal is a fitted with 'co-acting' arms, the upper arm being visible when the engine is in the distance, and the lower arm when it is nearby. Usually co-acting arms are directly above one another, but for sighting purposes the lower arm is bracketed out. A similar signal was built for this reason at Paythorne on the GHR exhibition layout, and is illustrated in the Introduction.

a 'Rest of the World' is helpful to promote realism within the system. We call 'the Rest of the World' a fiddle yard.

Fiddle yards

The fiddle yard is the place where that giant crane in the sky is permitted to lift engines and do all the things at which we throw up our hands on the 'proper' parts of the layout. We do not worry about scenery, so space-consuming things like platforms, goods unloading areas and so on do not hamper us, and we can have facing points to our heart's delight.

There are many sorts of fiddle yard. One of the most convenient for exhibitions or small layouts is a fan of tracks spraying out from a 'king' point, ie the first point in the fan. It can comprise three or more tracks, and these can either merge at the other end or not. If they do, a turntable is useful. Even so, a loco will need to be put on the other end of the train, so it is important that the fiddle yard king point is not half an inch inside the tunnel mouth, or whatever scenic device is used to mask the end of the 'proper' world from the 'fiddle' world. If we do so, engines shunting in our fiddle yard will constantly appear in the proper world, which would look ridiculous.

A traverser, moving whole trains, is another possibility, but demands careful engineering to build. A loco traverser could be used to replace the turntable or points at the end remote from the layout. However, I prefer a turntable unless one is running tank engines that do not need turning.

A simple 'balloon' loop can have section switches to permit stacking of two or more trains, but they will

Above The Stephen Moor layout was a circle, with the station on show to the public and a screened fiddle yard at the back. This utilised the shorter yard from previous exhibition layouts, explaining the curious layout on the left. The long loops were sectioned to hold two trains, and the idea was to have two 20-wagon freights on one long loop, and two six-coach expresses on another. I was at a school, but as a treat was allowed up to London to unpack the stock. As no power was available, I coupled up 40 wagons, and pushed them round to the loop. When Dad had power, he was so impressed with the 40-wagon train that he decided to run that way. When the judging took place, the judge was impressed after 20 wagons appeared, but Dad said 'There's a little more yet'. After 40 wagons the judge was aston-ished, but Dad repeated his remark, for he had increased the train to 55 wagons. The express on the right, meanwhile, has reached the LMSR maximum of 15 carriages. *Dr R. P. Hendry*

Below By late 1965 Middleton loops had been installed in one of the eaves, though sadly no longer 28 feet in length. Middleton became a balloon loop with an entry road fanning out into a nest of loops and sidings. This is the arrival side, with the divergence of the passenger loops in the background. The freight loops merge in the foreground. As a fiddle yard the only attempt at scenery has been the overhung signal box, as the station is purely functional. The main lines into Granton are carried on a viaduct over the top of the fiddle yard.

The departure side of Middleton shows the crowded passenger loops and, at a higher level, the divergence of the main line and Granton lines at Swinden & Nappa station. In the early days of the LMS, when Derby was trying to force Midland ideas upon Crewe, it was not unknown for red engines to go into traffic with black tenders or vice versa, in an emergency. Until I studied this photo, I did not realise that we had photographic evidence of such practice on the GHR, for the goods train engine, a black 0-6-0, has a blue passenger loco tender. The passenger loco had failed, and the freight loco tender was defective, so in the best Crewe tradition we put one unit into traffic, rather than leave two stopped for repairs!

always return in the order they entered the loop. On the Granton line of the GHR we have a plain balloon loop; this was not by choice, but we could see no way to provide a fan of loops. It is not ideal, and one proposal in connection with our Bradford Extension is to divert Granton loop services on to the Bradford Extension.

A nest of parallel tracks going into a return loop is another option, and this can have as many tracks as you have space for. At Middleton on the GHR we have eight passenger loops, which can hold trains of between four and 11.5 coaches. There are also four freight loops, three of which can stack two trains, and a number of dead-end loco, miscellaneous and push-pull sidings. The loops are a job on their own, but unlike the other stations, where the layout and operating practices are prototypical, Middleton is purely functional. Some operators enjoy the challenge of serving the rest of the system efficiently from facilities that, although apparently generous, are in fact barely adequate, while others do not enjoy working in a non-prototype environment. If we are short-staffed, the Middleton operator may double up as the Granton operator, working a wayside station on a secondary route. He has little time to relax, but has a prototype job as well.

The kind of fiddle yard you need will depend on the sort of layout you want, and the space you have. For a branch terminus the fan yard is convenient, and efficient in space. For a main-line through station, balloon loops at either end will create a 'dumb-bell' layout. This may take up too much space, and the alternative is a 'circle', with a scenic station at the front and loops at the far side of the layout. Again this is an efficient use of space, but means that an up train will remain an up train for ever, or until you physically transfer it to the down side and put an engine on the other end. After *Flying Scotsman* has passed through on an up express for the tenth time, and *Mallard* on a down express for the eleventh, it becomes improbable that they always work back by a different route. If a simple balloon can be added into the track plan to permit up/down reversals, this is beneficial.

A circle with station and loops can be fun to work, but can become boring after a while, and one answer is to add a branch-line junction. Branch trains can come in and out, run round, through carriages can be added and detached, horseboxes transferred, and so on. The branch can run to a terminus or a small fiddle yard. If the branch is usually worked by a push-pull, it can be automated, and only switched to manual control when tail traffic is to be added or a freight train is to run. If we have very little space, we can take a leaf from the GHR book and copy our Coniston branch, which is a single dead-end siding. This is suited for operation by push-pulls or auto-trains, though one can have an outbound freight in the morning and a return train in the evening. We would prefer more generous facilities at Coniston, but there was no space, hence the Bradford Extension plans.

As can be seen from the accompanying plan, the Greenlane & Hillside Railway comprises a main line running from Hillside via a number of intermediate stations, of varying sizes, to the fiddle yard, which is a multi-track return loop, at Middleton. At Ponkeston, the first intermediate station, a single-track branch climbs into the hills at 1 in 28 to serve the small town of Hoggsnorton. The dead-end Coniston branch also commences at Ponkeston. At Buchanans Hill the double-track Granton line trails in via a burrowing

junction. Here too there is a facing connection to the Higher Paradise branch (we did not invent Higher Paradise - it actually exists). At present the Paradise branch is a nest of sidings acting as a mini-'Rest of England', but will form the basis of the Bradford Extension. Triple track extends via a small wayside station, Swinden & Nappa, to Slack, where there is a colliery and a chemical works. West of Slack there is another trailing junction at Newsholme; in theory, this comes from Hellifield, but it is in fact the other end of the Granton line, which left the main line at Buchanans Hill. While some trains return to the main line via Newsholme, others go round the Granton loop and back through Granton to Buchanans Hill. Paythorne is the last intermediate

This schematic route map, prepared by one L. Sheepspeak, believed to be an alias for a certain B. RamSay, unravels the GHR running lines. Sidings are shown representatively where this adds to clarity, but are otherwise omitted. The 'time gaps' on the Granton line are where trains pause in a balloon loop, or become a different service altogether. A train that goes through Buchanans Hill and Granton is heading for Skipton. If that train goes over Newsholme Junction, as far as Paythorne is concerned it has come from Hellifield.

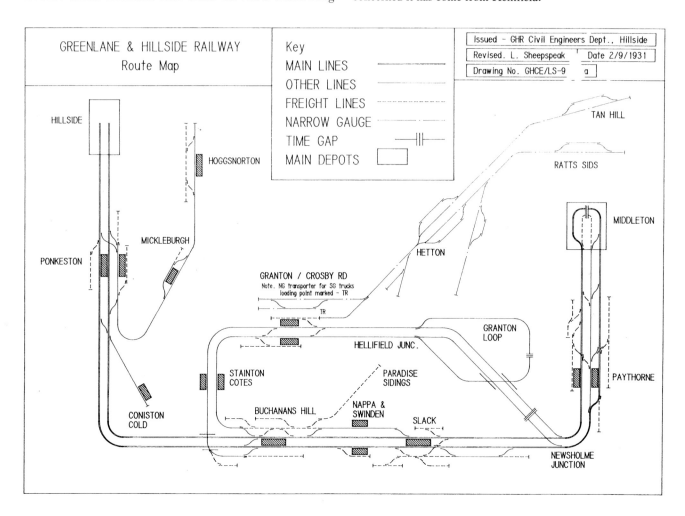

Above The Conway railway, built by Joe Griffiths, was one of the great operating model railways. This is Ganwick Town station with the lines to Ganwick harbour in the background. The Griffiths private owner coal wagon is indicative of the lighter side of railway modelling. *J. Griffiths*

Below The Conway layout was unusual in that it had a separate control office on a different floor! This was modelled on the LMSR District Control Offices, and was in telephone communication with the signal boxes, who reported the passage of trains. *J. Griffiths*

station before Middleton loops. This complex mix of routes, with various special route codes, permits an interesting operating pattern, and we need to know where trains are to go. It is rumoured that on at least one occasion, a train has gone to the wrong destination. As we have not received any written complaint from passengers actually travelling in the train concerned, these rumours are discounted.

When it is unwound from its spaghetti-like form, the GHR thus comprises a main line from station to fiddle yard, a couple of dead-end branches, a branch to fiddle sidings, and a loop diverging off the main line, and either returning to the main line at another junction, or recoiling on itself. The Gainsborough layout, which is one of the most spectacular club layouts in the country, has a similarly complex trackplan. Two other layouts that I was privileged to know were Joe Griffiths's 'Conway' model and Norman Eagles's 'Sherwood Section'. As with the GHR or the Gainsborough line, these could only be operated by a team, but if there is the space and the team, they can become a wonderful entity and a delightful challenge. My life has been centred on a 'team' railway, but for the modeller who does not have the space, or who prefers to work alone or with just one or two friends, any of the schemes we have discussed will still create a layout that can give endless pleasure.

A question of balance

Do you have balance? No, I do not mean 'Are you sane?'. If either of us were, I would not be writing this book, and you would not be reading it. Nor do I mean 'Can you walk without falling over?'. Trains run from A to B, and if the facilities at A are disproportionate compared to B, then however generous the facilities at A may be, they cannot be used to the full. If station A has 11 platforms and B has one, it is fairly obvious that the facilities at A cannot be fully used as B would be swamped.

The 'opposing' facilities do not have to be exactly balanced, for it may be that we will want a lot of trains in our fiddle yard, to send one after another to the branch terminus, where they shunt, then return, and another train appears. Here, we *could* have an 11-track fiddle yard and a one-platform terminus, and it would mean that a substantial time could elapse at the branch terminus before any train re-appeared. If the facilities were the other way round, it would not be so satisfactory; balance is important, but need not be exactly matched. If we have a junction, then the station that receives all services must be able to cope with what the individual lines can contribute.

Another aspect of balance is train size. I have seen layouts where one end can handle a six-coach train,

but the other end can only handle a two-coach train. The result is that only two-coach trains can run. If one end had been smaller, it is possible that the other station could have been larger, and four-coach trains might have been possible. In designing your layout, however magnificent one station is, if you find that the other end of the line can only handle small trains, think again, as you do not have balance.

Again, balance must be interpreted flexibly. At our main station, Hillside, we can accommodate 11½-coach double-headed expresses, and Middleton loops can accommodate a similar train. At Hoggsnorton, our branch terminus, if the operator received an 11½ coach train, he would probably ask for a double whisky, as he can only run round 5½ coaches. Usually the branch passenger service is a two-coach motor; a branch terminus does not expect to handle the same size of train as a main-line terminal. In this case the branch is working to a station much larger than it is, but that is because the larger station handles other services.

Another aspect of balance is that the various facets of our railway should be in proportion. For example, an eight-platform passenger terminus indicates an important town or city. If our goods yard will hold 10 wagons, it is out of proportion. We either need to have a goods depot in proportion to the passenger station, or a separate yard (in reality or imagination). On the Conway model railway, Conway Town station handled passengers, and freight was concentrated at Paxton yard. It was impracticable to have adequate passenger and freight depots together, given the permissible width of baseboards, so this was a sound alternative. To eliminate the yard altogether removes the diversity of freight traffic from the layout, so is not recommended.

'Balance' should also apply to locomotives, and our motive power fleet should be in proportion to our traffic needs. In other words, if we need 30 engines, we should have 30 engines, and not 90. As most model railway enthusiasts are loco fanatics, I am not writing this because anyone will pay any attention to it, but because it ought to be here. Once upon a time the GHR needed 28 engines in traffic to maintain its services. We had about 70, but as those of you who are familiar with O gauge equipment will realise, some of the motors of 40, 50 or 60 years ago were not inspiring when new, let alone after decades of service. Of those 70 engines, about 20 were almost fit for light engine duty on the rare occasions that they were capable of movement, and another 10 were spasmodic in their performance. We had a reliable fleet of about 40 locomotives. Many BR steam men would tell you that the ideal working ratio was a loco fleet of 140 per cent of daily requirements. With 28 engines needed in steam, that suggested an optimum fleet of 39.2 engines. Our fleet was in balance. However, traffic needs grew, due to increasing industrialisation (recession being unknown in the Hillside area), and current daily needs are in excess of 60 locomotives. We should therefore have 84 engines available for service, but many of the older engines were re-motored, giving them a new lease of life, and new engines acquired, the most recent as one chapter of this book was being written. The fleet therefore grew rather more than balance would have permitted. If you are a truly dedicated and fastidious being, devoted to balance, you will have a strictly balanced fleet. If not, then you have too many engines, but it's fun, ain't it?

The steam locomotive required a good deal of attention, including boiler wash, inspection of firebox, 'X-Exams' and so on. It also took a considerable time to light up before it could go into traffic. As most of us put an electric motor in our engines, we do not face these problems. We can run any engine we like, and put it in steam in one second. The same engine can appear forever on a train. This is not prototypical. With the opening of Hillside (Millbank) shed, it was made responsible for all LMS engines, and 'Wash Out and X Exam' sheets prepared. When we have an operator at Hillside 4/5 boxes, he acts as shedman at Millbank, and marks up which engines are stopped for wash-out or X-Exam.

In reality the frequency of wash-out varied depending on water supplies and treatments, and could be a few days or a couple of weeks. We opted for an eight-day cycle, with the rule that every LMS engine had to be stopped once every eight runnings for wash-out

and X-exam. We laid down minimum and maximum numbers to be stopped on any day to avoid fitters being idle, or shed facilities being overtaxed. We took a leaf from the prototype with a 'NOT TO BE MOVED' sign, but rather than attach it to the engine, we put ours over the on/off switch for the road where the engine is standing.

Engines for wash-out had to be worked into the shed. To begin with it was easy, but as one got into the cycle it was necessary to think ahead, for without care all motor tanks might fall due for wash-out on the same day. Engines stabled at out-stations had to be called in. By Day 7 of the first cycle, the shedman was sending out messages to summon 'defaulters'. Instead of 'flick the switch' motive power, the shedman has to estimate his needs. It helped us with preserving balance, too.

Finally there needs to be balance between track and the quantity of stock on it. In 1931 Dad met Frank Renshaw, the senior signal fitter at Rugby and a staunch 'North Western' man. He saw Frank's railway, and Frank visited the embryo GHR with friends, bringing a large quantity of visiting stock. Dad's recollections were twofold. In the past there had been a paucity of stock, limiting the service that could be run. Now there was a glut, and there was literally only one spare siding; when a train went to the station with the spare siding, it freed the space it had left for another movement. From lack of movement due to lack of stock, the railway had jumped to lack of movement through lack of siding space. During the week Dad laid in several more sidings, and the visiting stock came into its own the following week.

Although there was no possibility of modelling the whole 40 miles of the main line of the GHR (without winning the pools), the whole route was surveyed to fix the line into the Rest of the World. It has been an immense help in getting the 'feel' right. The assorted animal names - Bay Horse, Dolphinholme, Catshaw, Crowtrees - really do exist, and on the last extension surveyed by Dad he was delighted to continue the theme with Wild Duck!

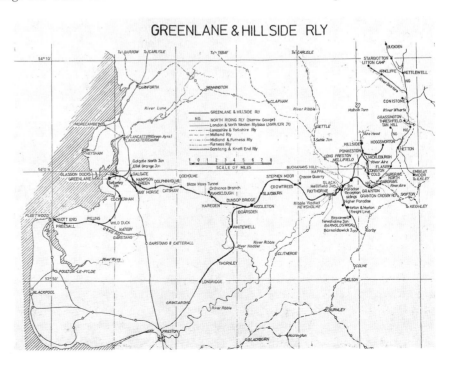

GREENLANE & HILLSIDE RLY

6.
BUILDING YOUR LAYOUT

This book is about creating a model railway you can live with and operate, so I do not propose to devote a few hundred pages to sawing up baseboards, and how to solder wire A to wire B. However, a few comments are in order, if for no other reason that we would otherwise have an almighty jump from 'think about your railway' to 'there it is, let's run trains'. In fact, there is a more serious reason. Just as a house depends on good foundations, so does a model railway. If the foundations are not sound, neither will give the owner any satisfaction.

The baseboard

The baseboard is the first step. Wood is normal, but one American modeller used rubble in a basement, rendering it solid with cement. When he came to move, what the next occupier of the house thought, when he found a miniature mountain range in concrete under the house, defies imagination. Moving away from such exotic baseboards, blockboard or plywood are customary. Some modellers swear by chipboard. I merely swear at it. With our wide baseboards, my father felt that on occasion a baseboard may have to take a modeller's weight, and opted for half-inch or three-quarter-inch ply or blockboard, well braced and with ample legs. Quarter-inch ply is sometimes used, but while this saves on one cost, more bracing is needed, increasing another cost. Open construction baseboards, with thin laths for the track, and wire mesh or other in-fill for scenery, are sometimes advocated. The average rabbit might go through such structures, but if you do not need to jump up and down on the baseboard, it is up to you; either method works.

Whatever the thickness of the baseboard, sufficient longitudinal and cross bracing is essential if it is not to sag between supporting legs. Without adequate longitudinal support you will end up with a series of valleys and peaks, which will make good running impossible. The longitudinal and transverse supports should be glued and pinned or screwed to the baseboard. Other writers have covered woodworking in detail, so rather than duplicate their words, I will merely say 'Consider what your maximum load is, and build accordingly'. If in doubt, make it twice as strong as you need, rather than half as strong. I have seen a layout where little bracing was done to the baseboards, and the result was frightening. A little money was saved to begin with, but at the expense of horrendous remedial work and deplorable running.

Track-laying

If your layout is multi-level, lay the lower-level track first, unless you have a masochistic streak or you can force someone you hate to lay the lower level afterwards. As the rule says, 'If it can derail in the most inaccessible place, it will', so make sure you can get at the inaccessible place. In O gauge, the size of the train is comparable to the diameter of the human arm, so we can put an arm down a tunnel, but in 4 mm or 2 mm it is not so easy. Unless you have trained hamsters to re-rail your stock, you will need access to the inside of these smaller-gauge tunnels, as something is bound to derail there sooner or later, or you will get a bad joint in the track. Lift-off hills are one answer, or, if the scenery is sufficiently deep, an access between the scenery and the baseboard. Loco and carriage sheds provide similar problems, and lift-off buildings are the easiest answer.

When it comes to track-laying, most modellers will buy proprietary track by the yard and ready-made points - they save a lot of time and effort. When my father started, in the 1920s, he could not afford commercial track, so he bought sleepers, chairs and rails, and became so used to making track that he continued to build it until a few weeks before he passed

My father used to prepare a series of scaled plans, and when the optimum layout was settled he would mark the baseboards accordingly. The baseboard for Hillside (Millbank) MPD was the first major extension to be commenced after he passed away, and I took a number of photographs of the process. The tracks are marked out using a straight edge, but auxiliary objects, such as hydraulic buffers, can be drawn in freehand. The run-round in the extension to platforms 4/5 was to accept a 'Royal Scot' but not a 'Pacific', and the mark between the rails indicates the clearance point between the stops and the escape crossover.

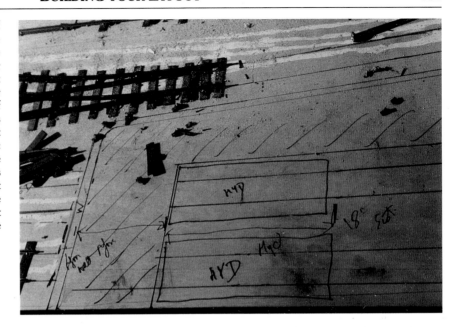

For drawing work and on the layout, Dad produced templates giving various curves, and they were invaluable in marking in points. Here I have placed the curve template over one of the running rails in the shed yard.

away, by which time he had created some hundreds of points and thousands of feet of track. I have followed suit. Making your own track has advantages over the ready-made item, as individual pointwork can be fabricated to your requirements rather than what the manufacturer churns out. Care in laying is repaid a hundredfold in operation.

In O gauge, the pre-war commercial track was mounted on quarter-inch-deep wooden sleepers, carried on quarter-inch-deep longitudinal battens. To ballast this formidable track called for a half-inch depth of ballast. Most modellers didn't bother, and the track looked awful. Dad decided that this was no use, and ordered 1 mm wooden sleepers, which, like modern 4 mm proprietary track, required only a light surround of ballast. It transformed the appearance of

the pre-war layout. When track-laying began again in 1947, the stock of pre-war timber sleepers was soon exhausted. Wood was in short supply, so some thousands of pre-cut creosoted card sleepers were ordered. The last of the 1947 sleepers are still in store as this book is written. The Bradford Extension will call for the third order for sleepers for the GHR since 1934.

In laying track, a small mirror, of the sort ladies carry around in their handbags, is invaluable. If you place the mirror on the track and look into it, imperfections, both laterally and vertically, become apparent and can be corrected prior to ballasting. Distortion of the baseboard is most likely where baseboards join, so this is *not* the ideal place for points. In determining the position of points in a layout, and the cutting point for wood in making the baseboards,

The GHR was in existence long before the British Railway Modelling Standards Bureau produced a set of standards. To secure the best running from Bassett Lowke, Leeds Model Co, Milbros and other wheels, before the official standards had been thought of, Dad carried out extensive tests, and then built his own track gauge. It is the most important and irreplaceable tool on the GHR. It is also very simple.

try to avoid a point on, or immediately adjacent to, a join. This is important on a permanent layout, but even more so on a portable one, as a point on a baseboard join on a portable layout is a guaranteed headache.

Proprietary track is customarily joined by fishplates, which may be conducting, or insulating for track section breaks. Many modellers rely upon these for electric conductivity, but they are a 'dry joint', and Dad preferred to solder bonding wires from rail to rail. In the long term it minimised dead spots and poor running through loss of power at each rail joint. It adds to the work, but I would recommend it.

If you have followed all this excellent advice (well, I think it is excellent advice, or I wouldn't have said it), you will now have a nice trackplan, marked out and laid on a baseboard that you can jump up and down on, or which a rabbit may fall through.

Curves and clearances

Railwaymen talk of the '6 foot', which is the space between adjacent lines. On model railways we also have a '6 foot', but it is scaled down appropriately. Dad and I were asked by a friend to help design his layout, and on our first visit he had laid some track, and as we were looking at it I asked 'Do coaches sideswipe one another on that curve?'. He replied 'Yes, but how did you know?'. On model railways we use much sharper curves than the prototype, and the tracks looked too close for the radius of the curve. This layout had been started paying great heed to a standards manual produced by one railway association. This standard set out track separations, but it did not give a proper explanation of the effect of

overhang on sharp curves. I suspect that other modellers will have made the same mistake.

The overhang of our stock is much greater on our sharp curves than on the prototype. On a curve a bogie coach overhangs outwards at the ends, but the worst overhang is to the centre of the curve, between the bogies. A 'Pacific' or similar loco, with a long overhang in front or behind the rigid wheelbase, overhangs to the outside of the curve, while a diesel loco is like a coach. If a bogie coach on the outer track meets a 4-6-2 on the inner track, and the clearance is to scale, it can be embarrassing. In real life the clearance on curves is increased, and engineering formulae exist to calculate the additional clearance needed between tracks, and between tracks and any fixed structures. Those with a mathematical bent may be interested.

A = the overall length of the carriage; B is the distance between bogie centres; R is the radius of the curve

$$v \text{ (versed sine of chord A)} = R - \sqrt{R^2 - \tfrac{1}{4}A^2}$$
$$V \text{ (versed sine of chord B)} = R - \sqrt{R^2 - \tfrac{1}{4}B^2}$$
$$D = v - V = \text{outside additional allowance}$$

The formula comes from Molesworth's engineering formulae, and is, I trust, clear to every reader. If not, you had better take a degree in mathematics, or use a rule of thumb. We increase the separation on our curves by about 10-15 per cent, but the best answer with proprietary flexible track is to lightly pin down two pieces of track in the approximate position in which they will be secured, and select the longest coach you will run and the loco with the worst overhang. Simply try it out, and if they sideswipe, your tracks are too close. Even if they just clear, increase the clearance, as you may decide to run longer vehicles later on, or you may have some side sway, and if two vehicles happen to sway in the wrong way, oh dear. . . If you do not have a model of your longest planned carriage, make a mock-up with a couple of bogies and a piece of card cut to size. You can work out the 'swept circle' by following round with a pen.

Dad laid out our line for 57-foot LMS stock, but many years later we acquired some 60, 62 and 65-foot vehicles. These take our clearances to the limit, and if a coach is not riding centrally or sways, 65-footers can sideswipe one another. Had we anticipated running 65-foot stock, more generous clearances would have been useful, but at the time Dad commenced work the stock he had been used to was 40 or 48-foot pre-war litho or tinplate, and the 57-foot stock represented a step up in quality and size.

Strange though it may seem, you may need to increase clearances on straight track for curves! Imagine three parallel lines, with a crossover between two of them. A 4-6-2 using the crossover will overhang towards the third road, and if the track is too close it could sideswipe a vehicle in the siding. Structures present a similar problem, and at Hillside No 2 box, ie the goods depot, we had two ground signals near a crossover. When the line was built our

largest freight locos were 0-6-0s or 0-8-0s, which cleared the signals, but the steps on locos with leading or trailing bogies did not, and after trying to prevent locos with bogies using the crossover, the problem was solved when a 4-6-0 swept the signal out of the way! When building platforms on curves, you will need to carry out clearance trials with coaching stock, and where there is an escape crossover, even on straight platforms, check the throw-over of the loco, and widen the gap between platform and track as necessary. If not, you will not be able to use the escape crossover. Clearances with lineside structures, eg overbridges and signals, may also need to be increased on sharp curves. Having carried out clearance trials, make a note of the clearances and stick to them.

As No 6157 *The Royal Artilleryman,* on the down main line, overtakes a '4F' on a through freight at the east end of Slack station on the Benger's Exhibition line, we see the overhang on sharp curves and can appreciate how sideswiping of other stock or structures will occur if clearances are not increased. In the case of bridges on a curve, this means that the arch may need to be widened, and Dad used to build such bridges to 8 mm rather than 7mm scale, to keep the proportions correct. The trap point in the foreground protects the main line from trains over-running, and is often overlooked on a model; passenger lines were protected from freight and even slow lines by traps, sand-drags or headshunts. *Dr R. P. Hendry*

Curves also present another problem. As they are sharper than those of the prototype, we can get bogie wheels fouling the backs of the cylinders on our locos, and six- or eight-coupled locos may not negotiate the tightest curves if all wheels are flanged. Many proprietary locos are built with flangeless centre wheels for this reason. You sometimes hear a modeller say 'My tightest curve is X, except in a few places where it is Y'. Unless the curves at Y are only negotiated by certain stock, and are not for general use, this is a recipe for trouble, for the old proverb that a chain is as strong as its weakest link applies. The ruling curve *is* the sharpest curve that all stock traverses. If by having a 5-foot radius curve at A you are compelled to have a 3-foot radius curve at B, your ruling curve is 3 feet, and you would be better to have 4-foot curves at A and B, so that there is a common ruling curve.

A vexed question is 'What is a reasonable curve?'. When Dad started in O gauge in the 1920s, 2 ft 6 in radius was regarded as normal, and 3 ft 0 in as generous; he opted for the latter as our standard curve. I was speaking to a modeller who expressed horror at such a ridiculous curve. I asked what radius he used. Six feet, came the reply. I asked if his curves were continuously check-railed, to which he said no. I pointed out that BOT rules called for any curve on a running line of 10 chains or less to be continuously check-railed. In O gauge a 10-chain curve is a 15-foot radius. I also enquired what locos he used. He had an LMS 'Jinty'. This was very worrying, as the minimum curve for the 'Jinty' was about 4.5 chains, or 7 feet in O gauge. At this point the conversation ended. His 6-foot curve was no more 'prototypical' than our 3-foot one - both were far too sharp. As many will be modelling in 4 mm, a 10-chain curve, which should be check-railed and subject to severe speed restriction, is approximately a 9-foot radius (ie 18-foot diameter), and the minimum curve that a large engine should work round is approximately half that. For the majority of modellers, such curves would preclude all but the simplest layout. Compromise is therefore unavoidable. The gentler the curves you use the better, but the harder it is to get a reasonable trackplan into a given space. The key is to recognise that it is a compromise, unless we go to 9-foot radius curves in 4 mm, or 15-foot in 7mm.

Some modellers opt for a 'realistic' - or at least a relatively gentle - curve on the scenic sections, and a sharper curve in the fiddle yard. This can enhance the appearance of the scenic area, but should not be at the expense of curves that will give trouble on the hidden section.

It is desirable to follow prototype practice and rather than go directly from straight track to curve, to provide a transition curve, becoming gradually sharper.

This does improve running, but if this makes the heart of the curve too sharp, the benefits are outweighed by the drawbacks. A left-hand curve followed immediately by a right-hand curve is a potential source of trouble, especially if one is using very sharp curves and prototype three-link couplings. A short length of intermediate straight track, which need be no more than 2-3 inches, will make a big difference in running.

Railway civil engineers will say that a good PW man used to bend the rail to the curve using a 'jim-crow', rather than relying on chairs or spikes to hold it to the curve, as that led to dog-legs at the joints. In O gauge this holds true. With smaller gauges and lighter rail, or proprietary flexible track, it is not so significant, but I still believe it is better to lightly bend the rail to the curve. Vertical curves, ie a change from level track to a gradient, should be made gently, otherwise long-wheelbase locos will lift their wheels. A change from level to inclined track on a curve is particularly sensitive. Dropped joints or dog-legs are further sources of trouble. Once you have laid your track, test it thoroughly, first by moving carriages or wagons by hand and remedying any bad spots, then with a locomotive.

Electrical connections

The control system you adopt is up to you. In Chapter 1, 'A Visit to Hillside', I outlined the signalling control system devised by my father, which has stood the test of time. It is complex to design, and takes a good deal of work to install, but once it is operational it permits complex train movements with the minimum of work and the maximum degree of security from conflicting movements. We operate to a split potential system, with one rail as common earth, with a heavy earth cable running around the system, to which there is regular cross-bonding. Forward and Reverse bus bars go from the two central power packs to a feeder section panel. This divides the system into five power supply areas, so that if there is a short on any given area, and the circuit-breaker trips, we can narrow it down to one of the feeder sections. The same system was adopted by tramways a century ago. Having isolated the feeder section, which will cover a couple of stations, we can operate the rest of the system normally while the fault is identified. It may be a derailment, or an object on the track, or it can be more obscure, but the on/off switches on each controller permit us to identify which controller is affected, and we can usually locate the problem within moments. That having been said, there can be problems that defy tracing for hours, for no system is perfect.

The GHR was departmentalised, and for many years I was Chief Mechanical Engineer. If it was on wheels, it was my responsibility. Dad was Chief Civil Engineer, responsible for track, point repairs, signalling, electrical circuitry, block systems and so on. If there was a 'wheel-to-rail disorientation', the CME would say in the best railway tradition that the vehicle ran OK elsewhere, so it must be a track fault. The Civil Engineer would point out that other vehicles ran over that spot, so it was undoubtedly a vehicle fault! Such discussions between the CME and CCE were not unknown to railway history, as readers of any of the accounts of railway accidents will recall! When Dad passed away, I was aware of the basic principles of the Civil Engineers side, and had done periodic work on it, but I had to learn the ins and outs. Fortunately Dad prepared comprehensive circuit diagrams, and at times I and other members of the team have pored over these to trace obscure faults.

The moral is to prepare detailed circuit diagrams, and make sure they are kept up to date. Provide facilities for isolating sections of the layout so that a short can be narrowed down to a limited area. Finally, make sure your soldered joints are good when you make them, and that there are no loose wires floating about. In almost 50 years, repairs, replacements and alterations have led to a few loose wires on the GHR, and sometimes they can give problems. Our hardest fault to trace was a piece of duff insulation on a low-grade early-post-war wire, which was the best Dad could get at the time. It had been taken out of use but left in situ, and the other end had come loose, and sometimes touched something else. It was great fun tracing it!

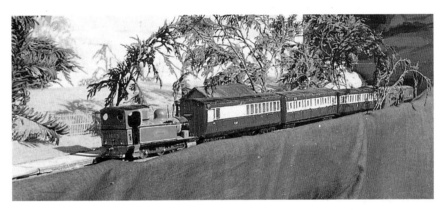

Right The GHR has been under construction for over 70 years, but once Dad and I were asked to build a layout in a *week*! At the time, the IOM Railway was under threat of closure, and it needed all the good publicity it could get, and an IOM layout had been promised for an exhibition. At the last minute the organisers were let down, and asked if they could borrow our IOM section. As this was decidedly non-portable, they then asked if we could build an exhibition layout in the next week, please! We thought about it, and decided that if Crewe could build an 0-6-0 loco in 25$^1/_2$ hours, we ought to be able to build a complete railway in seven days. (Blair insists I add that Stratford built an engine even faster - in under 10$^1/_2$ hours!) A week later, Peel Road station was ready for collection. It was a circle with the station 'up front', and four loops and sidings at the back. It was operated with a pre-recorded tape programme, saying what the trains were, and adding authentic IMR sound effects. No 15 *Caledonia* is pulling away from Peel Road with a Douglas train. *Dr R. P. Hendry*

Right IOMR No 3 *Pender* is entering Peel Road station with a train for Ramsey. The building was constructed from a single oblique photo, and although it captured the character of the original, with its quaint wooden porch to the right and partial wooden framing to the front elevation, the toilet area details to the left were wrong. We subsequently replaced it with a more accurate building, and this model was re-used as an enginemen's shanty at Hillside North! There is an ironic postscript to the story, for although the layout was ready, the lorry collecting it got stuck in a snowdrift, and in any case the exhibition was cancelled due to blizzard conditions in the North of England! *Dr R. P. Hendry*

7.
SIGNALLING YOUR LAYOUT

One of the biggest mysteries to many modellers is the function, purpose and positioning of signals, and I have seen many fine layouts with no signalling at all, or signalled in a way that would never have met BOT approval. Railway practice differed over the years, and from company to company, and it has been said that if two signals were needed, the GWR or North Eastern would provide four and the LNWR one. There is some truth in this, but broad principles evolved, and the modeller will not be far out if he applies them.

Prototype signalling explained

We will begin with a short station with a long name. Llanfairpwllgwyngyllgogerychwyrndrobwllllantysiliogogogoch, otherwise Llanfair PG, is on the Chester & Holyhead line and retained the classic early type of

goods yard radiating from a wagon turntable. The signal box was also of great age, but its 18-lever frame typified many small stations. Levers 1 and 2 locked the pedestrian wicket gates to the level crossing when a train was imminent. No 3 was the down Distant, and in order for it to be cleared the remaining down signals had also to be cleared, which in turn meant that the train had to be accepted by the next box. In other words, when the Distant signal was off, the driver could expect all the running signals in that section to be clear, and to have an unimpeded run to the next block post. He still had to look out for signals, in case an emergency had arisen. Signal 4 is the first stop signal, and is called the Home signal, protecting the level crossing and the station platform. On the accompanying signalling diagram it is shown as a tall signal with two arms. Before bracket signals evolved, with their arms side by side, running line signals for

The signalling diagram for Llanfair PG.

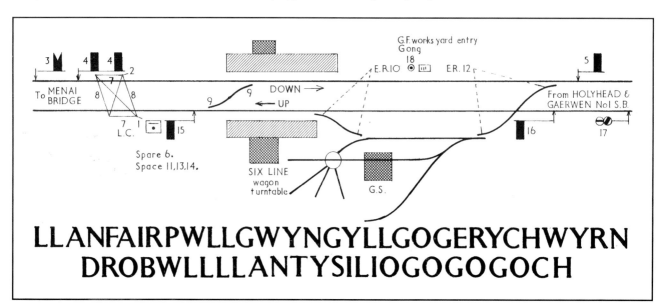

Above The signal box at Llanfair was typical of the 1870s Chester & Holyhead district boxes, but was re-equipped with a new 18-lever frame, as per the diagram, in 1893. Built for fewer levers, it was very cramped inside. *Dr R. P. Hendry*

Below The goods yard still retained its archaic radial tracks, fanning out from a wagon turntable, in BR days. The crane, of 1.5 tons capacity on a fixed radius with a shaped wooden jib, was common at wayside stations until the 1960s. *Dr R. P. Hendry*

different routes were placed one above another, but this is *not* such an instance, as one arm is near the top of the post, and one low down. Called 'co-acting' arms, they worked together, the driver seeing one at a distance, and the other much closer. The LNWR was especially fond of such signals, but they declined in popularity after the Grouping. The next down signal, 5, is at the far end of the layout. This is called the Starting signal or Starter, and controls the starting of the train into the block section between signal boxes. This arrangement - Distant, Home and Starter - was the pattern around which signalling was built.

On the up side, the Distant, 17, is a colour light. The Home, 16, protects the trailing crossover that runs from the goods yard into the down main. This crossover is not worked by the signal box, but by a separate local ground frame. If a shunter at the ground frame were free to pull these points without the knowledge of the signalman, catastrophe would be likely, as a train could be shunting from the yard to the down main as an up express roared through. The crossover is 'released' from the box by lever 12, and until this is pulled the ground frame cannot move the points. Once it is pulled, the signalman cannot clear 4 or 16 signals, as they will authorise moves that would conflict. The connection from the yard to the up main is also worked from a ground frame, but as this connection does not affect the down line, it is unnecessary to lock lever 4. A separate release lever, 10, is used, which will lock 16, which therefore 'protects' both connections into the yard; if either release lever is pulled, 16 cannot be cleared. In the days before telephones, signal boxes and ground frames used to communicate by means of gongs worked by levers. The gong lever is 18.

The up Starter, 15, protects the level crossing, and, like 5, admits trains into the next section. The level crossing gates are controlled by two further levers, 7 and 8. These are interlocked with 4 and 15 signals, so that the gates must be 'proved' in the correct position before the signals can be cleared. The signal box only controls one pair of points directly, platform crossover 9. One spare lever is provided, 6, along with three spaces, 11, 13 and 14. If necessary the spare could be used without much alteration, and three levers could be fitted to the frame in the vacant positions.

The signalling at Llanfair is as simple as possible at a double-track station with a level crossing and goods yard. No shunt signals are provided, and for the modeller the two ground frame releases, 10 and 12, could work the points directly. The gong lever would not be needed, so the station could be worked by a 13-lever frame. If the wicket levers, gate stop and lock levers were dispensed with, nine levers would suffice.

Claydon L&NE Junction, connecting the LNWR Bletchley-Oxford branch with the GC main line near Calvert, was built as a precaution in the event of bomb damage disrupting the rail network during the Second World War. In the up direction there is a Distant, 2, and a Home, 3. Off the branch there is again a Distant and a Home. The main line is protected from trains over-running off the branch by a sand-drag, lever 12. As this is a facing point on a passenger line, it must be locked. Sometimes the 'facing point lock' (FPL) is on the same lever as the points, but here it is a separate lever, 11. In order to route a train off the branch, the signalman must set 12 and 13 points and lock 12 points with the FPL, 11; only then can he clear 6 and 5, the distant 5 not coming until all other levers are set properly. Once he has set that route, indeed as soon as he has pulled 13 points,

The signalling diagram for Claydon L&NE Junction.

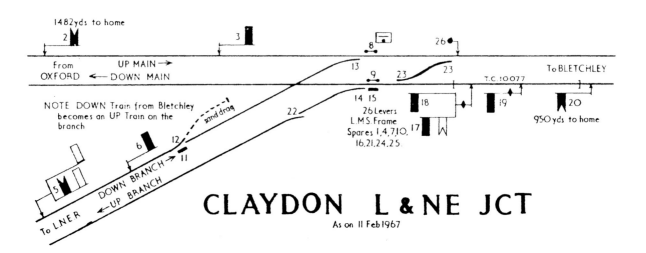

Above Claydon L&NE Junction was a standard LMS all-timber box, even down to the coxcomb ridge tiles, and was built to control a connection on to the LNER near Calvert.

Below Although a wartime precaution, Claydon L&NE Junction typified the rural junction. The GC embankment is visible on the skyline.

the up main Home, 3, will be locked at Danger, so no train can be signalled from that direction. As the train from the branch will pass over the down main line, 18 signal, on the down-line bracket, will also be locked at danger. No 19 will not be locked, but as 18 cannot be cleared, the Distant, 20, will be locked at Caution. At junctions, 'up' and 'down' can become confusing, for on the LNWR line 'up' is to the main line at Bletchley, whereas on the GC 'up' is towards Marylebone. The branch follows the GC 'up', so a 'down' branch train becomes an 'up' Bletchley train when it passes over the junction points!

On the down main, the single Distant, 20, cannot be cleared unless 18 and 19 are off. The bracket signal, 17/18, controls the junction, and the more important route is normally indicated by placing the arm slightly higher than that of the inferior route; 17 is lower than 18. The Distant arm under 17, which is not blacked in, is physically on the 17/18 bracket signal at Claydon L&NE Junction, but is the Distant for the LNER at Calvert. The down main is protected from run-backs off the up branch by the trailing trap 22. As this is a trailing point, no FPL is needed. The junction point, 14, *is* a facing point, so there is an FPL, 15. There is also a trailing crossover, 23, and a solitary shunt signal, 26, for setting back from the up main. The 'dumb-bells' 8 and 9 are detonator-placers for use in emergency and worked by levers from the box.

The down branch Distant, 5, is on a bracket signal with two arms, the higher arm on the left-hand post being for the GC main line to the north and worked by the Calvert box, while the arm above 5 is the starter from the LNER to the branch, and is also worked by the LNER box. If the LMS man at Claydon L&NE Junction sets his route and pulls 5 lever, but the LNER man has not pulled off his Starter, it would be confusing for the driver to see a Distant 'off' but the stop signal above it at Danger. To avoid this, a system of 'slotting' exists, whereby 5 lever can be pulled but the arm will only come off if and when the LNER signalman has pulled his Starting signal also. Claydon L&NE Junction provides the basic signalling requirements for a double-track junction.

Oakham Junction was on the MR route from Kettering to Melton Mowbray. Although called 'Junction', there is no actual divergence of routes, but the Midland sometimes classified a box as a junction where a line went from two to four tracks. Four tracks approach Oakham from Langham Junction to the north, merging to two before the station. As there is a level crossing at the south end of the station, and in mechanical signalling days it would have been impossible to work the 'junction' points and the gates from

one box, there is a second small box by the level crossing. Taking the up main, the Distant, 4, is on a bracket signal. As Langham Junction box is quite close, as with Claydon L&NE Junction and Calvert, that Distant shares the same post as Langham's Starter. On the accompanying diagram the Distant has an uncoloured arm shown in the 'off' position; this is a convention in signalling when a Distant is shared by two boxes. In this case it is shared with Oakham Level Crossing, and is that box's No 1 lever. For that Distant arm to come off, Junction and Crossing must pull their levers 4 and 1 respectively, and as the Distant arm will still not clear unless the stop signal above it is clear, (see explanation re Claydon No 5), that lever must also be pulled at Langham Junction.

We next encounter another 4, on a simple post but with a Starter above it. Because Langham Junction box is so close, if Oakham Junction's Distant were placed above its outermost stop signal, it would be too close to Junction's first stop signal; therefore inner and outer Distants are necessary; both outer and inner Distants are slotted by Oakham Level Crossing.

Oakham Junction's 5 is the first up stop signal controlled by Oakham. The unfilled Distant below it is a *third* Distant for Oakham Level Crossing, which therefore has outer, middle and inner Distants (all controlled from lever No 1), an unusual arrangement necessitated by the closeness of the three boxes mentioned. No 5 is the only stop signal on the up main at Oakham Junction, and protects 7 facing crossover from the up goods, and 23 and 24 trailing crossovers.

We will look at the up goods for a moment. The Distant, on the same bracket as 4, has 'F' against it. This means that it is fixed at Caution, which was common where secondary lines merged into a more important running line. Oakham Junction controls one crossover from the up goods to the up main, 7, which also has an FPL, uncommon on a goods line. Signal 3 controls movements from the goods over the crossover, while subsidiary signal 17, by the foot of the 3/5 bracket, permits trains to continue along the extension of the goods line. The un-numbered crossing short of the up platform on Junction's diagram is Level Crossing's 5 points; the latter box's signal 4 controls movements over this crossover. For better sighting, this is positioned on the other side of the down main line, as is 2 signal, which controls movements from the up main into the platform; on the diagram they are dotted to their appropriate tracks. The gates are protected by Level Crossing's 3 signal. As at Llanfair PG, there are up and down wickets, 14 and 15, but only one gate control lever, 16.

The down signalling follows a similar pattern. The divergence on to the down goods is worked by

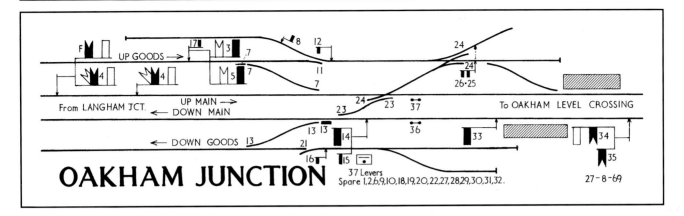

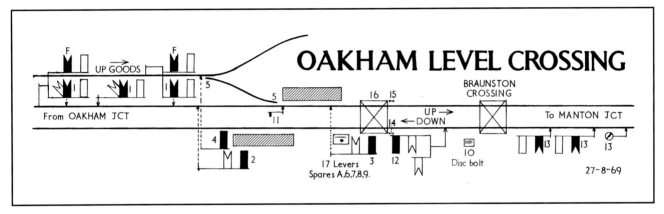

Top The signalling diagram for Oakham Junction.

Above The signalling diagram for Oakham Level Crossing.

Junction's lever 13, and unlike Claydon, where the facing point and lock were on separate levers, this is an 'economical facing point lock', with both on the same lever. The down main line signal is 14. This is unusual, for better practice is to group points and signals so that a signal relates numerically to the adjacent point. In this case, 14 can only be cleared if 13 is normal, and 15 is pulled when 13 is set for the down goods. On the 14/15 bracket, 15 is lower, and the arm is somewhat smaller, as it is to a freight line. On the GWR a ringed signal arm would have been used, a survival of a practice once adopted by many companies for signals on slow or goods lines. There is a single Home signal, 33, but worked splitting Distants 34 and 35.

The trap, 21, protects the down goods from movements from the down sidings, such movements being authorised by shunt signal 16. On the GWR or NER, shunt signals would also have been likely to control movements over crossover 23, but none are provided here, and the only shunt signals control movements from sidings on to the running lines. The double shunt signal, 26 and 25, controls moves from two siding roads, hence the double arrow. Yard signals were

often placed vertically, rather than side by side, and there is a simple way to remember how to read them, BR, British Rail, also stands for Bottom Right, and LT, London Transport, for Left Top. The top signal reads to the left, the bottom to the right. If there are three, it is left, middle, right, reading down. The bottom signal, 25, reads to the right, which is in fact a backing move along the up goods. The top signal, 26, reads to the left, which is over 24 and 23 crossovers to the down main, or over 13 as well to the down goods.

I have described the functions of many of the signals and their placing, as this should enable the modeller to signal his own station convincingly. The basic principle is that points that join a running line, or a diamond that passes through it, are protected by a stop signal. If it is a divergence, there will be splitting signals, one for each running line. As at Llanfair, one signal can protect a number of sequential points, although it is common to have each connection protected by a separate signal. Level crossings receive similar protection. Connections from sidings to passenger running lines are always trapped, and sometimes also if they lead on to freight running lines. Movements from such sidings are usually controlled by ground signals. Where there is a running line signal, as with Oakham Junction's No 3, and a divergence into a subsidiary route, ie the continuation of the up goods, there is a subsidiary signal, 17. This can

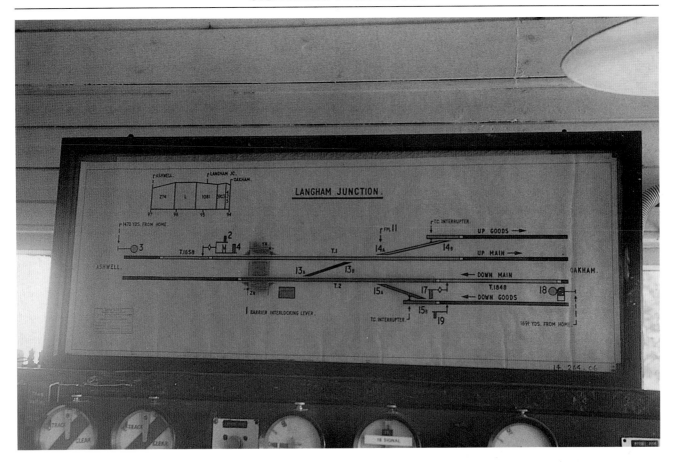

Above left Oakham Level Crossing is typical of Midland signal boxes, yet achieved fame as the prototype for the 4 mm Airfix plastic construction kit that has appeared on so many layouts. Note the fire buckets and the wooden walkway over the point and signal connections in front of the box.

Left BOT rules provided that roof columns, nameboards and other obstructions should be not less than 6 feet from the edge of the platform. Modellers sometimes overlook this, but at a few stations, usually early ones, predating the rule, there were exceptions. Oakham is such a location.

Above Langham Junction is the next box to the north, and we supplement the Oakham signal plans with a photo of the actual signal box diagram. Note how it corresponds to the left-hand end of the Oakham Junction diagram.

be a small arm on the bracket below any running signals, or a separate ground signal by the base of the bracket, as in this instance. Shunt signals were sometimes provided for backing moves on all running lines, but practice varied.

If one wished to signal Oakham Junction in the most pedantic manner, a four-arm vertical shunt signal could have been provided on the down goods by 13 points. Reading top to bottom, the arms would have controlled movements over 13, 23 and 24; 13 and 23; 13; and setting back into the down sidings with 13 normal and 21 pulled. A triple shunt signal

could also have been provided on the down main, and a quad controlling set-back movements on the up main in the vicinity of 23 points. The reader may care to work out the routes for himself. We have added eleven signals already, and more could be included. The signalling devotee will comment about 'Limit of Shunt' and other complexities, but these are outside the confines of this chapter. My objective is to show where you must put signals, and where you can put further signals if you wish.

A number of books have been published on prototype railway signalling that give extensive information on signal boxes, signals and other hardware. Signalling plans are less plentiful, but in the two volumes my father and I wrote on LMS station plans, about 100 signalling diagrams appeared for stations varying from the smallest to the largest. If you work from a lever frame, as the prototype did, and as I would recommend, it is sensible if you paint your levers in the same colour as the prototype:

Distant levers: yellow
Stop signals: red
Points: black
Point locks: blue
Combined points/point locks: black lower half,
    blue upper half

Above Finally, a treat for the signalling devotee. Pull-plates, giving details of a lever's function, were commonly fixed to a board at the back of the frame or, in the case of Midland Railway frames, to the quadrant plate. At Langham Junction a different and very rare alternative was employed, with brass plates bolted to the sides of the levers themselves.

Below This is an actual LMS signal box diagram. Points worked from the box are shown as continuous lines for the position in which they are normal, and broken for the route where the lever must be pulled. Points worked by ground frame are shown differently (as at the left-hand side of the diagram). Signals are coloured red or yellow, passenger lines were usually pale blue, and other lines orange-buff. Multi-colour diagrams, with colours changing for each track circuit section, came in later years.

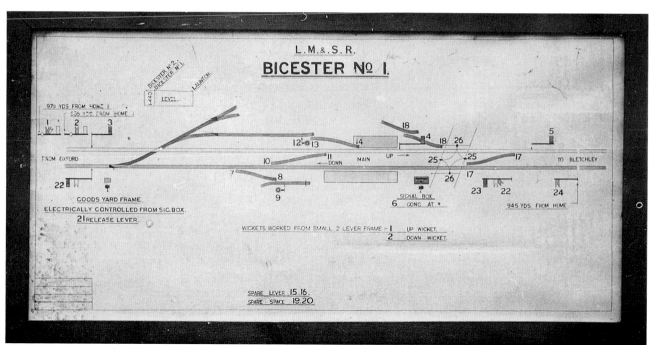

This splitting home at Ely Dock Junction, with its replacement colour light in the foreground, typifies the changes that are happening in railway signalling. The colour light has a multiple-aspect head (with a white 'not in use' 'X' on it) and two route 'feathers', ie a series of small white lights indicating a diverging route. The bracket signal has three separate posts - or 'dolls' - the relative heights indicating the importance of the routes. As the arms are too high above the bracket platform for maintenance, each doll has a subsidiary ladder.

Ground frame releases, gate stops, gate locks and
    wickets: brown
Gongs: green

Traditional semaphore signals survive in a few places, but multiple-aspect colour light signals now predominate. Unlike the semaphore signal, which customarily stood at Danger except when cleared for a train, the automatic and semi-automatic colour light normally shows green, except when a train has passed, when the signal changes to red, followed by single yellow and double yellow until it returns to green when the train is a sufficient distance away. In station areas the traditional approach, with signals normally at Danger, prevails. Some colour-light signalling is worked from

mechanical boxes, but much of the rail network is now controlled from Power Signal Boxes, or Signal Centres as they are often called today. The PSB dispenses with levers in favour of a track circuit panel, and routes are set by turning individual point switches, or on an entry-exit system.

Track circuits

Modern signalling relies upon track circuiting, which is sometimes thought of as a recent invention, but the first track circuit was installed at Crystal Palace station in the 1860s. However, it was not until 1901 that track circuiting made serious progress in the British Isles, the LSWR leading the way. In the simplest installation, the circuit comprises the continuous earth rail, the insulated block rail, and a battery connected across the rails. The circuit is completed by a relay in the signal cabin, which in early installations worked an indicator showing 'Track Occupied/ Unoccupied'. Subsequently, bulbs were installed in the signal box diagram, which made it easier to follow the path of a train. Examples of both are to be found on BR, and on the GHR! When a locomotive, carriage or wagon came on to the section, electricity flowed from rail to rail via the axle, as this was a lower resistance route than the relay. This tripped the relay and the indicator went to 'Track Occupied' or the bulb came on. In addition to working relays, a track circuit could work signals, semaphore or colour light, and lock block instruments. This system met the requirement of 'fail safe', for if the circuit was interrupted, for example if the battery failed, the track circuit went to 'Occupied'.

When Dad began to electrify the GHR in 1947 he decided on continuous track circuiting over much of the main-line system, and with three-rail, and later stud contact, electrification, this was easy to achieve. One rail became the common earth for traction and track circuits, the centre rail, and later the studs, provided the traction supply, while the other rail was the track circuit rail. We adopted a system whereby the axle completed a circuit rather than broke it, energising a bulb on the track circuit diagram. While this lacked the 'fail safe' facility of the prototype, any 'fail safe' system would require many relays. For a modeller working in three-rail or stud contact, track circuiting is simple.

Today most modellers use two-rail electrification, and as the track circuit has to share both rails with the traction supply, it is much harder to achieve. Roger Amos, in his *Complete Book of Model Railway Electronics*, describes a number of track circuit systems. One problem with these systems is that while they can detect the presence of a locomotive, the average carriage or wagon, with its insulated wheels, is invisible to the track circuit, so a 10-coach rake of carriages simply does not exist. This can only be overcome by circuitry in the coaching stock, adding to the cost and complexity. As track circuits form so essential a part of our operations, I do not regret the decision that Dad took to go to three-rail, and later stud contact, in 1947, and I would not dream of changing to two-rail, particularly as the studs developed by Dad were so inconspicuous. Few modellers would make the same choice today, so the simple track circuit is ruled out for the great majority of layouts, but as with so many things in this delightful hobby, you must decide what suits you best.

Track circuits can be made to do many things, from working track circuit indicators or red track circuit lights on a diagram, to controlling signals, power supply to sections in rear, so preventing tail-end collisions on the layout, or being interlocked with the block system. It is really up to the operator how far he takes it. If you wish to operate a modern signalling system in a prototypical manner, then track circuiting becomes essential.

This was the world in which my father grew up - yes, it is the legendary 44-arm double-deck Rugby 'Bedstead', built by the LNWR at GCR expense to provide a clear view of the signals when the GC's London Extension crossed the West Coast Main Line just outside Rugby station; it lasted until 1939.

Standing on the upper deck of the gantry is Frank Renshaw OBE, a dedicated North Western man and Chief Signal Fitter at Rugby for 30 years; he guided Dad's early interest in signalling, and made a model of the gantry. The engine is 'Prince of Wales' 4-6-0 N0 25673 Lusitania.

8.
OPERATING YOUR RAILWAY

After blood, toil, tears, sweat and sawdust, you now have your baseboards up, the tracks in place and the wiring connected. In the words of the best Hollywood film directors, 'Roll 'em!'. That was how railways started, and trains wandered off into the blue yonder, and no one knew where they were, or when one was expected the other way. Although railwaymen soon discovered that this was not the best way to work a railway, as it tended to produce collisions, many modellers still seem to favour the working practices of 1830, even though they may run 'Britannia' 'Pacifics' or Class '60s'.

The railways developed what in modern military jargon is termed '3C' - Command, Control, Communication. By the early 1840s they had the most sophisticated '3C' system the world had yet seen, and it was not until 20th century that military and government systems replaced the railways as the most advanced communicators on earth. What has this to do with railway modellers? My father said it was not sufficient to have tracks, rolling-stock and scenery. The railway needed to operate, and do so realistically. Trains do not start at random, because the driver feels like a trip to Blackpool or Brighton - they run to timetable. They are not going 'anywhere' - they are going somewhere specific. They do not go because someone feels like it - they are offered from one place to the next, and until the man at the next location has accepted the train, it doesn't budge. Even as a youngster Dad appreciated this, and wrote an amusing account of a visit to another layout:

'From 1925 until the beginning of 1927, the railway slept. I was then invited to tea with a school friend, with a third friend to make up an operating trio. I was asked to bring any railway bits I had. There was a spaghetti of track with about eight points and two diamond crossings. Operation was equally unconventional. We each wound up an engine, coupled on one or two vehicles and on the word "go" we set off, changing points as we approached them to wherever we wanted. Deliberate collisions were strictly prohibited, but accidental ones were frequent, in fact very frequent, and even if you stopped in time to avoid another train, you were liable to attack from the third train. After a time I suggested that someone act as signalman to authorise movements. The other two wanted to drive, so I was appointed, and we ran without accidents for a period, but the absence of excitement soon bored them. We did not have any more joint sessions, but we did have a very nice tea, and remained friends, and more important, my railway interest was rekindled, but with a very different modus operandi.'

Dad reasoned that if our trains worked as the real ones did, it would be more enjoyable, and kinder to the stock! In 1927 he took the first steps towards safe operating techniques, just as the prototype had some 90 years before.

The first step was to ensure that the operator at A would not send a train until the operator at B was ready. Having worked a layout where no such system was used, and A sent trains whenever he felt like it, and, being at B, I never knew when a train was going to bear down on me, I can appreciate the feeling of security that the block system must have given many railwaymen. If the block telegraph was good enough for the prototype, it was good enough for Dad.

Block instruments

The railway is divided into 'block sections', controlled from signal boxes or 'block posts'. When the signalman at box A wishes to send a train to box B, he must 'Call Attention' on the block telegraph instrument. This comprises a bell tapper for A to send coded bell messages to the operator at B; a bell to receive B's messages; a handle or commutator that controls a telegraph instrument needle at B to give B a visual indication when A has accepted a train, with a repeater needle in A's instrument; and a second telegraph that the man at B controls to give A a visual reminder of when a train has been accepted by B.

The procedure is simple. Once A has called attention, with 1 beat, B acknowledges similarly. A then offers the train he wants to send by sending an 'Is Line Clear?' code. This is a group of rings, 4 for an express passenger train, 3-1 for a local, 1-3-1 for a parcels, 3 for a wayside freight, and so on. If B can accept the train, he repeats the code back, and turns the commutator on his block instrument to 'Line Clear'. This works the corresponding telegraph needle in A's instrument, and the repeater needle in his own instrument. When the train is departing from A, the signalman there calls attention again and gives 'Train Entering Section', 2 beats, to B. This is acknowledged, and B turns his commutator from 'Line Clear' to 'Train on Line'. This switches the needle at A to 'Train on Line', and the repeater needle at B. When the train has arrived at B, and the signalman has checked that it is complete by seeing the tail lamp, B sends 'Train out of Section', 2-1, to A, and returns his commutator to the off (vertical) position, which is called 'Line Blocked'. He is now ready to accept another train, using the same procedure.

When worked properly, the block system ensured that there could never be two trains moving in the same direction in the section at the same time. In reality, signalmen sometimes forgot that a train had not passed, and 'blocked out' (sent 'Train out of Section'), or drivers ignored signals, as the books on railway accidents reveal. Various safeguards evolved, such as the interlocking of the block instrument with the Starting signal controlling entry into the block section ahead. Signals and block instruments were also locked with track circuits, but on much of British Railways the simple block telegraph functioned until the introduction of modern panel Power Signal Boxes, and it was only in the 1960s that the traditional signal box with its brightly painted levers, polished block instruments and permanently boiling kettle began to disappear in large numbers.

Dad adopted the block system early in 1928. Nowadays you can buy prototype block instruments, but as an LNWR block instrument is a collector's item, and will set you back over £100, that is an expensive addition to the model railway, especially as you will need two instruments for each block section. In 1928 the railways were not inclined to sell working

Swinden & Nappa is the smallest station on the GHR main line, but it is worked by the largest block instrument array, in this case a pair of standard LNWR wood-cased instruments, and one of the iron-cased needle repeater instruments. Some of the signals are indicated by prototype signal repeaters as well.

The lamp hut and platform railings at Hoggsnorton give an indication of the size of the standard GHR miniature block instrument, which are 3.25 inches tall; the oldest was built more than 60 years ago. The controllers are also purpose-built, with an on/off knob controlling a wiper arm to about 40 contact studs connected to a resistance mat.

block instruments, as they were expensive pieces of equipment that were required to run their services. In any case, a schoolboy's pocket money provided insufficient capital to pay for block instruments as well as locomotives, track and so on!

Dad decided to build his own miniature block instruments. The telegraph needles on the prototype are worked by electric solenoids, but these are large and cost money, so the repeater needle in the instrument was controlled by a mechanical linkage, and the remote needle in the other man's instrument was replaced by a green light for 'Line Clear' and a red light for 'Train on Line'. The first GHR instruments were built early in 1928. At the time Dad was unaware that the Westinghouse Brake & Signal Co had been commissioned by the LMS to carry out an extensive resignalling of Manchester Victoria/Exchange. It was an all-electric system with miniature levers, using block instruments built into the console. Red and green lights replaced the needles of the traditional block instrument. The system, representing the latest technology, was commissioned in 1928-29,

some months after the first GHR instruments on the same principle had been introduced. Many years later it gave Dad a good deal of amusement to think that the Westinghouse engineers had been exploring the same approach as he had simultaneously, but that the GHR got there first!

We now have over 30 block instruments in use, mostly of the GHR standard miniature style, but including three genuine LNWR instruments, which work to GHR standard instruments, and some intermediate ones built by another modeller. It is amusing to reflect that the GHR block system was actually capable of being linked in to genuine block instruments that had signalled real trains on the real railway. Triang Hornby produced a miniature block instrument for some years, based on the standard BR block, but this has long been out of production, so is itself a collector's item. It is possible to buy the most obscure RTR locos and kits, but the modeller finds it no easier to buy a block instrument today than 60 years ago.

Earlier in this book I spoke of an accident in Hillside No 6 platform, when a verbal train message was misinterpreted. Installation of the block system had not kept pace with civil engineering, and the result was a collision. Both operators had many years experience of railway working, and made the classic mistake. If your line will be operated by more than

GHR first, LMS second! A few months after the first GHR illuminated block instrument appeared, Westinghouse installed these illuminated block instruments at Deal Street signal box as part of a comprehensive re-signalling at Manchester Victoria and Exchange. Note the miniature levers in this Westinghouse all-electric system. *Author's Collection*

one person, then a means of communication is vital. 'OK for a coal through six' let us down, and sooner or later your message will be as clear - and as ambiguous. For well over a century the majority of British railways used the block telegraph system, and it adds to the realism and the pleasure of operating in an authentic manner.

Our block instruments were built using traditional small light bulbs and a mechanical linkage for the repeater needle. Had my father been starting today, I am sure he would have used the modern LED, which cuts down work when bulbs burn out. The LED is so cheap that the repeater needle could also have been replaced by lights, as was the case with the Westinghouse instruments at Manchester. The instrument would require two green LEDs, two red LEDs, a three-way switch, with centre off, and a tapper for a bell or electronic buzzer at the far end. Any modeller

who is capable of wiring in a control panel could manufacture his own block instruments quickly and easily.

Telegraph bell codes

This then gives us a communication system, and all we need to do is to use it. I have outlined the block system, and reproduce here some pages from the 1929 LMS Block Telegraph regulations, which set out the bell codes in more detail. The GHR timespan is somewhat elastic, as we have an LNWR 'Precursor' and a BR 'Britannia', but the predominant period is late 1930s/early 1940s. We should use the LMS 1930s block codes, but when construction work resumed after the war several of the operating team were professional BR signalmen, and were used to the current BR block codes. It would have been confusing, indeed dangerous, for them to work BR block by day, and have to revert to LMS codes in the evening, so Dad opted for BR codes. With Power Boxes now controlling so much of British Rail, it is no longer a problem, but our team are so used to the BR codes that we have retained them. For the modeller starting from scratch,

GENERAL REGULATIONS FOR TRAIN SIGNALLING BY TELEGRAPH BELLS.

BELL SIGNALS.

See Regulation	Description	Beats on bell	How given
1	Call attention	1	1
	Passenger train, breakdown van train, light engine going to assist disabled train, or fire brigade train entering section	4	Consecutively
	Parcels, newspaper, fish, meat, fruit, milk, horse, or perishable train, composed of coaching stock entering section	5	1—1—3
	Empty coaching stock train entering section	5	2—2—1
	Fitted freight or cattle train with the continuous break in use on NOT LESS than half the vehicles entering section	5	Consecutively
	Express freight or cattle train with the continuous break on less than half the vehicles but in use on four vehicles connected to the engine indicated by ✠ in the Working Time Tables entering section	7	2—2—3
4 and 5	Express freight or cattle train not fitted with the continuous break, or with the continuous break in use on LESS than four vehicles entering section	5	3—2
	Through freight train, or ballast train conveying workmen and running not less than 15 miles without stopping entering section	5	1—4
	Light engine, or light engines coupled together (see Regulation 7) entering section	5	2—3
	Engine with one or two breaks entering section	5	1—3—1
	Through mineral, or empty wagon train entering section	5	4—1
	Freight train stopping at intermediate stations, or ballast train running short distance entering section	3	Consecutively
	Branch freight train entering section (where authorised)	3	1—2
6	Bank engine in rear of train	4	2—2
	Engine with one or two breaks in rear of train	6	2—3—1
	Cancelling bank engine in rear of train signal	8	4—2—2
	Cancelling engine with one or two breaks in rear of train signal	8	4—3—1

BELL SIGNALS—continued

See Regulation	Description	Beats on bell	How given
10 & 12	Train out of section or obstruction removed	3	2—1
12	Obstruction danger	6	Consecutively
17	Stop and examine train	7	Consecutively
18	Cancelling Train entering section signal	8	3—5
19	Train passed without tail lamp	9	Consecutively to box in advance : 4—5 to box in rear.
19A	Tail light out, tail lamp in wrong position, or improper side light exhibited	9	7—2
20	Train divided	10	5—5
22	Vehicles running away on wrong line	12	2—5—5
	Vehicles running away on right line	14	4—5—5
23	Cancelling vehicles running away on right line signal	8	3—1—4
24	Opening of signal-box	15	5—5—5
	Closing of signal-box	17	7—5—5
	Testing sections switched through	6	3—2—1
27	Testing bells	16	Consecutively
28	Time signal	18	8—5—5
29	Lampman or fog-signalman required	19	9—5—5
30	Testing controlled or slotted signals	20	5—5—5—5

All BELL signals must be acknowledged by repetition.

USE OF TELEPHONIC COMMUNICATION.—Where telephonic communication is provided on the Telegraph Bell circuit, the Call signal is two beats on the bell without the Call attention signal preceding it.

In cases of emergency a special bell signal 3—3—3—3 may be given on the bell, without the Call attention signal preceding it, and a signalman receiving this signal must immediately attend to the Telegraph.

REVISED AND ADDITIONAL BELL SIGNALS.

See Regulation.	Description.	Beats on Bell.	How given.
4 and 5	*Additional—* Train conveying special horse traffic and composed of coaching stock entering section (where authorised)	5	3-1-1
19 A	*Revised—* Tail light or side lights out, or improper side lights exhibited	9	7-2

(1-10-31.)

there is much to be said for adopting the correct block codes for the company and period he models. The Southern and Great Western had highly idiosyncratic codes, and modellers should check the appropriate reference books, etc. The LMS and LNER codes were generally similar, and BR followed their practice, except on the Western or Southern Regions, which retained their old systems. I have not attempted to list all block codes for all companies at all periods, as it would run to a volume in its own right.

The signalling purist may complain that I have forgotten 'Obstruction Danger' (6 bells), 'Shunt into Forward Section' (3-3-2), and many other codes. I haven't. At the box I often work, I can expect to receive 3-3-2 from the next box at least twice during a running. In the other direction, Hillside No 6 platform is now worked by block, but not the usual Absolute Block. Instead it is under Station Yard Working, which was used between boxes at large passenger stations, and permitted two or more trains into a platform under carefully devised rules. Few modellers will need such refinements, and the first day we worked it I had to get out a copy of the BR Regulations for Train Signalling, as I had never worked some of the provisions before.

If this sounds too daunting, don't worry. Station Yard Working is something you are unlikely to need, and at least three of our operators have brought their youngsters aged 10 or under, and they have mastered the block system. They were late starters, for I could offer a train before I could do the multiplication tables! My mother used to go shopping in Leamington once a week. We had a 1946 Hillman Minx car, and while the wipers were power-worked, they had handles projecting through the dashboard to permit occasional wipes by hand. When Dad and I were waiting, we would put the block instrument needles - sorry, the wiper blades - to the vertical 'Line Blocked' position. As Hillman had inexplicably omitted to provide bells between the driver and front-seat passenger, we had to rap on the dashboard, but once I had accepted a train, I turned my needle (alias wiper) to 'Line Clear'. When I received 'Train Entering Section', I would turn to 'Train on Line', and after the train (which was sometimes round and edible) arrived, I would send 'Train out of Section', and turn my needle to the vertical again.

I soon became proficient at block working, and when I was about six I was taken to a signal box. After initial disbelief at a six-year-old who knew the block system, the signalman asked if I would like to ring the bells. This was splendid, but there was one drawback. BR, with as little imagination as Hillman, had failed to provide for six-year-old signalmen, and the block instruments were out of reach, so a chair

was called for. In later years it became necessary to learn far less useful and interesting things, and I have always felt that it is a grave reflection on the education system that not once in my school career was I asked an exam question on 'Train Running Away Wrong Line', or 'Blocking Back outside Home Signal'.

Single-line working

On a single-track line there is always the risk that stations at opposite ends of a section may both dispatch trains, and the Americans coined the phrase 'a Cornfield Meet' for such mishaps. In America reliance was placed on a 'Train Dispatcher' system, whereby a centrally placed officer, in telegraphic contact with the stations, ordered all train meets. A comparable approach was used in Britain briefly, on lines such as the S&DJR, but fell out of favour and did not re-appear until the modern radio-controlled dispatcher system introduced in recent years on long single-track sections of British Rail, such as the Highland line north of Inverness.

The British approach was to divide a single-track line into 'Staff sections' between crossing points, with each section being provided with a suitably inscribed wooden baton or 'Train Staff'. The driver was not allowed to enter the single-track section without the staff. As there was only one staff for any section, there could never be a head-on collision. A moment's thought will reveal the inflexibility of the system, for trains must go alternately A to B, B to A, and so on. Two trains cannot follow one another. The answer was to *show* the driver the Staff at Station A, but to give him a ticket, which said that, having seen the staff, he was entitled to proceed from A to B, and the staff would follow by a later train. This was the 'Staff and ticket system', and by the 1880s virtually every single-track line in the British Isles worked in this way.

In theory the system was foolproof, for if the signalman handed the driver a ticket without showing the staff, the latter was supposed to demand to see the staff, so that a ticket could *never* be issued from a station when the staff was at the other end of the section. In reality I have seen a driver accept a ticket without the staff being displayed, so human nature conspired to thwart the safety precautions. Moreover, sudden unexpected fluctuations in traffic may arise, or an engine may fail, when the staff is at the far end of the line, and it must then be collected before any trains can move.

Various inventors subsequently set out to design electric train staff instruments. These consisted of a block instrument that also housed a locked rack of

Right The Hoggsnorton Train Staff shows evidence of hard usage over the years, for like all wooden Staffs it takes plenty of knocks. It is about two-thirds the size of the traditional prototype wooden train staff - the slot in the end to hold the train ticket was an idea of my father.

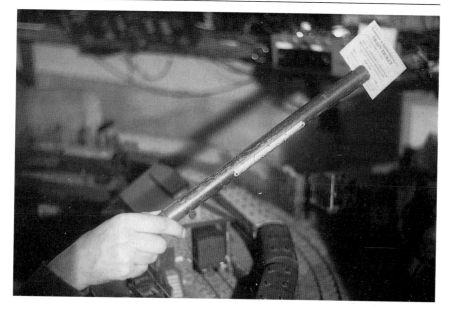

Below GHR train tickets for the single line from Ponkeston to Hoggsnorton (left, coloured pink), and for the return journey (right, green).

a281 100 5/94 HPC

Greenlane & Hillside Railway Co
TRAIN TICKET
To Engineman or Guard ....
of Train ....
YOU are authorised to proceed from
HOGGSNORTON to PONKESTON
and the Train Staff will follow by a
later train
Date ....199......
signature...
·(To be given up by Engineman on arrival at the Station to which he is authorised to proceed).

a280 100 5/94 HPC

Greenlane & Hillside Railway Co
TRAIN TICKET
To Engineman or Guard ....
of Train ....
YOU are authorised to proceed from
PONKESTON to HOGGSNORTON

and the Train Staff will follow by a
later train
Date ....199......
signature...
(To be given up by Engineman on arrival at the Station to which he is authorised to proceed).

Left The Tyers electric token system utilised steel or aluminium tokens, much smaller than the wooden staffs, and they were inscribed for the section concerned. The Stourbridge Junction to Stourbridge Town section was unusual in that there were two parallel single lines, one to the passenger station, one to the goods depot, hence the 'passenger train staff' inscription.

'tokens', the token replacing the staff as the driver's authority to proceed. If A wished to send a train to B, he offered it in the usual manner, but unless B depressed a plunger, A could not withdraw a token from his instrument. Once the token had been withdrawn, no further token could be withdrawn from the racks at either end of the section until it had been put back into one or other instrument. Although there could be a dozen or more tokens at each end of the section, only one could be 'out' at any time. The electric train staff system appeared in many different guises, and remains in use on a few parts of BR today.

In modelling a single-track section, you should adopt some form of staff system. The simplest is staff and ticket working, which has been used on the GHR for over 60 years. On the Hoggsnorton branch our earliest staff was a magnet, which could be attached to the tinplate cab roof of the engine or sit in the bunker. The signalmen were responsible for putting the staff on the engine, and taking it off at the far end of the single-track section. Train tickets were also devised, but as these were too big to put on the engine, they were handed across to the signalman at the next station. In the 1960s one of my mother's household brooms was pensioned off, and it occurred to us that the remains of the broomstick would provide a couple of prototype-sized wooden train staffs. The broom handle was forthwith cut up and reshaped. Staffs were 'coloured' for easy recognition, and the Hoggsnorton-Mickleburgh staff received yellow bands at each end, and the Mickleburgh-Ponkeston staff received white bands. The staff should also be 'inscribed'; readers in their mid-40s or above will remember the stamping machines on railway stations that would stamp out a name tag on aluminium strip. I paid a hurried visit to Rugby station and returned with suitably worded strips. Dad contributed the suggestion of a saw-cut in the end of the staff into which a train ticket could be slotted. I do not know of a prototype for this, but it would have been a wise improvement to the 'Staff and ticket' system. GHR rules provide that on the Hoggsnorton line, the staff must either be handed over when a train is dispatched, or a ticket must be passed over by means of the staff. The operator at the other end is entitled to reject a ticket unless it is handed over by this means.

Two members of the pre-war team built miniature electric train staff instruments for a single-track branch on that line. Sadly these went astray during the war, but the local college of further education recently produced a pair of miniature ETS instruments as part of a 'design and build' project for students, and these are awaiting installation. Whatever form of staff system you adopt, you will find that it adds a further dimension of reality.

Signal control

The block system copes with communication between signal boxes, but the signalman still needs to communicate with the train driver. The answer was the semaphore signal, and later the colour light. Dad decided on proper signalling in the 1920s. Through an advert in *Model Railway News* he met the chief signal fitter at Rugby, which gave him an entrée to the Rugby boxes, and his knowledge of signalling rapidly developed. On the clockwork layout the signalman controlled the routes and drivers had to obey the signals, as on the prototype.

A similar system was adopted by Joe Griffiths for his Conway model railway. This commenced as a clockwork line, and before a recruit could drive an engine he had to accompany a qualified driver for a number of trips, 'learning the road' and the signals. The signals were worked from enclosed signal boxes that were just big enough to accommodate a full-sized human being. The signalman had a miniature lever frame, some LNER one-third size-training block instruments, and red and green flags. Each station required a signalman, and each engine needed a driver, so a dozen operators could soon be swallowed up, but for realism it had much to commend it. When clockwork mechanisms became scarce, the system was electrified, with power permanently on, and rheostat control knobs in the tenders or bunkers to control the engines. Dad and I had many delightful visits to the Conway railway, where he was passed as a full driver.

On one occasion one of the GHR team came with us, and he talked his way into one signal box while I talked my way into an adjacent one. The friend, Robert 'Bill' Cave, was used to GHR block working,

Above right Paythorne is equipped with a standard GHR lever frame, although the electrics are not presently worked through the lever contacts as is normal. The levers are umbrella spokes, as they have a nicely engineered pivot at the base. The frame comprises a wooden base and sides, with a tin-plate or steel quadrant plate, notched to hold the levers in the pulled, or 'reversed', position, and the levers themselves. The levers will return to the 'normal' position when released from the notch through the action of counterweights, springs, etc. The pull-plate in front of the levers gives their numbers and, in prototype style, lists which other levers are required. For example, signal 20 requires crossover 19 to be reversed. When the original 29-lever frame at Paythorne required extending, this could only be done at the left-hand end, so an extra seven levers, A to G, were added. If it is necessary to extend a frame at the low-numbered end, this is the usual procedure, and in the previous chapter you may have noticed that Oakham Level Crossing box boasted an A lever.

Right The Conway model railway was operated from enclosed signal boxes. Here the signalman at Conway station looks out over the four-platform passenger station as he works his frame. *J. Griffiths*

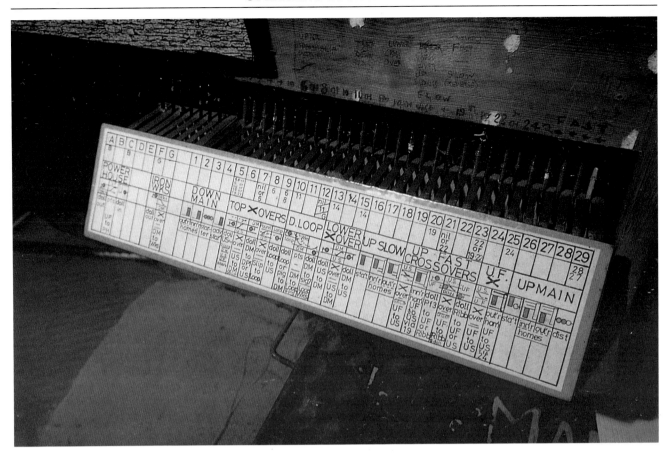

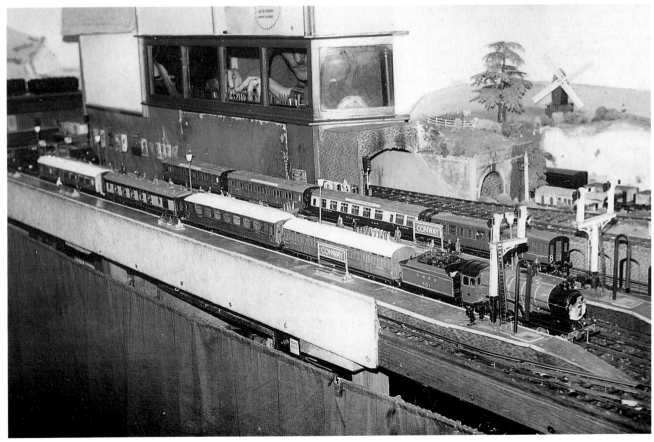

where 1-5-5, 'Shunt Train for Following Train to Pass', is sometimes used to liven up an operator who seems to have forgotten to 'block out' for the previous train. I was allowed to watch what was happening in the box. Suddenly 1-5-5 rang out loud and clear, and the signalman turned to me with an injured expression, asking 'What was that?'. I explained that Bill might be responsible, and he suggested that I deal with any future block messages in that direction, as I knew the Philistine at the other end. By the end of the evening the Conway signalman had accepted Bill's barbarous ideas, and even adopted them himself on occasion. I might add that Bill, who joined the GHR when he was at school, and joined BR after he left school, did the BR signalling exam for interest, although he was on the admin side, and received a pass far in advance of the standard expected of professional signalmen. He said that after a session on the GHR, the pace of BR operation was quietly soothing.

Dad and I both greatly admired the Conway system, but it required an enormous room, very few duck-unders, as drivers had to accompany their engines, and a large staff to operate. When the GHR was electrified after the war, he opted for signal box control of points and signals, with power being fed through the lever frame contacts, so that signals and points had to be set correctly before the train could move. If there were sufficient operators, at most stations there was room for a separate driver, but the controllers were placed so that the signalman could work them as well. Signals and points were worked mechanically by waxed twine, and the mechanical interlocking of one lever against another is simply achieved in this way. With the availability of point and signal motors nowadays, many modellers may prefer an all-electric approach, rather than our electro-mechanical system. Happily the principle is so flexible that it can accommodate almost any mechanical or electrical preference. Some of the mechanical frames are now over 60 years old, and with around 500 levers in the various frames, the 'down-time' through major faults is minimal.

The GHR occupies two rooms, a passage, two attics and the passage between them, and while the block system is used for train messages, some verbal contact is needed in the event of derailments, etc. As with BR, we have our own internal phone systems. If the railway was in one room, this would have been a luxury.

In writing this chapter I have concentrated on the team approach where there is at least one other operator, for a good part of the fun is teamwork. Some modellers prefer to work alone, or may have to, and offering block messages to yourself is rather pointless. The Rev Peter Denny, whose Buckingham branch has

been an inspiration to countless modellers, created an amazing electro-mechanical computer to control routes, power and bell codes at his fiddle yard; it was described in Railway Modeller some years ago. It could respond to bell codes, offer trains, set up routes and apply power. With the advances in computer technology, and the drop in prices compared with just a few years back, a computer program to manage a fiddle yard would be feasible. It might not be as good or flexible as a good human operator, but it might be better than a poor one, and you can always tell it what a twit it is without hurting its feelings!

Clock on!

We now have the tools to run the trains safely. The next thing is to run them sensibly. We can just 'run trains' as the mood takes us, and for testing, training, or when we are very short-staffed, we have done so on the GHR. However, timetable operation is more fun, for each move then has a purpose. We are not just driving a model engine from A to B, but are preparing the stock for the 9.10 am Hillside to Liverpool (Lime Street) express. It is an LMS working, so the engine is off Hillside (Millbank) MPD, and the stock comes from the carriage depot by Hillside (Exchange). It is platformed at 8.55 am. A through coach should have arrived on the back of the 8.24 am motor ex Hoggsnorton, due in to Hillside at 8.41 am. If the motor is late, it may delay the express, as the train engine is diagrammed to pick up the through coach from the motor and attach it to the front of the express, allowing the motor to leave at 9.00 am.

In the next two chapters we will look at building up a timetable, but the timetable is merely an operating tool, like the block instruments or lever frames. If we opt for timetable working, each station will need a timetable sheet listing that station's moves. Alternatively we could work by train sequence, at a pace that suits us or the other operators. This means that we never have a late departure, as time does not move on until the train moves. I am sure BR, or its privatised successors, would welcome such an idea, and I have found it enjoyable working to sequence on a friend's layout.

Personally, though, I prefer speeded clock operation. In the 1940s Dad decided that a three-hour operating session was as long as most operators would want, and if we used an eight-times clock, a 24-hour day would be covered in three hours. An initial eight-times clock was built, and as the railway expanded into two more rooms, further clocks were added. They were independently controlled, and upon the ceremonial bellow 'Clock onnn!', three hot little hands would start the clocks. The modifications to speed them up had some odd side effects, one being that the clocks would run as happily backwards as forwards. They were fitted with a pawl to prevent this, but on one clock the pawl did not work, so it would often start off backwards. If the operator did not spot this, time was marching forwards eight times as fast as reality over two-thirds of the layout, and backwards at the same speed in the remaining area! This did not help smooth timetable operation.

Dad explained one reason for the eight-times clock. On layouts the distance between stations is usually limited, and if we used real time the train might leave A at 12.00, leave B at 12.01 and reach C at 12.02. This was more appropriate to satellites or jet aircraft than trains, as stations are seldom that close together. With an eight-times clock, a train left A at 12.00, left B at 12.08 and reached C at 12.16. As well as permitting a 24-hour day in three hours, running times were thus more plausible.

For over 40 years we operated to these eight-times clocks, but their foibles, such as reverse time, prompted one of the team, Blair Ramsay, to suggest a modern digital display controlled from a central computer, with slave monitors in all operating areas. Blair said that he could program different speeds into the system, and four, five, six, seven and eight times were agreed. As there is a Tidal boat train on the GHR, the

tide-tables were consulted, for while it is said that time and tide wait for no man, on the GHR the tides seemingly waited on the needs of the Hillside yard master who had to make up the Tidal. With the tide on the clock, the tide controls the operator, rather than vice versa. It was suggested that the Blair Ramsay Award for Making Life Difficult take the form of a statue of King Canute. A day-selecting feature allows for Tuesdays and Fridays-only trains. If we are short-staffed, the seven-times speed can be a welcome relief. It is also a remarkably polite clock, and when the running comes to an end, and you wish to switch off, it says 'Goodbye Master'.

Apart from improving running time between stations, the speeded clock allows us to sample the different phases of the day in a three-hour running, with the morning rush-hour, the quieter midday period, the evening rush, the night freights being sent out, and the sleeping car expresses. It also means that the pace of operation on a branch line is more enjoyable. If we ran straight time or two-times, the Hoggsnorton branch, with motor trains at most once at hour, would not be terribly interesting to work. With the eight-times clock, an hour passes in 7.5 minutes. If there is a horsebox to add to the train, or a fitted wagon to detach, the time can pass quickly. Without the clock the only way we could have an interesting operating pattern would be to run a service that would be more in keeping with Clapham Junction than a country branch.

You may do something quite different, but if you enjoy it, all well and good. I have explained how our block system, signalling, timetable working and clock dovetail together. I know it works, and it has given us years of enjoyment in a realistic environment.

In adopting a speeded clock, it is important not to go too fast, for while many operations are quicker on the model, some still take a good deal of time. One of the most demanding is shunting, and if one is fighting the clock it can take away much of the enjoyment. Here BR Standard Class '4' 4-6-0 No 75067 shunts a selection of wagons at Brockenhurst in 'real time' in the mid-1960s.

9.
PASSENGER TIMETABLING

Passengers are a nuisance. They expect railways to say when they will run their trains from A to B, rather than to see what turns up in the way of passengers and run a train when there is a suitable cross-section of humanity to cart around. They expect that the railway will send the trains at the time it says it will, and if it does not, they write letters of complaint. About three days after writing this chapter, I shall be going to Crewe, and I shall be most upset if the train does not travel at the appointed time. Thankfully our model passengers do not indulge in this sort of unreasonableness, so we can run trains when we feel like it, but it is more satisfactory if we follow the prototype and operate to timetable. How do we go about it?

Following the prototype

If we are modelling the GC London Extension in 1932 or the Great Northern main line, we need to obtain a copy of the appropriate timetable. Passenger services are detailed in two sorts of timetable, the public timetable, which is on sale to the passenger, and the working timetable, or WTT for short, which is confined to railway staff. Traditionally the WTT listed not just the passenger services, but empty coaching stock (ECS) movements, parcels trains, light engines (LEs) for passenger purposes and so on. There was a similar volume on freight services. In pre-Nationalisation and pre-Grouping days many companies issued just one WTT, covering all passenger and freight services, and the GWR continued to do so in some of its Service Time Tables (STTs) into early BR years. We will follow majority practice by separating passenger and freight.

The public timetable gives us a lot of information if we are modelling a specific line, but does not cover parcels, fish, milk, ECS and LE movements, so we must either guess these, or obtain a WTT. Many leading railway antiquarian/second-hand booksellers offer public and working timetables in their lists. Sadly a genuine pre-Grouping timetable can fetch £50 or more, but a number of publishers have reprinted historic timetables from the 1860s to the 1930s, including company public timetables, working timetables and even copies of Bradshaw, which covers the whole of the British Isles. If we wish to model a specific branch, we need the timetable for that branch. The GWR, for example, divided its services into some 16 STTs, and if we model the Chippenham-Calne branch there is little benefit in buying any of the 15 volumes we do not need. Of course the volume we need may be the one the dealer does *not* possess. That presents a problem, but until the mid-1950s BR service patterns closely mirrored pre-Nationalisation practices, so if we cannot get a 1938 GWR timetable, an early 1950s BR version is a fair substitute. Having spoken of the Calne branch, I will illustrate a page from the Western Region STT for June-September 1951. It details auto-services, mixed trains, passenger trains, freights and light engines.

Above right The pre-Grouping era has receded beyond the direct recall of all save a dwindling number of octogenarian enthusiasts, but as we look at the gleaming paintwork of GNR No 1341, an Ivatt 'D2' of 1898, as she enters York, we can understand the appeal this era holds for so many modellers, with its graceful locomotives and panelled stock. It must have been a glorious sight. Obtaining details of train formations of long ago is not easy, so such illustrations are a valuable source of data. The diamond crossing through the points at the end of the platform is an extraordinary piece of trackwork. *H. J. Stretton Ward*

Right LYR No 1126, an Aspinall '11' Class goods, takes water on Lea Road troughs as she hurries along with a Blackpool excursion comprised of six-wheel stock shortly before the Grouping. On summer Saturdays, when tens of thousands of excursionists and holidaymakers presented themselves at the city stations, it was a point of honour to get them all away, and 0-6-0 goods locomotives, spare at the weekend, were pressed into service, along with rakes of stock that might only venture out of the sidings on peak days of the year. *Author's Collection*

BROOM JC., STRATFORD-ON-AVON, BANBURY AND BLISWORTH.

WEEKDAYS ONLY.

184

Stations (Down):
BROOM JUNCTION — dep.
Bidford-on-Avon
Binton
Stratford-on-Avon
Ettington
Kineton
Burton Dassett
Fenny Compton
Byfield
Woodford West Junction
Woodford & Hinton (L.N.E.)
Morton Pinkney
Blakesley
BANBURY
Farthinghoe
Cockley Brake Junction
Helmdon
Wappenham
Towcester
BLISWORTH

c—Arrives Wappenham 11.10 a.m.

BLISWORTH, BANBURY, STRATFORD-ON-AVON AND BROOM JUNCTION.

WEEKDAYS ONLY.

Stations (Up):
BLISWORTH — dep.
Towcester
Wappenham
Helmdon
Cockley Brake Junction
Farthinghoe
BANBURY
Blakesley
Morton Pinkney
Woodford & Hinton (L.N.E.)
Woodford West Junction
Byfield
Fenny Compton
Burton Dassett
Kineton
Ettington
Stratford-on-Avon
Binton
Bidford-on-Avon
BROOM JUNCTION

A—Advertised 8.45 a.m.
K—This train may make one stop between Stratford and Bidford (in addition to the booked stop at Binton Station) when required for the purpose of setting down and picking up Engineers' Dept. workmen. The necessary instructions to the trainmen will be issued by the Station Master at Stratford-on-Avon.

A page from the LMS Passenger WTT for October 1942 for the former Stratford-upon-Avon & Midland Junction Railway.

No. 4

277

CHIPPENHAM AND CALNE.

Single line, worked by Electric Train Staff.

DOWN TRAINS. — WEEK DAYS.

Stations:
Chippenham B.H'lt
Stanley B.H'lt
Bl'k Dog Sid'g
Calne

DOWN TRAINS — WEEK DAYS—continued.

SUNDAYS.

UP TRAINS. — WEEK DAYS.

Stations:
Chippenham
Stanley B. Halt
Black Dog Siding
Calne

UP TRAINS. — WEEK DAYS—continued.

SUNDAYS.

Down Trains.—Ruling Gradient 1 in 60 F. Stanley Bridge Halt, 90 R. Black Dog Siding and Calne, 109 F.

In addition to above, special trips are arranged as desired with live stock, meat and urgent traffic.

WELLS. TRANSFER TRIPS BETWEEN WESTERN AND SOUTHERN OPERATING AREAS

East Somerset
Priory Road
Tucker Street

Tucker Street
Priory Road
East Somerset

The Calne branch timetable from the Western Region STT for June-September 1951.

The timings shown on this page WILL NOT APPLY ON SATURDAYS, 20th June to 12th September, 1959

J 10 WEEKDAYS Salisbury, Exeter, Plymouth, Ilfracombe and Torrington

DOWN		1.0 pm Waterloo			LE		ECS	4.40 pm Exmouth		1.5 pm Waterloo	To Padstow and Bude	5.15 pm Exmouth			5.45 pm Taunton	
					SX	FO Q	Q			Q						
		PM	PM	PM	PM	PM	PM	PM	PM	PM	PM	PM	PM	PM	PM	PM
SALISBURY .. .. arr	1	2 39								2 51						
dep	2	2 45								2 57						3 5
Wilton South	3															3a12½
Dinton	4															3a22½
Tisbury	5															3a30½
Semley	6															3e41
Gillingham	7															3c48½
TEMPLECOMBE .... arr	8	3 19							3 19	3 31						3 57½
.. dep	9	3 23							3 34	3 34						4 1½
Milborne Port	10															4a 7½
Sherborne	11	3a35														4c15
YEOVIL JN. .... arr	12	3 43							3 52	3 52						4 22
.. .. dep	13	3 46							3 55	3 55						4 31
Sutton Bingham	14					Until 11th September inclusive	FX until 10th September SX commencing 14th Sept.									4a37
Crewkerne	15								4a 8	4a 8						4a48
Chard Jn. .... arr	16								4 20	4 20						5 0
.. .. dep	17								4 21	4 21						5 1
Axminster .... arr	18								4 28	4 28						5 8
.. .. .. dep	19								4 32	4 32						5 9
SEATON JN......... arr	20								4 38	4 38						5 14
.. .. dep	21								4 42	4 42						5 15
Honiton	22					4‖35	4†35		4c58	4c58						5c32
SIDMOUTH JN. .. arr	23					4‖43	4†43		5 4	5 4						5 38½
.... dep	24				4‖35				5 6	5 6						5 40
Whimple	25								5a13	5a13						5a47
Broad Clyst	26								5a20	5a20						5 53
Pinhoe	27								5a25	5a25						5a57½
Exmouth Jn.	28	4 38			4 52			5 4	5 29	5 29		5 38				6 1
St. James' Park Halt	29							5a 6½	5 31	5 31						6 3
EXETER CENTRAL arr	30	4 41			4‖55			5 8	5 33	5 33		5 41				6 5
dep	31	4 43	5 5											5 52		
Exeter St. Davids ...... arr	32	4 51	5 8											5 55		
.... dep	33	4 54	5 12											6 1		
Cowley Bridge Jn.	34	4 57	5 15			Runs during school terms only	Runs during school terms only							6 4		
Newton St. Cyres	35		5 20½											6a10		
Crediton	36		5a26½											6a16		
YEOFORD .. .. .. arr	37	5 10	5 33½											6 23		
.... dep	38	5 12	5 35											6 24		
Coleford Jn.	39	5 14	5 37											6 26		
Bow	40													6a34		
North Tawton	41	5a27												6a41		
Sampford Courtenay	42													6a48		
OKEHAMPTON .. arr	43	5 39												6 56		
.... dep	44	5 43									5 51					
Quarry Halt	45															
Meldon Jn.	46										5 59					
Bridestowe	47	5a58														
Lydford	48	6a 5								Mondays to Fridays only stops at St. James' Park Halt						
Brentor	49															
TAVISTOCK NORTH ..	50	6c18							Through Coach, Waterloo to Lyme Regis, until 11th September inclusive and Through Coach, Waterloo to Seaton				6 55			
Bere Alston .. .. .. arr	51	6 28½											7 5½			
.... dep	52	6 29½											7 7			
Bere Ferrers	53												7a13			
Tamerton Foliot Halt	54												7a18			
St. Budeaux, Victoria Road	55	6a42½											7a23			
Ford	56												7a27			
Devonport, Kings Road	57	6d50											7c32			
Devonport Jn.	58	6 52											7 34			
PLYMOUTH arr	59	6 54											7 36			
NORTH ROAD dep	60	6†57											7†37			
Lipson Jn.	61	7 1											7 41			
Mount Gould Jn.	62	7 2											7 42			
Friary Jn.	63	7 2½											7 42½			
PLYMOUTH FRIARY arr	64	7† 5											7†45			
Copplestone	65		5 42½						Mondays to Fridays only stops at St. James' Park Halt Will not run when 1.5 pm Q Waterloo runs							
Morchard Road	66		5 46													
Lapford	67		5X50½													
Eggesford	68		5 57													
Kings Nympton	69		6gX7												Commences 14th September	
Portsmouth Arms	70		6a13													
Umberleigh	71		6a20													
Chapelton	72															
Barnstaple, Victoria Rd. arr	73														7 26	
dep	74														7 34	
BARNSTAPLE JN. .. arr	75		6 29												7 39	
.. dep	76		6 35	6 40												
Barnstaple Town	77		6a39													
Pottington Box	78		6 40													
Wrafton	79		6a47													
Braunton	80		6c51													
Mortehoe and Woolacombe	81		7a 9													
ILFRACOMBE ...... arr	82		7 17													
Fremington	83			6a46												
Instow	84			6a53												
BidefordGoods	85															
Bideford	86			7c 0												
TORRINGTON .. arr	87			7 9												

A page from the 1959 BR Southern main line timetable for stations west of Salisbury.

However, a modeller relying on the public timetable would have to guess the freight services, etc. While it may not be right to run a 1938 layout with a 1951 timetable, in most places the changes will be minimal. When we find that illusive 1938 timetable we have the right answer, but until then this will keep us going.

Cross-country routes have a fascination for many modellers, and I have chosen the LMS Passenger WTT for October 1942 for the former Stratford-upon-Avon & Midland Junction Railway, which became part of the Midland Division of the LMS (page 140). We discover (column 14 of the upper table) that a Saturdays-only (SO) train left Stratford at 9.27 pm for Kineton, where it expired. With only the public timetable we are left wondering whether it went on to Blisworth, or returned to Stratford. The WTT gives the answer. It ran round at Kineton and returned ECS to Stratford, and was due in at 10.14 pm.

We see a limited passenger service by 1942. Five trains each way between Blisworth and Towcester, of which two went to Banbury via Cockley Brake. Three continued on towards Stratford, but two of these got no further than Byfield! The workings at Byfield were complex, as certain trains terminated, then ran via a short chord to Woodford & Hinton on the GC London Extension. Unless we have sufficient freights to make up for it, it does not offer much operating potential. In 1942 the freight service was extremely heavy with through trains and military specials to the military depot at Burton Dassett, but we will have to find a freight timetable to obtain those details. Having studied two routes, we have one with a reasonable branch service, and another with a derisory passenger service, but from other sources we know that freight will make up for it.

Moving to the Southern main line west of Salisbury in 1959 (page 141), we see westbound departures at 2.45 pm, 2.57 pm and 3.12 pm. We also discover LEs and ECSs, so the data is there to build up an accurate service for any station on the line. If we model Seaton Junction or Sidmouth Junction, we will need to look up the branch services as well.

The imaginary timetable

We may wish to model an imaginary station, so S&MJ or Southern main line timetables are not strictly relevant to us, but if we are to develop a service for an imaginary station, we need to know what sort of services were provided at real stations on comparable routes serving similarly sized communities. If we add an imaginary station to an existing line, the WTTs for the line will give the service. On the LSWR west of Salisbury there are locations where a small station could have been built. If we add a junction with an imaginary branch to some small town lying off the main line, we are blending an actual route with 'King Arthurs' and Bulleid 'Pacifics' on genuine timetabled services with perhaps an 'M7' or an 'O2' on our hypothetical branch. The main line service is hardly likely to be significantly altered because of our invented station, but within reason we can shape the branch as we like.

From Axminster to Exmouth Junction a series of lines run south to little holiday resorts such as Lyme Regis, Seaton and Sidmouth. Is our imaginary branch another resort? If so, the service will be similar, and if we work on that basis we will have a convincing 'story' to tell. Do we move further west, and take a line from the vicinity of Crediton or Okehampton into the wilds of Dartmoor? The service will be different from that to coastal resorts, and the GWR services to Moretonhampstead or Princetown would be more appropriate. Perhaps we fancy a junction east of Salisbury. Bulford Camp, Tidworth and Ludgershall already serve the army, so should we have a branch to an army camp? If so, those are the lines we need to study. I have taken just a few examples of how we may blend fact with fiction to produce a convincing result. If we just build a branch to Somewhere, with no idea of what Somewhere is like, we are shooting without aiming, which is not a good way of scoring a bull's-eye.

In adding an imaginary station to an existing line, we have the sheet anchor of a real service, and only need to create the subsidiary service. This could be busy, and we could ask what would have happened had the Somerset & Dorset Joint built a line from south of Templecombe to Weymouth? This would have given the S&DJR access not just to the Bournemouth/Poole area, but also to another important holiday resort and the Channel Isles services. It would not have been popular with the LSWR, one of the S&DJR owners, but might have found favour with the Midland, which showed itself quite ruthless as regards its partners' interests elsewhere. Indeed, we could postulate a Midland Railway connection, if the LSWR balked at funding a line competing with itself! This could have carried almost as heavy a service as the S&DJR main line, and to build up a service pattern we would need to consider the S&DJR services, and the GWR and LSWR routes into Weymouth.

If our station is on an existing route, then we know what service to provide, and it is only the subsidiary service that we need to develop. Common sense tells us that our branch trains would connect with main-line services, so that the trains on our imaginary LSWR branch will be influenced by the services on the main line. If we move away from the main line, and model a purely imaginary station, the branch services will still

The South Western lines in the West Country provided some delightful contrasts, with short branch-line trains in the charge of 'Pacifics', banking engines, and delightful scenery. Here 'Pacific' No 34058 *Sir Frederick Pile* heads the 'Atlantic Coast Express' over the long curved bridge at Barnstaple on 21 September 1954. *R. E. Tustin*

Although the load is not particularly great, the difficult terrain necessitated severe gradients, and a Drummond 'M7', No 30250, is banking a service from Braunton up to Mortehoe on 15 June 1957. The platform Starter gives a much better 'off' than the Distant below it (which is for the next box). *R. E. Tustin*

With the exception of the Southern, 'Pacifics' and branch lines did not go together; No 34026 *Yes Tor* is depicted at Ilfracombe on 13 June 1952. A fan of carriage sidings reminds us that the station, though remote, served a seaside community, with excursion traffic in summer. *R. E. Tustin*

Above 'Pacifics' seemed more 'at home' on the main lines, and Doncaster-based 'A3' 'Pacific' No 2544 *Lemberg* drifts past York Road platform into King's Cross with the up 'Yorkshire Pullman'. The inner city character is recalled by the tall buildings to the right. York Road always looked like an intermediate station that had been built in the wrong part of town, as it was not the kind of building one associated with a major terminus, but the Suburban and York Road platforms at 'The Cross' made it another example of a terminus with through trains.

Below Meanwhile, on the GHR No 5939 *Clio*, a Bowen Cooke 'Claughton' 4-6-0, accelerates past Hillside South Shed with the 9.10 am Hillside-Liverpool (Lime Street) express. Providing a logical destination makes operation much more satisfying.

want to connect with the main line, so the key timings are not the arrivals or departures from our station, but from the junction that we may never model. What we need to do is to work out when trains will call at the junction, and build up our pattern from the genuine main-line service.

Until the Beeching era, through carriages operated from all sorts of obscure places on to the main lines, and the LSWR was a past master at the art. If we have a seaside resort, a through portion to and from Waterloo is feasible. This could be a single coach tacked on to the back of the usual local, hauled by an 'M7', or it could be a separate two- or three-coach corridor set. On a summer Saturday we could run excursions from Waterloo, or if we model our hitherto unsuspected extension to the S&DJR, they might come from the Midlands and the North of England. Although we are talking of a hypothetical model of a hypothetical railway, it is beginning to develop a character. I suspect that the reason why some layouts fail to develop a character is that their builders do not ask 'Could it have existed, and if it had, what would it have been like?'

When construction started on the post-war GHR, the theoretical venue had not been settled. In due course two options emerged. One was a cross-country line running inland from Glasson Dock for about 40 miles to the vicinity of Skipton, of which the last 10 miles would be modelled. Dad's other option was to copy the Dutch, with the reclamation of the Zuider Zee, and reclaim The Wash. The predominance of LMS Western Division motive power in our fleet militated against this, as 'Royal Scots' on the Norfolk/Lincolnshire coast would be unlikely. Another problem was the limited industrial potential of the area. In the event, a friend filled in The Wash, so our omission has been remedied!

Once the location for the GHR was settled, we had to connect with the various lines that the GHR would encounter. Foremost was the West Coast Main Line near Lancaster and Preston. The service at Preston was sufficiently heavy to provide plenty of connections; indeed, as Hillside grew, and through coaches became six- and seven-coach expresses, running independently, the problem was to find times when the WCML would have a path for such workings!

One working where connection is imperative is the West Coast Postal, for Dad decided that the rising town of Hillside would merit a TPO detached off the Postal at Preston. The Up Postal left Glasgow for many years at 6.25 pm, and was due into Preston at 10.55 pm. The 'Evening Hillsider', which is a mixed passenger and mail service, is timetabled to leave Hillside at 9.10 pm and arrive at Preston at 10.30 pm,

an allowance of 80 minutes for the 40-mile run. At Preston the passenger portion, which includes two sleeping cars, is attached to the 8.30 pm Windermere-Euston express, departing from Preston at 10.39 pm and due into Euston at 3.32 am. The mail portion is attached to the Postal, departing Preston at 11.05 pm, and due into Euston at 4.00 am. The Hillside station announcer has been known to say 'The next train to depart from Platform 6 is the 9.10 pm "Evening Hillsider" to London Euston, calling at Buchanans Hill, Middleton, Preston, Warrington (Bank Quay), Crewe, Rugby and London (Euston)'. We have taken a slight liberty by adding the Rugby stop. In the down direction the workings are more protracted, for while the 8.30 pm down postal ex Euston is at Preston at 1.20 am, the 'Evening Hillsider' does not leave for a while. This is to make connection with the 10.52 pm passenger ex Euston and the Manchester newspaper train, providing a mail, newspaper and passenger service.

Another connecting working is the 9.10 am Hillside to Liverpool (Lime Street), which conveys a through coach from Hoggsnorton and Hillside to Euston. This is attached to the 10.00 am Blackpool to Euston, due into London at 3.05 pm. These services were worked out by Dad with the help of LM Region working timetables of the early 1950s. We would have preferred a late 1930s timetable, but as I commented at the start of this chapter, a BR WTT of the early 1950s is often the best available. As our timespan was flexible, with the 'Britannia' 'Pacific' I mentioned, I see no particular need for change. The service evolved along these lines, with trains slotting into the Midland services at Skipton as well as the WCML.

Trains and traffics

We have discussed services on a variety of routes, from main lines such as the WCML or LSWR Salisbury-Exeter route, to branches such as Calne, a modest market town with a dozen trains a day, mostly auto-workings, and the rural S&MJ with its three to five workings. Some principles evolve. Dead-end branches carried between two and a dozen services each way. On a busy branch, the earliest trains were around 6.00 to 7.00 am for workmen and other early starters. Trains would arrive a little before 9.00 am for shop and office staff and school children. A mid-morning service was common, with the next train about lunchtime. There might be an early afternoon working, with a couple for the rush-hour, taking school children, workmen and shop/office staff home from 4.15 to 5.45 pm. Later services would be sparse, perhaps two or three at most, with the last train around 10.30 pm. The busier the route, the more

The 'motor train', push-pull or auto-train was common on many branches. No 6669, a Webb 5 ft 6 in 2-4-2T makes a dramatic start out of Leamington Spa (Avenue) in 1947. Motor trains ran from Leamington to Rugby, and via Daventry to Weedon. A cattle wagon is attached to the rear of the train. *H. J. Stretton Ward*

intensive the pattern became, but the peaks were the morning and evening rush-hours, with a reduced rush ran on a Saturday morning in-bound, with the return at midday as many workers worked a half day on Saturday. The Saturday evening rush was very light.

Express services varied dramatically. Small communities rarely had a good express service, but places such as Windermere attracted influential residents as well as tourists. Southport, Blackpool and Brighton were smart dormitory towns for the city businessman. Flanagan & Allen, of the 'Crazy Gang', immortalised the 'Brighton Belle' with their Second World War song capturing the Home Guard spirit: 'Who do you think you are kidding, Mr Hitler, when you say Old England's done?. . . Mr Jones goes into town on the 8.21, but every evening when he comes home, he's ready with his gun. . .'

What did the trains look like? My childhood was spent beside the West Coast Main Line, and when I was regretting that we did not run 13-15-coach

expresses, Dad reminded me that 13-15-coach expresses might be common on the WCML, but they were not the rule in most places. As I researched train formations, I discovered how true this was. Train formations were not made up at random from the coaching stock that happened to be lying around. Detailed passenger train marshalling circulars were issued, and one of the most interesting books I have seen is *Passenger Train Formations 1923-1983 (LMS/LM Region)* by Clive Carter. This lists selected train formations over 60 years, and shows that many five-, six- and seven-coach expresses ran on important main lines. Even if you are an LNER or Southern fan, this book is invaluable for the background to passenger train formations that it provides. I have reproduced overleaf the cover and two pages from an actual 'Passenger Train Marshalling' book of 1957.

Passenger train services include mails, parcels, milk and similar passenger-rated traffic conveyed in stock complying with passenger requirements. Sometimes parcels and milk were worked on routine passenger trains, often they were worked separately. Cows are milked twice a day, early in the morning and in the early evening. When milk was conveyed by churn, the evening milk usually stood overnight, and the two milkings were taken by the farmer to the station for collection as soon as the morning milking was completed. The churns would arrive at the stations from 7.00 am onwards, depending on train times and the distance of the farm from the station. They would be collected by a milk train, stopping at each station over a distance, then taken to the urban area for sale. In the 1920s the railways experimented with glass-lined milk tank wagons, and these carried large quantities of milk at high speed over long distances, for example from Cheshire or the Settle-Carlisle line to London.

One such working was the Independent Milk Supplies run from Dorrington, south of Shrewsbury, to Marylebone. At one time running in the evening, by the late 1930s this ran down the GW Birmingham main line as far as Banbury, arriving about 5.30 pm, where it met an LNER engine with empty milk tanks that had worked up from the IMS depot at Marylebone to Woodford, where the train had reversed and run over the GC link to Banbury. The trains were handed over, and went their respective ways, loaded tanks to London, and empties back to Shropshire. The train usually consisted of three or four tanks and a six-wheel or bogie brake for the guard, plus any residual churn traffic.

The odd horsebox was once common on the back of a passenger train, but horsebox specials, perhaps in conjunction with race meetings or with the hunt, provided added variety. Such a train could arrive at our station, adding still more operating potential.

As we ask these questions, the diversity we can build into a simple layout becomes remarkable, and my father used his powers of observation to find further interest. At Kendal he noticed a couple of bogie parcel vans in a bay platform, being loaded with boots and shoes from a nearby factory. At Ponkeston, the first station out of Hillside, the plan had been to pro-

vide a track at the back of the platform, but to fence it off, as there was no need for passenger services to terminate there, and it would serve purely as a yard track. The Kendal boots eliminated the idea of the fence, and a boot and shoe factory appeared at Ponkeston. That was over 40 years ago, and to this day an engine arrives from Hillside with a couple of empty BGs in the morning, drops them off in the bay platform, then crosses over to the dairy to pick up the milk tanks. With our 1 in 55 main-line grades, light duties such as these provide welcome employment for some of the smaller engines, such as a Johnson 2-4-0 or a Webb 'Jumbo'.

I have outlined how to develop a passenger timetable, what sort of services to operate given a particular route or community, and what the trains look like. I have also covered special traffic such as horse-boxes, milk and special parcels movements. The list is enormous, and the challenge facing the modeller is to build up a comprehensive pattern that makes sense. Large numbers of horsebox specials and milk trains on the Highland Railway 'Farther North' line would not make sense, while a race or hunt special in Snowdonia is unlikely. It is often a matter of common sense.

Creating your timetable

In your timetable you should cover train times, the make up of passenger train formations, the addition of through coaches and the combining or splitting of trains. Once that is done, you have a pattern to work to. On the prototype, train services were arranged using a master graph, with stations marked out at the correct distance down the page, and time across the page. Conflicting movements were immediately apparent, though on one occasion BR did timetable one train to

A 'Bulldog' 4-4-0 climbs through Whitnash Cutting with the IMS Dorrington milk in 1936, with the usual three tanks and brake. Sometimes the latter was a six-wheeler, but it could be a bogie vehicle, and on this occasion is a former GC 'Extension' bogie. Such duties, where limited loads had to be moved quickly, provided turns for the 4-4-0s in their latter days. *H. J. Stretton Ward*

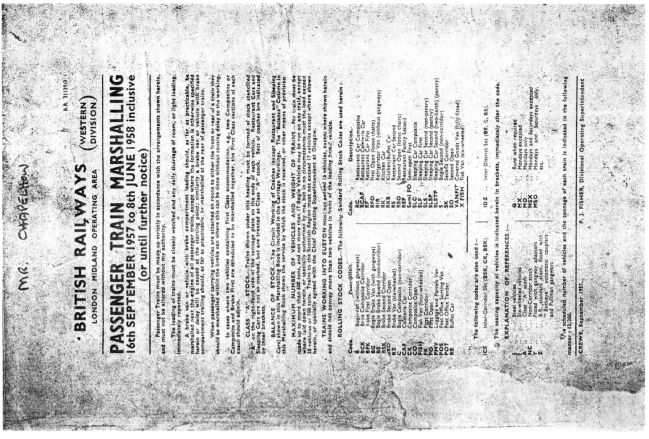

Above Having spoken of the WCML with its 15-coach trains, let us go to the opposite extreme, to Torrington in North Devon, with 'E1R' No 32610 on a single-coach mixed train in September 1954. As not all the wagon stock is fitted with the vacuum brake, the last vehicle is a goods brake, in which the guard rides. Such mixed trains were more common on the SR or GWR than on the LMS, but offer fascinating prototypes. *R. E. Tustin*

Right and below 'Passenger Train Marshalling' circulars were produced economically, using type-written masters rather than fully typeset pages. The cover lists the standard vehicle codes, and shows evidence of hard wear! We see four-, five-, six- and seven-coach corridor services, which are more practical for the modeller than the 13-15-coach trains on the WCML. In building up GHR passenger train formations we found the marshalling circular invaluable. In the services shown, there are eight-car formations with a catering vehicle, and in Carter's book quite a few six-car formations are so equipped. The standard express on the GHR, whether LMS, LNER or GHR, is six or seven coaches, so a restaurant car is permissible.

The circular reveals a characteristic of the Steam Age that has since declined, the combining and splitting of trains *en route*. Portions could vary from one coach to half the train. The 9.20 am Birkenhead to Bournemouth (West) (top right, right-hand page) picks up a portion at Chester, and detaches a portion at Shrewsbury. Other trains are equally complex. This offers further scope, for if we model a junction, a train can divide, with portions going in different directions; in the reverse direction trains will need combining. Until the 1950s horseboxes were common, and our express could convey a couple of these as 'tail traffic'. If it splits, these may go with the rear portion, but they could be for the front portion, so the station pilot will need to detach them and add them to the front portion after the train has divided.

Upper section

Marshalling	Balance	Marshalling	Balance	Marshalling	Balance

9.20am BIRKENHEAD TO BOURNEMOUTH (West)
(Reverses at Chester)

- Wa BCK (12/32) }
- Ws SK (64) (MFSO) } Cardiff
- B 12/403 (SO) }
- B BSK (32)
- B FK (42)
- B GAP
- B SO (56) } Bournemouth
- B SK (64)
- B BSK (32)

Balance: 9.20am

Attach front Chester :-
- ED SK (64) (FSO) } Bournemouth
- B BCK (12/32)
- B BSK (32)

a. Transferred Shrewsbury to 9.15am Manchester (L.Rd.) to Swansea (H.St.)

B. W.R.(B.R. Standard) Stock (MFO)

C. S.R. Stock (ThSO). 8.55am from Cardiff, 12.0nn from Shrewsbury, 2.26pm from Chester.

D. Runs daily until 5th October and commencing 19th May 1958.

W. W.R. Stock.

8/272 (MFSO), 7/241 (MFSX)

10.50am (SX) BIRKENHEAD TO CREWE.
- Z BSK (24) }
- Z SK (48) } Crewe
- Z OK (24/18) }
- Ia SK (64) } Euston
- Za BSK (24) }

Balance: 5.55pm (SX), 2.30pm (SX)

a. Transferred Crewe to 10.0am Blackpool to Euston.

5/165.

7.35am BIRKENHEAD TO MARGATE
(Reverses at Chester)

- BSK (32) }
- SO (56) } Margate
- GAP }
- BCK (12/24) }
- BCK (12/24) } Ramsgate
- BSK (32) }

Balance: 9.18am, 8.56am

Attach front Chester :-
- BSK (32) }
- SK (64) } Hastings
- CK (24/24) }
- BSK (32) }

Balance: 9.25am

W.R.(B.R. Standard) Stock (MFO)
S.R. Stock (ThSO).

6/210

7.50am BIRKENHEAD TO PWLLHELI
- EZ }
- 2SK (64) }
- BCK (12/32) } Pwllheli
- CK (24/24) }
- RB }
- SK (64) }
- BSK (32) }

Balance: 12.45pm, 4.17pm

a. Transferred Chester to 8.38am to Cardiff.
W.R. Stock

9/263

11.45am BIRKENHEAD TO PADDINGTON
(Reverses at Chester)

- Y BCK (12/28) } Wolverhampton
- ES (30)
- Z BSK (32)
- Z SK (64) } Paddington
- Z FK (42)
- Z 2SK (64)
- Z BSK (32)

Balance: 5.4pm

B. 4.10pm (Sun) 2.10pm (SX) from Paddington, Work 8.10pm Paddington to Shrewsbury.

W.R. Stock.
8/274.

8.55am BIRKENHEAD TO PADDINGTON
(Reverses at Chester)
- Y BSK (42) }
- Z CK (24/24) } Paddington
- Z 2SK (64) }
- Z BSK (32) }

Balance: 6.10pm

W.R. Stock
6/198

2.10am (SX) BIRKENHEAD TO CHESTER
- 2a CK (24/18) } Euston
- 2a BSK (32) }

Balance: 5.35pm (SX)

a. Transferred Chester to 7.30am Holyhead to Euston.

2/67

Lower section

Marshalling	Balance	Marshalling	Balance	Marshalling	Balance

12.10pm BANGOR TO MANCHESTER (Exchange)
- A BSK (24) }
- A CK (18/24) } Manchester (Ex)
- A SK (42) }
- A BSK (24) }
- A SK (42) (SX) }
- A ICS (18/24) (SO) }

Attach rear Llandudno Jn. :-
- Aa BSK (24) }
- Aa CK (18/24) } Llandudno
- Aa SK (42) } Manchester
- Aa BSK (24) } (Ex.)

Balance: B

a. Received off 12.30pm from Llandudno.
B. 5.45am from Chester. Work 5.7pm (SX), 4.30pm (SO) Manchester to Chester.

12.50pm BANGOR TO EUSTON
- Z BSK (24) }
- Z CK (24/18) }
- RP (24) }
- SO (56) } Euston
- Z BCK (12/18) }
- I CK (24/18) }
- Y SK (42) }
- SK (42) (SO) }

Attach front Chester :-
- A SK (42)(SO) - Euston

a. Received off 1.5pm from Llandudno.
B. Until 4th October and commencing 2nd May.
C. 11.0am from Holyhead, Work 10.50am Euston to Holyhead, 11.0am from Holyhead, Work 5.5pm (FSX) 6.5pm (Sun) Euston to Preston, 4.10pm (Sun) Euston to Holyhead.

Continued :-

12.50pm BANGOR TO EUSTON (Continued)
BANGOR - 7/242 (SX), 8/273 (SO)
LLAN.JN. - 10/341 (MSX) (B), 12/403 (FO) (B) 11th Oct. 11/372 (FO) to 25th April. 11/372 (SO)
CHESTER - 10/341 (FSX) (B) 12/403 (FO) (B) 11/372 (FO) 11th Oct. to 25th April. 12/403 (SO)

6.20am BARROW TO PRESTON
- Y BCK (12/21) (SX) }
- Z CK (24/18) (SX) } Preston
- ICS (18/96) }
- S (108) }
- S (108) (MO) }

Balance: C

B. 5.5pm (SX) from Euston, Work 9.47am (SX) Preston to Blackpool (C).

8/233 (MO), 7/206 (MSX), 5/242 (SO)

6.58am BARROW TO MANCHESTER (Victoria)
- Z BSK (24) }
- Z 2CK (18/24) } Manchester
- Z BSK (24) } (Vic.)
- Y SK (42) }

Attach rear Lancaster :-
- Aa BSK (24) }
- Aa CK (18/24) } Morecambe
- Aa SK (42) } Manchester
- Aa BG (MX) } Heysham
- a BG (MX) } Manchester (Vic.)

Balance: D

a. Received off 8.3am from Morecambe (E.Rd.)

BARROW - 5/165
LANCASTER - 9/289 (MO) 10/314 (MX)

6.30am BIRKENHEAD TO PADDINGTON
(Reverses at Chester)
- Z BSK (32) }
- Y FK (42) }
- Z 3SK (64) } Paddington
- Z BSK (32) }

Balance: B, 4.10pm

W.R. Stock
6/198

overtake a previous train between Northampton and Roade on a section where there were no loops or refuge sidings! On a single line, where trains must pass, a train graph is particularly important.

It is possible to diagram trains on a master working sheet, but conflicts are less obvious than with a graph. The GHR timetable had been developed by Dad in the 1950s, and updated by myself in the 1960s, and with another member of the team in the '70s. These updates were needed as new industries appeared and extensions were built. In 1991 Blair Ramsay offered to put the timetable on computer, producing a printed WTT book and individual station sheets, samples of which are shown in the accompanying illustrations. Dad was thrilled, and just a few hours before he passed away was discussing Blair's latest sheets.

The WTT, although a vital tool, is not the easiest item to use when working a station, and on prototype and model it is common to produce a station time sheet, listing up and down trains, and all necessary data, including any shunting, combining or splitting. Page 2 of the Paythorne timetable is depicted, covering midday to midnight. We have followed Midland Railway practice by showing 'am' times as 11.01, and 'pm' times as 11/01. Down trains are listed in the left-hand columns, an arrow indicating their direction as the operator stands at the station. Up trains are on the right. Train numbers make it easier for different stations to know which train they are talking about in a phone discussion, for Paythorne may not recognise the 12/42 pm ex Hillside as his 12/58 pm, but both can recognise train 110. A time appearing only in the 'Depart' column indicates a non-stop service. To identify trains that start or terminate at Paythorne, a black circle appears in the unwanted time column. A Maltese cross appears against some trains, and after reading the freight chapter you will know why! The central column provides identification data.

For example, train 104 is a Hellifield-Paythorne LMS motor that terminates at Paythorne at 12/18 pm, leaving Paythorne for Hellifield at 3/00 pm. Train 112, the down pick-up, arrives at 3/40, and is away at 4/06. If the Tidal 'Q' (ie optional) freight runs in path 132, the Paythorne signalman must shunt the pick-up to the up line to permit the faster train to go through. There are no up trains scheduled between 3/36 and 4/05 pm, by which time the pick-up should have shunted back on to its proper line.

'Q' paths were the conventional way of showing trains that were sufficiently regular to be timetabled, but might not be needed on all occasions. A basic timetable can be prepared, providing sufficient activity to keep you happy, but if you fancy an extra-busy operating session, or the team are very experienced, you can add the 'Q' workings to the running.

Readers who are accustomed to block working may recognise the down-line codes, 4, 3-1, 3-1-2, etc, but some of the up codes, 4-3-4, 3-1-3-4 or 1-2-2-4, may not be familiar. Where routes diverged, a signalman had to know where a train was to go, and special route codes were adopted. A branch express, instead of being a 4, became a 4-4. If there were further routes, still more codes were needed, and an express might become a 4-3-4. BR adopted standard codes, known as the A1, B1 and C1 route codes, giving three additional route options, and we have adopted the A and C codes with some modifications. The GWR and Southern pursued a somewhat different course.

Although most of the GHR's operating practice is LMS or LNER, we have adopted the LB&SCR idea of route code discs, for if our train gets out of course the signalman cannot ask the driver where he is going! Only trains to and from the Granton section carry route discs, of which there are three varieties, a plain white disc, a white disc with a bar, or a disc with a cross. Train 141 carries a white route disc, and runs via Buchanans Hill, Granton and the Granton loop. Train 163, the 5/10 pm motor ex Paythorne, in theory runs over Newsholme Junction to Hellifield, but in practice gets on to the Granton line.

Even today, when the railways are less flexible than they used to be, extra trains are run, but in steam days vast numbers of extra trains ran, sometimes using 'Q' paths in the timetable, sometimes under timings given in Special Train Notices, and sometimes at short notice with little or no advance warning to staff. Tail traffic, for example horseboxes or strengthening vehicles to cope with a late rush of passengers, was frequent. Some modellers prefer a rigid adherence to timetable, but the reality was very different, and Dad always encouraged sensible initiative. Other than in the middle of the rush-hour, with Hillside short-manned as well, tail traffic is seldom if ever frowned upon. If the Middleton-Hillside local arrives with a couple of horseboxes for Hoggsnorton, the Hillside signalman adds them to the next available branch train. If I am working Hillside, I would be surprised if I did not get at least one horsebox or other special vehicle on the back of a train during a running. I have operated on the GHR for over 30 years, averaging something like 40 runnings a year. That adds up to many thousands of hours of train operation, but when the clock goes on, I can reckon that by the end of the day I will have encountered some new set of circumstances, which I could not have predicted at the outset. That is the ultimate test of the living model railway. If you can create that flexibility, you will have recaptured the vitality of the Steam Age, and provided a layout that will offer you endless interest and enjoyment.

PAYTHORNE 2. — Page 2

GHR — Down Trains ———>> to MIDDLETON. | <—— UP TRAINS to SLACK and

Q Runs if required
● Indicates a train terminating, commencing or held for traffic purposes.
MX Mondays Excepted

Train No.	Bell Code	Arrive Time	Depart Time	Operators / Notes	Arrive Time	Depart Time	Bell Code	Train No.
100	4 1		12|05	Ety coal HCY-MDN				
104	1 3 2 ⊗	12|18	●	Htd-PY motor terminates	12|47	12|48	3 1 2	119
110	4		12|58	[LUNE COAST EXP] HLL-KE				
108	3 1 3	1|06	1|07	Railcars HLL-MDN		1|16	4	121
						1	38	4 1	127
116	1 4		2|17	Htd-MDN Min/t(142 NJ)	2|47	2|48	3 1 2	135
120	1 2		2|30	[HILLSIDER] HLL-En LMS		3|00	1 3 2	137
124	3 1 2	2|57	2|58	HLL-MDN Railcar		3|13	4 3 4	141
132	1 2	3|40	3|40	HYD-MDN Spg g'ds shunts		3|13		145
112	3		4|02	Q (HYD-GDK Tidal frt Path 1)		3|36	4	
112	4		4|06	departs				
136			4|18	Nor'tham-KE LMS Exp	3|55	4|05	3	153
				Cattle train conveys accommodation for drovers TuO	3|55	4|05	3 1	155
138	1 3 2 ⊗	4|36	4|36	Htd-PY Motor LMS	4|37	4|38	3 1 3 4	157
140	4 1		4|48	SK-MDN Coal		4|50	1 1 3	159
142	1 2	4|59	5|00	HLL-Htd Motor LMS		5|10	1 3 2	163
148	4		5|26	[BOWLAND FORESTER] HLL-KE	5|23	5|24	3 1 3 5	167
150	3 1 2		5|39	Skipton-MDN Motor	5|33	5|33	4	169
160	3 1 2		5|59	HLL-MDN Dsls	5|47	5|48	3 1	173
154	1 2 2		6|05	Railcar Htd-MDN		6|13	4 3 4	175
162	3		6|10	Q (HYD-GDK Tidal frt Path 2)				
166	3 1	6|16	6|17	Brad-Lcr Psr				
166	1 4	7|00		SK-NJ-PY L'stone trip for PIW+RSC	7|03	7|03	4	183
174	4		7|16	[ULSTER BOAT] LNER KK-KE				
180	3 1 2		7|59	BDN-PKN Milk Tanks	7|51	7|51	1 3 1	189
178	1 2 2		8|10	Q (HYD-GDK Tidal frt Path 3)				
186	4 1	8|48	8|25	Ety coal PYW-MDN S.M. Colly	8|31	8|31	3	191
188	4 1		8|48	GNL-HLL Dsls	8|47	8|48	3 1 2	197
				Lbs-HLL LMS + En HGN TC	9|13	9|13	4	199
190			9|33	[EVENING HILLSIDER] Express	9|27	9|28	1 3 1 4	203
				Lcr-Leeds Psr via BH				
194	3 1 2	9|58	9|59	GDK-Htd gds add S&C traff	9|58		3 2 2	205
192	1 2 2		10|10	[BOWLAND FORESTER] KE-HLL		10|13		205
196	1 2 2		10|25	GDK-Leeds Goods via BH		10|21	3 2 2	207
200	4		10|35	Leeds-Lcr Psr		10|33	3 2 4	213
202	3 1 1		10|50	HYD-Crw frt		10|42	3 2	215
206	3 2 ⊗		11|00	Leeds-GDK frt		10|58	3 1 3 5	217
208	3 2 ⊗		11|09	Htd-GDK frt (322NJ)		11|07	1 2 2 4	219
210	4 2		11|23	MDN-HLL railcars		11|28	3 1 2	221
214	3 2		11|32	GDK-Skip Pul Exp		11|51	3 2 4	223

RIBBLESDALE Sand and Cement Co. Ltd.
Works day 6.45am to 5|15pm, 4|45pm FO.

Issued GHR. scheduling office, Paythorne
by authority of A. Lamb-Charter, Chief Clerk.
Commences 1/3/1931, ref 920411

Printed by Inkett and Press (Printers) Ltd. Paythorne, Lancashire.

Note: These headcodes ⊕⊖ although shown in the timetable may be missing from down trains.

The station time sheet for Paythorne on the GHR.

A page from the GHR WTT showing passenger and freight movements, and giving train numbers, signal box bell codes, stock and loco diagrams and any other useful information.

10.
FREIGHT OPERATION

The inspiration for this book was a humble four-wheel goods wagon, or rather a number of them, and the manner in which they were shunted. Dad and I visited an exhibition and watched a freight arrive at a branch terminus. The engine ran round, and shunted the goods train into the yard. The coal wagons ended up in the goods shed, which did not please the local coal merchant, particularly as he discovered two or three cattle wagons by his coal stack. Unless they were winged cattle, it was going to be difficult to unload them. There were a couple of tank wagons, but as the station had no apparent facilities for discharging rail tank wagons, they had presumably arrived merely because the shunter at the local yard thought it would be a pleasant outing for them. After a few minutes 'on shed', the engine collected the train it had brought in, and departed with exactly the same wagons as had arrived. The cattle wagons must have been empty on departure, as they were at the back of the train now, which would ensure a rough ride and possible compensation claims if they had contained livestock.

The modelling was excellent, but the operator, who may or may not have been the builder, had given little thought to how freight was worked. Some wagons take longer to unload than others. A cattle van will be unloaded quickly, as there were rules on how long beasts could be kept without water and feed. A side-door 12-ton coal wagon took considerable manual effort to unload, for while coal would spill out when the door was released, there was also a lot of back-breaking shovelling. On the NER, with its coal drops and bottom-door wagons, a 20-ton wagon could be spotted over the cell when the daily shunting goods arrived, and long before it was ready to depart the wagon was empty and awaiting collection. Some wagons were emptied by railway staff, others by traders, and while a free period existed, after the free period demurrage, or wagon hire, was charged, as the railway companies did not want their wagons standing idle under load day after day.

Wagons were worked to where they could be unloaded, and coal wagons in the goods shed were a

Cattle were once moved by rail, and virtually every station had its own cattle dock. I have included this illustration of that at Moreton-in-Marsh as it provides useful detail for the modeller.

nuisance to the goods porters, as they stopped them doing their proper work, and were no use to the coal merchant. Livestock was handled at a cattle dock, and any attempt to do otherwise would risk broken limbs, and damage claims, as animals crashed to the ground. Petrol and chemical tankers, although colourful, were only seen at stations that had facilities to handle them, *or en route* to or from such stations. On

'How to shunt your yard'. The 'operator' obviously knew what he was doing when he positioned this Conflat A next to the yard crane. The 5-ton container would be beyond the capacity of many yard cranes, but the Moreton crane was rated at 6 tons. The wheel in the foreground is an unusual sight in a goods yard, but clearly a wagon was in difficulties and the yard crane was used to lift it for attention to the journals. Incidentally, the white quadrant plate at the back of the signal arm in the background is to give the driver a clear view of the arm, as the background would be confused otherwise.

'ROD' Class 2-8-0 No 3024 drifts through Leamington Spa on a stopping freight. The leading vehicle is a cattle wagon, correctly marshalled at the front to give the least jolting to the livestock. *H. J. Stretton Ward*

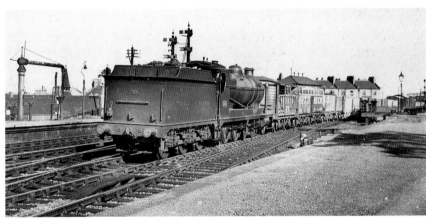

The curved frontage of the Holgate foundry, a part of the Arley Coal & Iron Co, dominates Paythorne station. Apart from helping with the scenic backdrop, the foundry provides useful traffic for the railway, and permits us to use wagons that would otherwise be inappropriate; it therefore meets operational as well as scenic needs. The foundry is named after a member of the team whose dental training is put to excellent use in casting various parts for the railway in dental resin. While grey or black would be more suitable for iron castings, Chris tells me that there is surprisingly little call for grey or black dentures, so castings come in a fetching shade of pink! The advertisement hoarding with its 'If YOU can invent it, WE can cast it' slogan, attests to the diversity of the foundry's output. The booking office, carried at right angles over the line, draws inspiration from Brinklow, and saves space.

a main line, or even a wayside station on a secondary route, tankers are permissible, as they can be going to or from a handling station, but at a branch terminus they are only sensible if the station has handling facilities. The same applies to other wagons, for example a bulk grain wagon would be appropriate at a station where there is a grain silo or granary, but not otherwise.

Traffics and wagons

A theme that runs through this book is that we are doing something because we enjoy it. Our model railway is *fun*. Real railways were built for more mundane reasons, to carry passengers and goods and earn money. In a previous chapter it was pointed out that sinuous curves may look pretty, but they cost money, and railway engineers did not install sinuous curves for aesthetic reasons. If we do so on a model, we court derision, unless there is a reason for them - I suggested a venerable ruin or an historic 'henge' as possible excuses for such a curve. The same principle applies to freight traffic. If it is to make sense, there should be a reason for doing it.

On the prototype wagons were built to convey goods, freight trains ran to move the wagons, and that was it. Unless someone made a mistake, a tank wagon did not go to a station without facilities to handle it, any more than an engineer would build a 'fun' curve. We can get a good deal of fun out of running our freight trains, even if what we do is not actually commercially or economically based, but it is more enjoyable if we make sense of it.

If our freight services are to be convincing, we have to ask a number of questions at the layout design stage, when we buy or build wagons, and as we operate. On the GHR my father took a number of decisions in the 1940s that shaped our freight services to this day. He wanted a sawmill, and there was space at Ponkeston. Felled trees arrive on bolster wagons, and are shunted into the mill. The sawn timber is sold locally for road distribution, which does not involve the GHR, while other timber is forwarded by rail to timber merchants, builders, etc, who do not have their own sawmills. When the yard master at Hillside (Preston Road) yard is making up the down 'pick-up', he knows that Ponkeston is the first stop, and that the Ponkeston timber traffic should be marshalled at the head of the train for ease in shunting. Thus the decision of over 40 years ago shapes the kind of traffic and the make-up of a train, but unless the Hillside yard master does his job properly, the effect is lost. Similarly, the Ponkeston operator needs to detach the wagons to the sawmill siding.

There are two fundamental questions you need to ask in designing your layout. As is often the case, the answers may conflict, and you will have to find a compromise, or change your ideas. The first question is 'What sort of freight do I want?'. The second question is 'What would be reasonable for the place I am serving?'. If you adore GNR 40-ton bogie brick wagons, and with their red oxide livery and prominent GN lettering they were attractive vehicles, would a GW branch terminus in the West Country be a likely destination? The answer is no, as the wagons spent most of their life on the GN main line between the Fletton brick fields near Peterborough and London. If you are building a GW West Country branch terminus, a fleet of GN brick wagons is *not* logical. Having told you what you should *not* do, I must confess that we *do* have a GN bogie brick wagon, but as it came from the pre-war GHR, and was rebuilt and improved by two of the team, I do not have the heart to dispose of it. As the GNR did get to the West Riding, and our Bradford Extension will make a connection to the GNR, I do have a tenuous justification.

If you want a particular type of traffic or wagon, for example the china clay trade around Fowey, then your location and other factors are fixed. Perhaps you remember the ironstone quarries in Oxfordshire and Northamptonshire, and this may be the feature you want to recapture. In my own case, there were family and personal associations. As I have already said, Dad was MO to the 1st Royal Tank Regiment, and had an affection for the Royal Armoured Corps. He had been stationed at Tidworth, and we spent a number of holidays in the area when I was a youngster. We visited the Royal Tank Museum at Bovington, and when he signed in the visitors' book 'late MO, 1st RTR', he was asked to wait for a minute or two, then a Sergeant arrived and asked if we would care for a guided tour, and if we wished to examine any of the vehicles not open to the public. . .! For a small child, the resultant visit was memorable, and I crawled in and out of Matildas, Shermans and all sorts of equipment used in the Desert War. When we were taking pictures of trains on Salisbury station, a Southern 4-6-0 arrived with a load of tanks (AFVs, not wagons). The combination of railways and tanks was irresistible, but it was many years before I could find some suitable O gauge armour. Even today it is

Above right To a small child, the combination of tanks and trains was irresistible. The arrival of a trainload of Second World War Comet tanks at Salisbury fired a determination to see similar trains move on the GHR. *Dr R. P. Hendry*

Right Maunsell 'S15' No 30841 heads her heavy load around the sharp curve at the east end of Salisbury station. *Dr R. P. Hendry*

In case you wonder how tanks are secured to 'warwells' or 'warflats', here is the answer.

Grants, Lees and Shermans, and what I would really like are Vickers Light Tanks, Matildas and Churchills. The 'military' connection to explain the survival of the GHR into the Grouping came as a side effect of the wish to see tanks and railways together.

In order to clarify your ideas, list the freight traffic you find interesting. Is it china clay, iron ore, armoured vehicles, coal or something else? If you have a location in mind, does that traffic make sense for the location, as some wagons can only be handled where there are suitable facilities? A branch terminus is much more restricting than a through station. If the traffic is appropriate to the location, then all is well. If not, you must either change your ideas as to the traffic, or change your location, or accept that what you are doing is not strictly logical.

When you have an answer, you can develop the layout and wagon fleet in sympathy. Of course, you may have a layout already, and want to adapt and improve the realism of your working practices, or you may have lots of wagons, but no layout. The wagon fleet may not make sense for the layout - for example you may have a dozen tankers and a branch terminus with no petrol discharge facility. On the other hand, you may have a score of our friends the GNR 40-ton bogie brick wagons and a wholly GWR loco stud. Can you modify the branch terminus to provide a petrol discharge facility? If so, all is well. If not, then logically you should either dispose of the tankers or the layout. Either is a painful choice, and you may prefer to take modeller's licence, which is your right.

We should carry this process further. Before the Second World War private owner wagons abounded on Britain's railways. Most were four-wheel timber-bodied coal wagons, owned by coal merchants, coal factors (a sort of super-merchant), wagon hirers and colliery companies. As the railways charged wagon owners for moving their vehicles about the country, coal merchants tried to get as much coal as possible from local collieries. In the case of London, with its enormous demand for coal, this included South Wales, the Warwickshire, Leicestershire, Derbyshire and Nottinghamshire coal fields, and even South Yorkshire. 'Local' can be interpreted quite widely, but coal wagons operated in broadly defined areas. Coal merchants' wagons worked between their home town and a colliery within reasonable range. This could be a substantial distance, and was not necessarily the nearest colliery in a straight line. Prices would vary as mining was competitive, and grades of coal produced by different pits and seams were suited to different purposes. A coal merchant would want a good house coal, rather than a gas or coking coal, and even if there was a pit 5 miles away producing a gas coal, he would tend to use a pit further away producing household coal. What is unlikely is that a London coal merchant would send his wagon to the Scottish coalfields for ordinary house coal, as the saving on any cheap purchase price would be eroded by rail carriage.

Some firms built up vast fleets of wagons, supplying colliery companies with vehicles, serving their own distribution points and individual merchants. Stephenson Clarke & Associated Companies Ltd operated 10,000 coal and coke wagons, which were to be seen throughout much of England and Wales. One 1934 wagon was marked 'Empty to Toton LMSR, Doncaster LNER or Aberdare GWR', so covering the Midlands, Yorkshire and South Wales coalfields!

Private owner wagons add colour and variety to any pre-Nationalisation layout, and, if selected sensibly, add realism. 1254 is a Clay Cross Co side-, end- and bottom-door seven-plank mineral wagon. It was built for iron ore, so has a 15-ton capacity, while a comparable coal wagon would have been 12 tons before the war, uprated to 13 tons during the war. Iron ore wagons had stronger axles and bearings, so were not placed in the 'general user' category during the war, hence the 'NON POOL' inscription. *R. E. Tustin*

While a coal merchant's wagon should only work into a suitable colliery or a station where the merchant has a depot, colliery company wagons were more widely distributed, as they might go to any customer within reasonable range of the colliery. We would expect to see South Wales colliery wagons, such as Ocean, Emlyn or Tredegar, over a wide area, including London, the South Midlands and the Home Counties. One wagon, which has been available in model form, is the Ystradgynlais & Yniscedwyn Collieries, and I bought an example for our friend Tom Hayward who rescued Dad and I when our car broke down. He promptly told us that he had a relation who had worked in the pit, and he had been down it as a young man! Yniscedwyn produced anthracite for shipping use, and while much of this would go to the South Wales ports, there is one recorded instance of a 24-ton shipment to Hull. A South Wales coalfield wagon in Hull must have been quite a surprise!

In selecting suitable coal wagons, the principle is clear. Coal wagons did not work at random, but in logical commercial patterns. In recent years any coal wagons we have acquired fit this pattern, but we have a number of wagons bought many years ago, some of which are fine models, and their justification is difficult. However, there is an answer. In 1939 all private owner coal wagons were pooled to help the war effort by minimising empty mileage. A Tredegar wagon might be loaded with 13 tons of South Yorkshire coal and end up on the East Coast. The wagons were never returned to their owners, but passed to BR in 1948. If you model the period from 1939 to the early 1950s, by which time most of the old private owner wagons had vanished, one well off its home territory is permissible!

'Pooling' of coal wagons brings us to another issue where modellers go wrong. I was looking at a GW branch at an exhibition one day, and except for the odd coal merchant every single wagon was Great Western. This modeller was not making the mistake of alien wagons, but he had gone too far the other way.

If a trader arrived at one of the Edinburgh goods depots of the North British Railway wishing to ship 6 tons of wares to a customer at Eastbourne on the Brighton line, the goods would be loaded into an NB wagon, which would wend its way south, being transferred from one freight train to another, until it

Modeller's license allows us to personalise a few wagons, so that friends can become coal merchants, or our local stations can be 'home' to specific wagons. With an 'independent' railway we have even more scope, and GHR Gunpowder van 2651 carries a paint date based on NB practice, and is to 'RETURN TO PARADISE'. If you look on the Ordnance Survey map you will find that there really is such a place, and it seemed the logical location for an explosives plant!

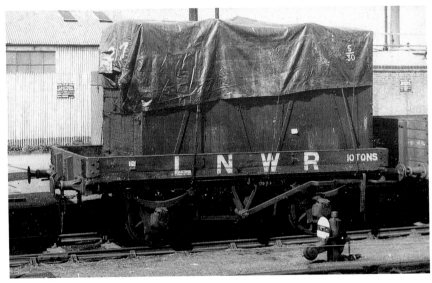

Considerable latitude is permissible over liveries, as wagons could go for many years without repaint. This LNWR lowside wagon, 17893, is conveying an early example of an LMS Type B wooden container, covered with a wagon sheet, carrying a May 1930 issue date. *H. J. Stretton Ward*

reached Eastbourne. The wares would be unloaded, and the goods agent at Eastbourne then had a NB wagon on his hands. What could he do with it? One thing he could *not* do was to load it up with goods for Littlehampton on the Brighton, or Plymouth on the GWR. Many companies permitted 'back loading' to the home system, or in other words if the Eastbourne goods agent had a consignment of freight for somewhere on the NB, he could use the NB wagon rather than send an LB&SCR wagon, but even this was not universal until the First World War.

Under the pressure of wartime conditions, the Railway Clearing House regulations were modified in July 1915 to encourage back loading to home system for ordinary wagons, but special vehicles, fitted stock, perishable vans, etc, were not covered. In December 1915 the GCR, GER and GNR pooled their ordinary open wagons of three-plank or larger construction, so that a GC goods agent at Rugby with an empty GN open wagon could now load it to a destination on the LSWR. This cut unproductive empty mileage dramatically. By June 1916 the GWR, LYR, LNWR, Midland, NER, NBR, Caledonian and GSWR had joined the pool. By January 1917 virtually all railway company-owned open wagons, other than special vehicles, were a part of the pool, and a Highland open wagon might now be loaded at a Cambrian station for an SE&CR destination. By 1919 non-fitted ordinary vans were in the pool, and it was so effective that the pool survived into the Grouping of 1923. A pre-1914 layout should include a proportion of 'foreign' company wagons, but these should only be worked *in* loaded, and should seldom go out under load. After 1915 the proportion of foreign wagons at any station would increase, as they could

Loads of Goods Wagons containing Traffic invoiced through Goods Department.

District.. Month of _July,_ 1910. Number of Working Days in Month 1909-27 ; 1910 26.

SECTION AND NAME OF STATION.	NORTH EASTERN AND PRIVATE WAGONS.					FOREIGN WAGONS.							(7) N.E. and Foreign wagons loaded with Live Stock.	(10) N.E. wagons loaded to Foreign Companies' Lines. (These wagons are included in column 1.)	REMARKS.
	(1) Loaded except Cattle (loaded with Live Stock) and Road Wagons. (See Column 10.)	(2) Weight Loaded in Wagons in Column (1)	Average Load, Wagons in Column (1)	Corresponding figures for previous years.	(8) North Eastern Road Wagons.	(3) Loaded to points beyond the Junction with N.E. (Cattle Wagons excluded).	(4) Weight Loaded in Wagons in Column (3)	Average Load, Wagons in Column (3)	(5) Loaded to N.E. Stations (Cattle Wagons loaded with Live Stock excluded).	(6) Weight loaded in Wagons in Column (5)	Average Load, Wagons in Column (5)	(9) Empty except Cattle Wagons.			
	No.	Tons.	Tons.	Tons.	No.	No.	Tons.	Tons.	No.	Tons.	Tons.	No.	No.	No.	
A	705	6306·3	8·95	8·78	...	...	...	...	...	...	...	3	...	12	
B	1,292	9581·4	7·42	7·26	...	...	...	...	...	...	...	167	...	107	
C	221	1041·8	4·71	4·12	4	17	36·9	2·17	...	...	...	8	64	50	
D	139	561·1	4·04	4·30	76	24	47·8	1·99	...	...	...	116	22	15	
E	568	2059·6	3·63	3·88	71	92	79·4	·86	...	...	...	216	7	6	
F	1,062	3044·4	2·87	3·16	258	142	232·6	1·63	52	106·6	2·05	283	8	84	
G	5,774	18672·0	3·23	3·12	573	2,327	3222·2	1·38	358	681·3	1·90	949	1,001	690	

In this return, which covers all loading points, the Stations are arranged in Branch order and the totals and averages shown for each District.

Numbers in brackets refer to paragraphs in Station returns.

Above Although back loading to home system was limited before 1915, it did happen, as this North Eastern Railway table of July 1910 reveals. Sadly the Section names are identified by letter rather than name, but we see a limited use of foreign wagons being back loaded home, often with quite trivial loads, but even the 0.86-ton average from Section E was better than an empty wagon, and an NE wagon being sent out also!

Right North British Railway four-plank drop-door open 7944 has strayed far from its parent system, for it was photographed at Rugby, an indication of just how far afield wagons could roam.

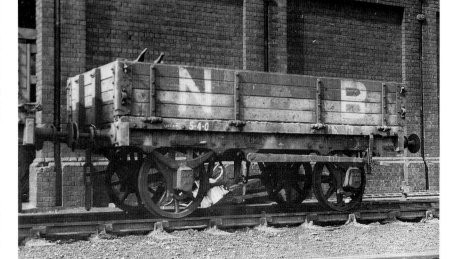

be used on internal movements. By the Grouping this meant that as the LMS and LNER had far larger general wagon stocks than the GWR or SR, even on the most remote GW branch line many of the ordinary wagons would be pooled LMS or LNER equipment.

One could multiply the list of dos and don'ts almost indefinitely, but there are several excellent books on railway company and private owner wagons (eg Essery/Rowland/Steel on _British Goods Wagons_ published by David & Charles, Bill Hudson on _Private Owner Wagons_, 4 volumes from OPC/Headstock, or the LMS, LNER, GWR, Midland and Southern wagon books by various authors). These give far more detail on what is appropriate to a given location or period than is possible in a single chapter in this book. I have aimed to set out the principles, and deal with the questions that the modeller needs to ask.

Freight trains

I have discussed wagons in depth, as they are the building blocks out of which we make our freight trains, and if the ingredients are wrong, the finished dish will be wrong. Let us now look at the trains. The traditional British freight train comprised a string of four-wheel wagons, and often no two were identical, and it might appear a haphazard mix without thought or purpose. Nothing could be further from the truth. The freight train was strictly utilitarian. Its wagons might have originated from 50 or 60 starting points, and might disperse to as many before they had completed their journey; on the other hand, they might have started from a single station, and be heading for a marshalling yard where they would scatter on to a host of other trains, as they travelled north, south, east and west. The train might be a through freight, travelling 50 or 100 miles from one large yard to another, or it might be a wayside goods, picking up and setting down at every intermediate station, and taking hours to travel a few miles. How does this affect us?

The way the train is marshalled and the stock it conveys will be determined by many factors, some contradictory. As wagons came in from the humble wayside freights, they had to be sorted and attached to the long-distance services. This was the purpose of the marshalling yard. A skilled shunter would group wagons for a particular destination on an outbound freight for two reasons. First, if he did not, the staff at the next yard might complain, and the complaints might reach head office. Second, if he did not look after his colleagues, they might not look after him, and it made life easier all round. There was a greater tendency to marshal well if the destination was a yard on your own system than if it was to another company. With a pick-up goods, the train would start with the wagons in station order, and would pick up wagons in batches from each station, so arrive in that sort of order. The longer-distance freights would be assembled in the yards with stock grouped as far as possible to simplify shunting at the next yard. All the traffic for one line would tend to be together, and the traffic for another route similarly concentrated.

So far shunting sounds nice and simple, but the traditional British goods wagon was four-wheeled, with no continuous brakes and loose coupled. As the train started, the slack had to be taken up in the couplings, so the train engine could be moving at several miles per hour before the last vehicles were snatched into motion. Goods guards had a rough ride, and were used to such violent starts. As they were only guards, that did not matter, but cattle were much more important, as any guard will tell you. A violent start to a loaded cattle wagon and you might have a compensation claim from the farmer. The best place to marshal cattle wagons was therefore at the head of the train, where the snatching was minimised. This was so even if the convenient place for shunting was at the rear. The same rules applied to pigs and sheep. If you see cattle wagons at the rear of the train, they are probably empties, or may have been converted to ale wagons when the livestock business began to decline between the wars.

Steam locomotives produce sparks and cinders. These are not strictly compatible with petrol and other inflammable substances, so normal practice was to marshal at least two barrier wagons not conveying explosive or inflammable goods between petrol tankers and the engine. It was common to do so at the other end of the train, but as the guard was not likely to set the train on fire, it was merely a courtesy, and not essential. Goods guards, you will have realised, ranked with, but probably after, black beetles. Anyone who has travelled in a goods brake van will agree that such instruments of torture are not fit for the conveyance of any item of value, such as a cow, but were clearly adequate for a guard!

Felled timber and long loads, liable to move in transit and warranting close supervision, were customarily marshalled immediately ahead of the brake van, so that the guard, whose means of stopping the majority of freight trains comprised a hand brake, could have a grandstand view of the impending disaster. Earlier in this chapter I spoke of the Ponkeston sawmill on the GHR, and that the leading wagons on the wayside freight would be felled timber for Ponkeston. This introduces one of the conflicts faced by shunters. On a long run, felled timber should be marshalled at the rear of the train. On a short run, it may be preferable, indeed imperative, to marshal it quite differently. This is such an instance.

Getting a freight train under way is hard work, but once it is moving the problems begin. An 80-wagon general freight could easily gross 1,200 tons, but the only brakes available for stopping it were on the engine, with a weight of perhaps 100 tons, and the brake van, which might be 12, 15 or at most 20 tons. Freight trains were thus difficult to stop, and the faster they went, the greater the problem. As the majority of freight stock was unfitted (ie had no continuous automatic brake) until the end of the Steam Age, the limiting factor in freight train working was

Above Cattle were a valuable commodity, with strict limits on transit times before watering and feeding. Where flows were regular, for example from the ports to major cities, scheduled fast trains were timetabled, and specials could run at short notice. A Stroudley 'E' tank, carrying Brighton & Portsmouth section route discs, dashes through Ham Bridge station on a short cattle train in 1911. For many years cattle wagons were disinfected with a lime wash, hence the whitened body sides and running gear. *H. J. Stretton Ward*

Below Fowler '4F' No 4514 heads a long freight off the Peterborough line towards the down goods at Clifton Road Junction, just south of Rugby, on 25 May 1939. As was customary, two barrier wagons have been marshalled between the engine and the tank wagons. Beyond the tanks are a number of Stephenson Clarke empties and the odd GLM empty. Space for a signal box can perplex the modeller, and the LNWR had a similar problem; Clifton Road Junction was thus perched atop the flyover on brick abutments. It was demolished a few weeks after this photo was taken. *H. J. Stretton Ward*

Loads such as this felled timber would ordinarily be marshalled next to the guard. As well as showing the 1920s LMS wagon livery to perfection, this study of 40-ton code BBZ bolster wagon 279173 recalls how long timbers were moved by rail; where the load extended beyond the end of the wagon a runner or match truck was necessary. The 'N' marks indicate a non-pool vehicle. *H. J. Stretton Ward*

not starting, but stopping. However fast the engine might be able to run, the freight train had to run slowly if it was to stop in any reasonable distance.

Following the Armagh accident in 1888, in which an excursion train without automatic brakes ran away when divided on a gradient, such brakes were made compulsory on passenger trains, but no such provisions existed for the humble freight wagon, let alone the hundreds of thousands of private owner wagons. If freight services were to be speeded up, more brake power was essential, and this was recognised in pre-Grouping days, but the cost of equipping the whole of the wagon stock with vacuum brakes was so high that little progress was made. Wagons that were likely to work on passenger trains and convey urgent or perishable traffic were the first to be fitted, but before the First World War the fitted wagon was still a rarity.

Attempts were made to operate fast freights, but differed from company to company. The LYR rules of 1907 set out the traditional position, with a fish, meat, fruit, cattle or perishable train composed of stock up to passenger requirements belled as a 5; the modern equivalent would be a parcels train. Empty coaching stock was a 2-2-1, while a Class A freight, of goods stock, for fish, meat, fruit or cattle, was a 3-2. The Class B express goods was a 1-4. By 1919 the LYR had developed a new and superior freight, the 'Right Away' goods, belled as a 1-1-3 and ranking ahead of

parcels or ECS trains. The LNWR developed two types of fast perishable train, composed of goods stock and both operating under the 5 bell code. The Class 1 was a fully-fitted train limited to 50 wagons, while the Class 2, also limited to 50 wagons, was composed of fitted or piped stock, with not less than half braked. For its period this was very ambitious. A name that was to enter railway folklore was born, the 'Maltese Goods', so named from the Maltese cross symbol in the timetable. A 'Maltese' was to have not less than four fitted wagons at the head, and could not be stopped for shunting purposes out of course without special permission from Central Control at Crewe.

The LMS inherited a variety of operating practices, and in January 1925 re-classified its freight services. Two fast freights were envisaged, the 5, which was an express freight with continuous brakes in use on at least half the vehicles, and the 3-2, on which the continuous brake was in use on less than half the train. The 'Maltese' did not rate too highly at this stage, and the LMS rules were premature, given the limited amount of fitted stock, and caused problems. The 1929 regulations listed three types of train. The 5 retained its place as a 'Fitted freight, fish or cattle train with the continuous brake in use on *not less* than half the vehicles'. The 'Maltese' gained wider usage, and the 1929 regulations demonstrate how it got its name, for it was an 'Express freight or cattle train with the continuous brake on less than half the vehicles, but in use on four vehicles connected to the engine, indicated by ✠ in the Working Time Tables.' It was offered as a 2-2-3. The 3-2 was retained for an unfitted express freight, or one with fewer than four vacuum-braked wagons. The 5 suffered a further decline of status with the 1934 rules, when it became one-third fitted, and this was still the case with the 1947 regulations.

The LNER followed similar principles with their Braked Goods Class 1 and 2. The LNER 1931 rules explained that a Class 1 braked goods was expected to average 40 mph or above, and consisted of vehicles conforming to coaching stock requirements if scheduled at over 45 mph. Wagons that otherwise met coaching stock requirements but had grease boxes could travel in trains diagrammed to average 40-45 mph. The proportion of fitted wagons varied from two-thirds for a short train to four-fifths in the case of a 60-wagon freight. A Class 2 braked goods would average 33-40 mph, and once again a table of fitted vehicles was laid down, varying from nil for an 18-wagon train to four in 34 wagons, eight in 46, 12 in 60, and 20 in 75. The GWR and Southern remained a law unto themselves, the Southern, with its more limited freight requirements, paying little attention to the developments on the northern lines.

As the LMS and LNER classification systems were close, they were unified under British Railways, and applied on the LM, E, NE, Southern and Scottish Regions. The blue riband went to the 3-1-1, which was piped throughout, with the vacuum brake operational on not less than half the vehicles. The 5 remained partly fitted, with the brake operative on at least one-third of the stock. The 2-2-3 'Maltese' goods had been replaced by a new code, the 1-2-2, which was either a limited-load train without automatic brakes, or a full load with four wagons as a braked head. The 'Maltese' symbol passed into limbo. The remaining BR freights were the unfitted express freight, or 3-2, the through freight or ballast, 1-4, and the mineral or empty wagon train, 4-1. A freight or mineral stopping at intermediate stations, ie a 'pick-up', was a 3.

I have explained these regulations in some depth, as they seem to be frequently misunderstood. In effect, freight trains were graded by braking power, which determined their permissible running speed, and they could be identified by the bell codes and head lamps under which they ran. Grease-axlebox wagons, even if owned by the railway companies, were not allowed on the fastest freights, and grease-box private owner coal wagons were not tolerated on fast freights at all. The fast freight that may roar through your main-line station with a mix of vacuum-fitted wagons at the head, then a string of coal wagons, is not convincing. The D-shaped axlebox on older wagons commonly indicates a grease box, whereas the more complex shape with the waist wider than the rest of the box, and ribbed, suggests a later oil box.

Apart from fitted and unfitted stock, another species of wagon had appeared. This was the piped but unfitted wagon. The reasoning behind this hybrid was that while it did not add to braking capacity, it could be marshalled in between vacuum-fitted wagons, its through pipe being coupled up so that vacuum-braked wagons behind it could still contribute to train braking; it could also work within the fitted head on fast freights. For the shunter it was a mixed blessing, for while it eased marshalling, if by chance he marshalled a large number of piped wagons and just a few vacuum-braked wagons in a train, it might look as if it had excellent stopping capabilities, but it was a sham. LNER rules provided that the pipes on fitted wagons were to be painted black, but on piped unfitted wagons were to be red, as a warning that these vehicles did not contribute towards the brake power.

Now that we know what kind of freight trains existed, when did they run, and where? Public goods stations opened in the morning, as early as 6.00 am in pre-1914 days, but latterly 8.00 am was more common. As some wagons were unloaded by consignees, and it was desirable not to risk injuring them or the railwaymen working on other wagons, shunting in the loading and unloading areas was limited from opening time until the goods depot closed to public business at around 5.30 or 6.00 pm. By then many of the wagons should have been dealt with. As well as providing rail haulage, the companies provided road cartage at each end, and carters, lurrymen or motor vehicle drivers came on for early and late shifts. Goods that had arrived at a large depot the previous night were sent out as early in the day as possible, and inward loads collected. At any large goods depot the early evening was a period of intense activity, as open wagons were sheeted and roped, and gangs of porters, checkers and loaders made up wagon loads of small consignments from the depot to large towns and tranship depots. As the evening progressed the wagons would be collected, shunted into the appropriate trains, and as the passenger service slackened off after 9.00 pm, the long-distance night freights would depart. While the fastest long-distance freights, such as the LNER Class 1 braked goods, might average 40-45 mph, most freights were much more sedate, and 15-20 mph averages were considered good. For mineral trains 10 mph was not uncommon - indeed, for many years a 10 mph average for a coal train would be regarded as excellent.

Although few modellers will build a large goods station, they were the hub of the operation, and as with a stone thrown into a pond, the waves rippled outwards. The night goods would run 125 to 200 miles overnight, though this distance increased as faster services were introduced. At centres such as Crewe, Whitemoor or Toton, freights were broken up and remarshalled, for while there might be adequate traffic between a few cities such as London and Birmingham, Liverpool or Manchester, freight was too disjointed to run large numbers of direct services between every small or medium-sized town in the British Isles.

When the freight came into the marshalling yard it was broken down, with wagons for local stations going on 'trip' workings or wayside freights, while wagons for distant places were added to further long-distance trains. Unlike the large freight stations, which were operating continuously although only open to the public in normal working hours, the small yards were only open during normal hours. On many branches there was no service before 6.00 am, or after 10.00 pm, and only a reduced station staff in the early morning and evening; freight to wayside stations would thus normally be moved in daylight hours. If a station regularly handled a lot of freight, say 20 wagons or more, a 'trip' working from the yard to that station, or to two or three stations, was common. For stations in rural areas with lower daily traffic flows, the pick-up might shunt at 10 or 15 stations during its journey, spending minutes or hours at each place. As we have seen, in theory, the pick-up would be mar-

Rugby Wharf was on the MR Rugby-Leicester line a short distance north of the junction with the main line, and provided a public goods depot for the Midland, and access to a canal wharf. No 43795 shunts the wharf on a pick-up freight on 19 July 1955.

shalled with the stock for each station grouped together, to speed up shunting on the road, but the presence of cattle wagons, to be marshalled at the front of the train, petrol tankers, not to be at the front, or timber or similar awkward loads, to be at the rear, complicated the picture. The pick-up would complete its work by the early evening, so that its wagons could reach a large yard for onward transmission later that day.

Coal and minerals tended to move in separate trains from general merchandise if travelling in bulk or over long distances. Such traffic was often marshalled separately, and even handled in separate coal yards in large towns and cities. At smaller stations, which is what the majority of modellers will build, coal was usually handled in a portion of the yard set aside for the coal merchants, and would usually come in with the general freight on the pick-up. Other minerals, such as iron ore or limestone, also used to move in bulk. Iron ore, limestone and coal or coke were the raw materials for the iron and steel industry, and many lines carried a heavy traffic. One thinks of the iron ore fields of the South Midlands, the steel plants of Corby, South Wales, the Black Country, Middlesbrough and the Clyde. Iron ore wagons were commonly seen at the ports, ironstone quarries or iron works, but not in wayside station goods yards.

Working timetables are vital in assessing your freight needs. Once again, pre-Nationalisation, let alone pre-Grouping, freight WTTs are hard to find,

Robinson 'O4' No 6323 heads a heavy coal southbound along the GC main line near Rugby Central in 1938. Most if not all the wagons, are private owners; there is an individual merchant's wagon, then a group of three of the same owner, followed by at least six Stephenson Clarke wagons. Such groups of wagons were common, and are often neglected on the model railway. Incidentally, the signal to the rear of the loco is a 'banner repeater', consisting of a white circle with a horizontal black bar that is rotated to give the 'off' position. As the line here is on a continuous curve and sighting of the home signal is poor, the banner repeats to the driver the indication shown by the as yet invisible home signal.

and expensive. There have been some reprints, but the most likely source for the modeller is the BR freight WTT of the 1950s. Once regional foibles had been dealt with, freight WTTs were readily identifiable by size alone, for while the passenger WTT was 11.5 inches in depth, the freight WTTs were 10 inches deep. A selection of freight timetables are reproduced on the following pages, and repay study.

Model freight - labelling and loads

So how do we recapture these freight services in miniature? We have looked at where wagons should be shunted, and appropriate stock for a specific station or locality, the kind of trains that ran, and how they were marshalled. On a layout with one station and a fiddle yard that is enough, but on a larger layout there are further possibilities. One of the greatest modellers of all time was an American, the late John Allen, whose Gorre & Daphetid was a stunning visual representation of railroading in the rugged West. Floor-to-ceiling scenery, the careful use of mirrors to provide false distance and skilled lighting contributed to a brilliant concept. However, John Allen was not just a scenery man, but an operator too. His was a large layout with numerous stations and private sidings, and rather than operate wagons at random a labelling system was adopted. As a genuine wagon label is only a few inches square and affixed to the side of the wagon, it would be impossible to read one even in 7 mm, let alone the HO, ie 3.5 mm, in which John Allen worked. Instead each station was colour-coded, and a minute hole was drilled in the roof of closed wagons or in the top of the side of opens. A pin with a coloured plastic head was inserted in the hole so that an operator, seeing, say, a red pin, knew it was for Great Divide, whereas a green pin might be for Gorre. This was simple to operate, and meant that a yard master sorting a freight would see a variety of red, green, blue, black, pink, etc, cars, and would have to sort them by route and in station order. Instead of gathering wagons at random, they were worked for some purpose.

Classification of Goods & Coal Trains to & from L. & Y. Line

5.15 a.m. Goods, Ordsall Lane to Miles Platting, to convey Traffic for Miles Platting, Beswick, and all Stations on the Ashton Branch, and when short of a load Traffic for other Stations on the L. & Y. Line.

6.25 a.m., Miles Platting to Ordsall Lane, to convey Traffic from Miles Platting, for exchange at Ordsall Lane.

10.55 a.m., Ordsall Lane to Miles Platting, Traffic for Miles Platting and Stations on the L. & Y. Line.

12. 5 p.m., Miles Platting to Ordsall Lane, Traffic for exchange at Ordsall Lane.

10.25 p.m., Springs Branch, to Oldham, to convey Traffic for Castleton Siding, Milkstone Siding, Rochdale, Milnrow, Shaw, Royton Junction, & Oldham.

10 20 p.m., Little Hulton Junction to Rochdale, to convey Coal for Castleton, Castleton Siding, Rochdale and beyond, and when short of a load to be made up with Traffic for Middleton. Will detach sufficient Middleton Traffic at Patricroft to give 11.30 p.m. from Tyldesley a full load. Other Middleton Traffic to be detached at Middleton Junction.

8 45 p.m., Tyldesley to Rochdale, to convey Traffic for Castleton, Castleton Siding, Milkstone Siding, Rochdale, Heywood, Milnrow, Shaw, Royton Junction, Hartford Works Siding, and Oldham. Not to convey Traffic for Ordsall Lane or transfer there.

1.35 a.m., Rochdale for Tyldesley, to convey Empty Wagons for Tyldesley Coal Company, Ramsden's Siding, Astley, and Tyldesley Siding, Leigh and Bedford, Sanderson Siding, and Atherton.

2.45 a.m., Rochdale to Springs Branch, to convey wagons for the Tyldesley Coal Company, Ramsden's Siding, Sanderson Siding, W. C. & I. Co.s Siding, and Atherton.

2 0 a.m., Middleton to Tyldesley, to convey Empties for Sanderson Siding, Tyldesley Coal Company, Ramsden's Siding, Leigh & Bedford, Atherton, and Hulton's Siding.

5 30 p.m., Atherton to Rochdale, will convey Traffic for Castleton, Castleton Siding, and Stations on L. & Y. Line between Rochdale and Oldham. This Traffic to be detached at Patricroft and sent forward by Through Rochdale Trains. When short of a Load, will make up with Traffic for Ordsall Lane and Miles Platting. That for Miles Platting to be taken through to Ordsall Lane. L. & Y. Through Traffic to be marshalled next the Engine.

Instructions respecting the running of the WOOL TRAIN.

During the time of the running of the Wool Train, the 4.0 a.m. Train, Stockport to Bradford, will be discontinued, the Engine and Breaksman working forward this Train instead.

The Special Wool Train will carry from Crewe a White Light at the foot of the Engine Chimney, and a White Light over the left-hand Buffer during the night time. With the exception of the 9.12 p.m. Broad Street to Leeds, this Train must have precedence over all other Goods or Mineral Trains, which must be shunted in time to prevent any detention to it.

The running of the Wool Train to be reported on the speaking telegraph from Station to Station, and a clear road kept for it.

The Wool Train will detach Halifax Traffic in the Contractor's Loop at Hill-house, and it will detach Leeds' Traffic at Heaton Lodge.

16 NED

A pair of pages from the LNWR NE Division WTT of 1 January 1885. There are several freights in the early hours, a midday working and an early evening service. The notes on train classification say what traffic the trains carry and where they shunt. Until the 1960s wool was an important commodity in the mill towns of Yorkshire.

Up. NEW HOLLAND, IMMINGHAM, GRIMSBY, and CLEETHORPES. 35

WEEK DAYS. — STATIONS. (Trains 1–14)

Distance from New Holland	Distance Station to Station	STATIONS		1 LE for 2.55 a.m. Goods Grimsby to Barnetby MO and Pilots.	2 8.44 p.m. Coal ex Firbeck Colly.	3 7.30 p.m. Goods ex Sheffield.	4 LE for 7.50 a.m. Grimsby to Boston.	5 9.0 p.m. Coal ex Castle Hills.	6 11.30 p.m. Goods ex Normanby Park. S.X.	7 Goods.	8 2.30 a.m. Coal Elies. Frodingham to Orgreaves.	9 1.13 a.m. Goods ex Retford.	10 LE for 3.55 a.m. New Clee to Markham Main.	11 1.12 a.m. Coal ex Worksop.	12 12.55 a.m. Coal Retford to New Holland.	13 1.56 a.m. Coal ex Heathorpe.	14 3.20 a.m. Mineral Frodingham to Whitemoor.
		Class.		C	C	B	C	B	B		B	C	B	C	C	C	C
M. C.	M. C.			MO	MX	MX	MO	MX	MX	MO	C	MX	SO	MX	MX	MX	
...	...	Wrawby Junction	pass	...	12 6	12 11	...	12 46	2 3	...	2 56	3 5	...	3 24	3 35	3 42	3 53
		BARNETBY	arr.		pass	12 15		pass	2 7		3 0	pass		pass	3 39	3 46	pass
			dep.		12 10	12 30		12 49	2 40			3 8		3 27	4 5	4 28	3 56
		Brocklesby	arr.		pass	pass		pass	pass			3 28		pass	pass	pass	pass
			dep.		12 30	12 53		1 9	3 3					3 47	4 28	4 51	4 17
		New Holland Pier	arr.		...	...		...	...					...	...	...	
...	...	New Holland Town 0|24	arr.		...	...		...	...					...	...	...	
			dep.														
2 16	2 16	Goxhill	"		...	...		...	...		West Marsh dep. 2.0 a.m.			...	...	...	
3 68	1 52	Thornton Abbey	"		...	...		...	pass				pass		pass		pass
6 37	2 49	Ulceby	arr.		pass				3 6				3 31		3 50		4 54
			dep.		12 35				3 20			3 44	4 3				
		Immingham (Reception) Sdgs.	arr.		12 52												
		Immingham East Jcn.	dep.														
8 13	1 56	Habrough	"		...	...		...	...					...	...		
11 77	3 64	Stallingborough	"		...	...		...	...					...	...		
12 78	1 1	Healing	"		...	...		...	...					...	...		
14 24	1 26	Great Coates	"		...	...		...	...					...	...		
15 0	0 56	Grimsby (Marsh Jcn.)	pass		12 38		1 24	2 25		2 5	Barnetby dep. 3.30 p.m.		2 13				4 42
		Grimsby (West Marsh)	arr.		pass			pass		pass			pass		pass		pass
16 23	1 23	GRIMSBY (Town)	dep.		12 43			2 30	1 43	2 10			2 18		5 4		4 50
16 55	0 32	Grimsby (East Marsh)	arr.		12§48			2§35		2 15							
17 15	0 40	Grimsby Docks	dep.					Loco.									
17 37	0 22	Riby Street Platform	"		...			1 56					2 28		5 20		
18 2	0 45	New Clee	"		...			...									
9 45	1 43	CLEETHORPES	arr.		...			...									

WEEK DAYS. — STATIONS. (Trains 15–31)

STATIONS		15 9.10 p.m. Goods ex Mexboro'.	15a 350 a.m. Coal Elies. Frodingham to Orgreaves.	16 Goods to New Holland.	17 LE for 5.25 a.m. Pass. to Peterboro'.	18 Pilot.	19 Goods	20 1.40 a.m. Pass. ex Manchester.	21 4.40 a.m. Goods ex Frodingham.	22 12.40 a.m. Goods ex Dewsnap.	23 1.40 a.m. Goods ex Ardsley.	24 LE for 7.30 a.m. Pass. Cleethorpes to Retford.	25 5.26 a.m. Goods Cleethorpes to Peterboro'.	26 1.16 a.m. Min. Orgreaves to Frodingham.	27 5.10 a.m. Min. Elies. Frodingham to Highdyke.	28 5.25 a.m. Normanby Park to Woodford.	29 LE for 6.55 a.m. Cleethorpes to Lincoln.	30 Pass. to Louth.	31 LE for 7.58 a.m. Pass. to New Holland.
	Class.	B	C	B			B		B	A	A				C	C			
		MX	MO					B	B	MO	MX			MX					
Wrawby Junction	pass	4 20	4 26	a.m.	a.m.		a.m.	5 5	5 13	5 29	5 31			5 41	5 48	6 16	a.m.	...	a.m.
BARNETBY	arr.	pass	4 30					5 5	pass	pass				5 45	5 52	6 20			
	dep.	4 23		4 50	a.m.		a.m.	5 8	5 17	5 31	5 33								
Brocklesby	arr.	pass		pass						pass	pass								
	dep.	4 43		5 11						5 47	5 48								
New Holland Pier	arr.	...																	
New Holland Town	dep.	...		Barnetby dep. 4.50 a.m.	West Marsh arr. 4.46 a.m.	West Marsh dep. 5.0 a.m.	4 30												Runs 5 minutes later M.O.
Goxhill	"	...																	
Thornton Abbey	"	...					pass					Arrives Grimsby Town 5.37 a.m.							
Ulceby	arr.	...		5 14			4 50												
	dep.	...		5 40															
Immingham (Reception) Sdgs.	arr.	...					pass												
Immingham East Jcn.	dep.	...					5 1												
Habrough	"	...												Depts. Barnetby 6.15 a.m.	Depts. Barnetby 6.31 a.m.	Starts from Frodingham (N.L. Jcn.) 5.45 a.m. M.O. passes Wrawby Jcn. 6.18 a.m., arr. Barnetby 7.20 a.m. dep. 6.49 a.m.			
Stallingborough	"	...																	
Great Coates	"	...																	
Grimsby (Marsh Jcn.)	pass	5 10		4 50	5 5		5 18		6 11	6 30	5 35							6 45
Grimsby (West Marsh)	arr.	5 13						5 30	pass						6 40		pass	
	dep.								6 40									
GRIMSBY (Town)	arr.			pass				5 50	6 47	5 40	5 55				6 10		6 50
	dep.			4 55	5 24		5 50	6 55									
Grimsby (East Marsh)	arr.				5 15	5 27											
Grimsby Docks	dep.						5 58		West Bank.								
Riby Street Platform	"				Pasture Street.	6 2											
New Clee	"					6 2											
CLEETHORPES	arr.			5 9				5§55							9§25		7§5

WEEK DAYS. — STATIONS. (Trains 32–48)

STATIONS		32 LE for 7.38 a.m. Pass. Grimsby Town to Louth.	33 Light Engine.	34 3.13 a.m. Mineral Orgreaves to Frodingham.	35 5.25 a.m. Pass. ex Lincoln.	36 Exp. Pass. to Peterboro'.	37 Pass. to Peterboro'.	38 1.0 a.m. Coal Warsop Junc. to Frodingham.	39 5.55 a.m. Pass. Grimsby Town to Frodingham.	40 6.19 a.m. L.E. ex Scunthorpe	41 11.15 a.m. SX Goods ex Ardwick.	42 6.40 a.m. Pass. ex Louth.	43 Goods to Marshgate.	44 Pass. to Louth.	45 Pass.	46 6.25 a.m. Goods Frodingham.	47 2.35 a.m. Coal ex Wath Yard.	48 1.15 a.m. Exp. Fish Elies. ex Woodford.
	Class.			C			C				A		D			B	C	No. 2
				MO			MX				MX					MX	MX	
Wrawby Junction	pass	a.m.	a.m.	6 20	6 25	a.m.	6 26	a.m.	6 34	6 40		a.m.	a.m.	a.m.	6 59	6 47	6 52
BARNETBY	arr.			6 24	6 27		6 30		6 36						pass	6 51	6 55
	dep.				6 30				6 43					7 2	7 6	7 7
Brocklesby	arr.				pass				pass					pass	pass	pass
	dep.				6 39			6 46	7 3					7 22	7 31	7 32
New Holland Pier	arr.		G.N. Yard dep. 7.0.	Depts. Barnetby 6.58 a.m.			Depts. Barnetby 6.58 a.m.	6 6					7 0			
New Holland Town	dep.							6 9					7 1			
Goxhill	"							6 7					7 3			
Thornton Abbey	"							6 14					7 9			
Ulceby	arr.											6 35	7 13			pass	7 36
	dep.							6 22	6 51			6 55	7 19	7 25	7 55
Immingham (Reception) Sdgs.	arr.											7 45		7 38	8 11
Immingham East Jcn.	"														
Habrough	dep.			6 43									7 23		
Stallingborough	"			6 50									7 30		
Healing	"			6 53									7 34		
Great Coates	"			6 57									7 38		
Grimsby (Marsh Jcn.)	pass	7 5								7 37				
Grimsby (West Marsh)	arr.												7 42		
	dep.													
GRIMSBY (Town)	arr.	7§10			7 1	7 15						7 17	7 38	7 47	pass
	dep.		7§5		7 6										7 58
Grimsby (East Marsh)	arr.				7 22							7 52		
Grimsby Docks	dep.				7 14							7 54		8 5
Riby Street Platform	"				7 18							7 58		
New Clee	"				7 22						7 30	8 2		
CLEETHORPES	arr.													

The Great Central handled a vast quantity of freight in the Immingham area, so here is a page from the LNER WTT for 5 July 1937. At times freights are passing at 10-minute intervals.

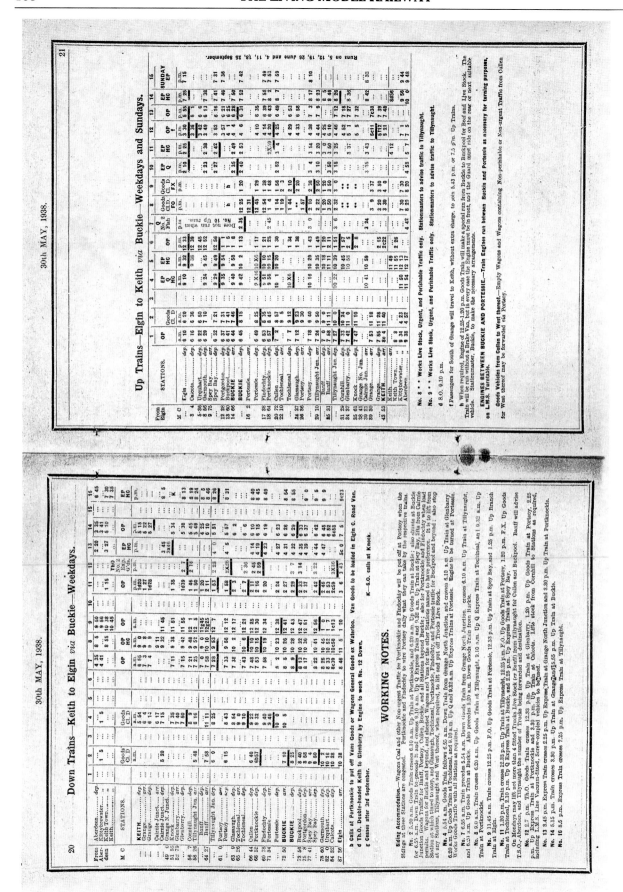

This second glimpse of the LNER takes us to very different territory, to the old Great North of Scotland section. OP stands for ordinary stopping passenger train, EP is an express, and, contrary to what one might think, HC indicated that horse-boxes an carriage trucks are not conveyed by this train.

Two pages from the LM Region WTT covering the Settle-Carlisle route for June 1955.
With the freight then moving north of Skipton, it would be hard to argue that the line was not earning its keep!

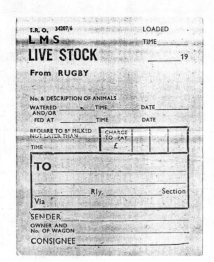 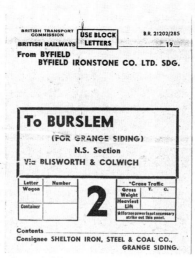 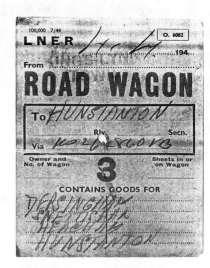

Wagons must be worked to their correct destinations, and the humble wagon label played a vital role on the prototype. Here are three different examples: an LMS 'LIVE STOCK' label from Rugby, with watering, feeding and milking times listed; a BR IRONSTONE label from Byfield on the S&MJ; and an LNER ROAD WAGON label. Road wagons conveyed traffic for a variety of way stations, in this case Hunstanton and three intermediate places. If we want to work our wagons logically, a labelling system is a help, but the 1930s standard wagon label was 4 x 5 inches, and in O gauge this is less than 3 mm square, and in OO about 1.5 mm. Reading all the fine print would be difficult, so some other method is needed.

Quite independently Dad developed a similar labelling system for the GHR. As UK wagons have convenient buffers to hang labels over, we did not need to drill holes in the roof of every wagon. Instead, an inverted U-shaped label was made out of tinplate (for durability) and painted. Dad could have given each station a different colour, but wanted to route traffic off the system too, for many of the wagons leaving a station will not be going to the next or next-but-one station, but may be going 200 miles away. The Allen system covers 'on line' stations, but not distant destinations. So instead of giving each station a colour code, each *route* was given a colour. The GHR main-line stations are blue, but as there are several stations on the modelled section, and more on the section we could not model, this was not enough. Each station was therefore number-coded, and labels similarly numbered. The theoretical termini, Greenlane/Glasson Dock and Hillside, are coded green and purple respectively, while the Hoggsnorton branch is coded pink. If the Hoggsnorton operator wishes to send a wagon to Slack, he puts a 'Blue 5' label over the buffer, and sends it out on the Hoggsnorton-Hillside branch freight. When the train arrives at Hillside yard, the operator does not need a

verbal message, 'Hey, will you send that LMS cattle wagon to Slack, please?', for the wagon label conveys that message already. He will transfer the wagon to a freight scheduled to call at Slack.

Thus far John Allen's system would have sufficed, but let us say that the Hoggsnorton operator wishes to send a consignment of furniture to a shop in Rugby (as there is a furniture factory at Hoggsnorton) and another consignment to Grimsby. The whole of the British Isles is colour-coded, as well as the GHR, so areas reached off the West Coast Main Line via Preston are grey, the East Coast southwards is orange, the West Coast north and Scotland is brown, etc. The coding is based upon the routes our freight trains can take, for in the evening the Hillside yard operator has to make up five night goods. A couple of these are for the GHR main line to Greenlane and Glasson Dock, another couple are for Preston and the WCML, and another conveys transfer traffic to be added to other trains at Middleton. As the yard operator is making up these trains, he will gather all grey-labelled traffic for the Preston trains. As both Prestons are part-fitted, one being a 3-1-1 and the other a 1-2-2, the yard master has to sort out fitted and unfitted stock, and ensure that there is a sufficient 'vacuum head' for the 1-2-2 (four wagons); all other fitted stock is sent on the 3-1-1.

In fact, the system is even more sophisticated, for BR introduced a numerical parcels sorting code, and each major centre was accorded a number. Rugby was 5, and Grimsby became 123, and Dad adopted the BR parcels numbers for freight purposes. As Rugby was WCML-South, it became label 'Grey 5', while Grimsby, via the LNER, was 'Orange 123'. The Hoggsnorton operator will go to the central label store, which is a multi-drawer unit divided into com-

A gleaming Rolls-Royce awaits dispatch from Hillside Bray Street yard on an LNWR carriage truck to Blackburn, its destination revealed by the 'Grey 33' wagon label over the buffer. This carriage truck may go by passenger train, or be sent out on one of the fitted Preston goods.

partments, obtain the correct labels and put them on his wagons. When the branch freight arrives at Hillside, instead of it being a random mix of wagons, which one could do anything with, the yard master has to shunt off the blue-labelled stock for the local pick-ups, set the grey stock aside for the Preston goods and the orange-labelled stock for the East Coast via Coniston and Skipton. When a wagon reaches its destination, eg Slack, the operator takes off the 'Blue 5' label and returns his incoming labels to the central labels depot, usually collecting his estimated requirements for the next running at the same time. Middleton, which operates as the rest of England, will do likewise with the various green, grey and brown labels that inundate him.

Some wagons operate on an out-and-back basis, loaded from A to B, empty back to A, and so on. Dual-coloured labels were made for such workings, and remain on the wagons for a prolonged period. An empty wagon returning home would carry an appropriately coloured but un-numbered label, and pooled empties would carry an un-numbered white label.

However, we found that this was unnecessary, and empties were later dispatched unlabelled. Sometimes a wagon might be running badly, suffer damage, or be a complete failure. Wagons that can work to destination, but not thereafter, receive a second dual-coloured red/green label, and have to be serviced on arrival at destination. Wagons that are unsafe to travel are red-labelled.

The labelling system has operated successfully for many years, and is still used, but not as much as I would wish, as we are often short of operators, and to shunt each freight into blue, grey, brown, orange, etc, labelled wagons is a full-time occupation for the Hillside yard master. If the passenger station operator has to do this when there is no yard master, while he can pull out rakes of stock, there is no time to shunt by label-coding. This is a pity as it loses one of the most brilliant operating concepts Dad devised.

The labelling concept altered freight working from the movement of random wagons into a purposeful exercise, and added a fresh dimension of realism. However, wagons move because there is traffic to be

Joe Griffiths adopted the same sort of wagon labelling system as my father and John Allen. In his case the Conway wagon stock was fitted with a small staple on the wagon solebar, and a wagon label was slipped into the clip. One of Conway's controlled clockwork engines is shunting a Franklin & Co private owner wagon into Franklin's siding on the main line between Paxton Junction and Ganwick; the wagon carries an 'F' label. The NE van on the pick-up carries a 'G' label, for Ganwick, so the pick-up freight has been properly marshalled. *J. Griffiths*

moved. A list was therefore drawn up for the GHR, detailing the local industries at each station - I have already referred to the furniture factory at Hoggsnorton - so that the operator would know what merchandise might go out, and operators at other stations would know what he would need to receive. At Mickleburgh, on the Hoggsnorton branch, there is a cannery, the Tinex factory. This receives tinplate for cans, printed labels for the outside of the cans, and the ingredients that go into the cans. The cannery produces meat and fruit products, but sometimes operators have flights of fancy; I am not convinced that canned bananas are common, but banana wagons have been known to arrive at Mickleburgh. If a working is too eccentric, then a suggestion that we try something more normal suffices.

When working properly, the labelling system has another attraction. As with the prototype, wagons will be originated from a variety of different points, creating a random element. It may happen that three or four operators independently send several wagons to the Hoggsnorton line stations. Due to the short passing loops at Mickleburgh and Hoggsnorton, and the 1 in 28 grade, the branch freight is limited to 12 wagons. If 15 or 16 wagons arrive at Hillside, the yard master does not 'forget' the surplus - he has to get them to Hoggsnorton. If some are vacuum-fitted, three or four can be added to a convenient motor train. A couple of trains are authorised to run 'mixed', with unfitted wagons and a brake van. If there is a flood of traffic, the yard master must ask Hillside Control for a special freight. Control must find a suitable engine, for with its tight clearances not all motive power can work over the branch, a restriction from which many branch lines suffered. If Control is doing *his* job properly, he will try to select an engine that is already 'in steam', or will be required later on.

Our freight system works by physical labelling of wagons, and we have found it satisfactory. Some operating systems, especially in America, use card order or computer-generated data, in which each wagon is matched by an individual card. The pack of cards are shuffled, and then so many cards 'dealt' to each station. The wagon must then work to the station. Under this system a petrol tanker could be dealt to a station with no facilities for handling it, so a 'bad choice' facility is necessary.

An alternative approach concentrates on the station. The pack is dealt out, and we find that station A needs three cattle wagons, two coal wagons, a horsebox, etc, and the yard master must find the appropriate wagons from the stock on hand. With modern technology the process could be computerised, and

with suitable programming 'bad deals' could be barred. A print-out would go to each station, listing what he needs and what he has to send out. I have not had personal experience of a card system, but this would achieve comparable results to the wagon-labelling system developed independently by John Allen and my father.

Dad disliked fixed loads in wagons, for a loaded coal wagon may look convincing arriving at the branch terminus, but looks ridiculous arriving loaded at the colliery. For mineral wagons he devised removable loads, with a rectangle of thin plywood cut to the size of the standard wagons, then covered with a suitably humped load of coal, limestone or gravel, etc. If the load was on a solid block of wood it would be difficult to remove without lifting the wagon off the track and tipping it upside down. A block was therefore fixed to the underside of the load, making it the right height, and all one needed to do was to depress one end of the load, and as the other end rose up, lift it out. It is difficult to achieve the same realism with removable loads as with fixed loads, as it is not practicable to chain vehicles properly, but on the other hand there is *no* realism in a loaded coal wagon arriving, then departing still loaded.

For mineral traffic, a couple of modellers arrived at a convincing answer to permanently full and empty wagons, by suggesting a colliery or sand and gravel pit at the station. Empties are propelled into the sidings, which connect directly to the fiddle yard. The engine then pulls out a separate rake of loaded wagons, which are shunted on to a train, and depart for the fiddle yard where they go back into the sidings to emerge from the colliery or sand pit once more. The empties circle in the opposite direction. For this to work, there must be a connection between the colliery, etc, and the fiddle yard, but it can offer excellent possibilities. On a circle layout with hidden loops to the station and back to the loops, the up coal could be permanently loaded, and the down coal permanently empty.

Loose minerals can look splendid, and I visited one layout where a working stone tipper was in use, recalling scenes from the prototype. At the other end of the line the wagons discharged their minerals. It was a giant leap in realism, *but* conveying loose minerals by model railway has its drawbacks. In the 1950s Dad did some cine-filming of the GHR, and 30 or 40 coal wagons were loose-coaled for appearance. They looked so good that they ran for some weeks, until the day when a wagon at the rear of the train derailed on a curve, and the engine kept on going! The running stopped while a couple of hundred scale tons of coal were removed from the permanent way.

EPILOGUE
'7-5-5'

When my father passed away in 1991, the GHR team were a wonderful support. With our family connections with the Isle of Man, the funeral was not in Rugby, but on the island. One of the team, Tom Hayward, went with me to attend the funeral. One of the floral tributes, from another member of the team, carried a message that might confuse the outsider, but would be understood by every member of the team, and indeed anyone who has worked block telegraph. '7-5-5' - 'Closing Signal Box'. It was a farewell message Dad would have appreciated.

Some weeks later there was a memorial service in Rugby, at which many members of the team were present. Some had travelled from Kent or Sussex, others from the Home Counties, yet others from the North of England. All had gained immense pleasure from a model railway, and had become friends. In front of the

pulpit there were tokens of Dad's life, his career in medicine, his sword as a regular officer in the Army, the nameplate of a locomotive that was to be named in his memory, and a much rebuilt Hornby 'Compound' of 1927, which had been given to him by *his* father for the model railway when he was in his teens. Fitted with an electric mech after the war, it is

A model railway often provides a focal point for a general railway interest. Many of us collect prototype railway artefacts, and my father stands beside some of the collection we have built up. The BNCR, MR NCC and LMS NCC wagon plates recall many happy visits to the railways of Northern Ireland, and are complemented by the rare oval RE NCC plate (ie Railway Executive - Northern Counties Committee). As the NCC was transferred from British Transport Commission ownership on 1 April 1948, this plate covered a three-month period only. *Rugby Advertiser*

still in regular use today, its service career exceeding the engines that were still emerging from Derby when it was built so long ago. At the suggestion of one of the team, there was a memorial running later that day.

As I write this, in a few hours time members of the team will be gathering for another running. One will have come over 60 miles. At the end of the running we will chat over the things that happened, that ought not to have happened, and the amusing side issues. We will make a note of what needs to be repaired, and so it will go on.

Not long before he died, Dad met one of Norman Eagles's 'Sherwood' team. Norman had passed away, and his railway, which had given pleasure to his gang, had been broken up. They chatted, but later Dad said how sad it was that Norman's line was no more. What cheered him up was that I would carry on the tradition after he had passed away. An idea at the back of my mind was that there was no reason why I could not form a charitable trust to continue the GHR after I had gone. I broached the idea with Dad, and it thrilled him. The Hillside Railway Trust was duly formed in 1994, to ensure the long-term survival of a model railway that has given enjoyment to the team for over 60 years. Long may it continue to do so.

When I started this book with a blank computer screen, I would have found it hard to define a living model railway. After many thousands of words I think I have the answer - it is a railway that will bring you pleasure and enjoyment, that will bring others pleasure and enjoyment, and build deep and lasting friendships. '7-5-5' was appropriate to the man, but not to the concept of a model railway that would live on and give pleasure to others. If, after reading this book, you can get as much pleasure from your model railway, and build such valued friendships, then my father's concept of what a model railway should be will live on, not just on the GHR, but elsewhere too.

In the Introduction to this book I quoted from the appreciation given by Philip Ingram at the memorial service for my father. He spoke of his commitment and thoroughness, whether it was in pioneering new and life-saving treatment for dysentery in the Army, or visiting a patient who was ill no less than three times on Christmas Day. Apart from his interest in model railways, he had a deep love for the railways of the Isle of Man, and was chairman of the Isle of Man Railway Society. When he was seriously ill in hospital, the Society decided to name Manx Electric Railway electric locomotive No 23 in his honour. This unique machine, which was rescued by the society when it was in danger of being broken up, is the oldest bogie locomotive in the British Isles. Sadly he passed away before the plates were ready, but the locomotive was named in his memory a few months later.

The final ingredient in creating a living model railway is commitment. The commitment that led to a mention in dispatches during the war, demanded safety-nets for high wire acts in the circus, or gave the railways of the Isle of Man an eloquent and skilled defender, was equally applicable to model railways. Ordinarily I do not like 'helicopter' shots of a layout, as our perspective of the real thing is usually near track level, but this is an exception. It is Paythorne station at the 'Doctors' Hobbies Exhibition'. The buildings are painstaking replicas of Clifton Mill station. Alas, Dad did not know what the roof details were, and there was no convenient road bridge, but with the signalman's permission there was a tall signal post to climb. He discovered the drainage channel and a row of transverse ribs. The building is illuminated, and as you peer into the waiting room, you can see through the ticket hatch into the booking office, just as you would have done on the prototype. *Dr R. P. Hendry*

INDEX